W9-ACB-343

JEAN-JACQUES ROUSSEAU

LONDON: HUMPHREY MILFORD
OXFORD UNIVERSITY PRESS

Selections from the Works

of

JEAN-JACQUES ROUSSEAU

EDITED WITH AN INTRODUCTION
AND NOTES

BY

CHRISTIAN GAUSS
Professor of Modern Languages in
Princeton University

Second Edition Revised and Enlarged

PRINCETON
PRINCETON UNIVERSITY PRESS
1920

First Edition

Second Edition

Second Printing March, 1921
Third Printing August, 1924
Fourth Printing January, 1926
Fifth Printing March, 1929

Printed in the United States of America

PREFACE TO THE SECOND EDITION

In preparing this enlarged edition of the *Selections from J.-J. Rousseau* I am availing myself of suggestions made by teachers who have used the first. The idea of giving complete works met with general approval. In the nature of things these could only be works of briefer compass. I have therefore retained *in extenso* the four complete selections of the first edition. To meet the request that all of Rousseau's important works be represented, selections have also been made from the remaining masterpieces. In arranging these I have attempted to choose such extracts as would, with the introductions to each, explain themselves, the purpose being to give in as brief a space as possible a general conspectus of Rousseau's contribution to the various fields of philosophy, politics and especially literature.

Students of Rousseau are still impatiently awaiting a definitive text. Since my first edition an excellent text of *The Political Writings of Rousseau* (1915) has been provided by Professor C. E. Vaughan. I have followed this for the selections from the *Discours sur l'Inégalité* and the *Contrat Social.* For the remaining selections I have used the Musset-Pathay

(1823-6) edition making a few changes which older or better authority seemed to warrant. In preparing this second edition I have been greatly aided in certain passages, especially of *La Nouvelle Héloïse,* by the *J.-J. Rousseau, Morceaux Choisis,* 3ᵉ édition, of that most learned of our Rousseau scholars, M. D. Mornet, to whom I wish to acknowledge particular indebtedness. For assistance in preparing this volume for the press my thanks are due to my colleague Professor Frank L. Critchlow.

CONTENTS

BIOGRAPHICAL NOTE

Jean-Jacques Rousseau was born in Geneva in 1712, the son of a watchmaker whose character, like that of his illustrious descendant, was somewhat unstable. He spent less than two years at the school of M. Lambercier and after various vicissitudes was apprenticed to an engraver who treated him badly and whom the "temperamental" lad repaid in kind. Seeing the gates of Geneva locked in his face one Sunday evening, at the age of sixteen he turned his back upon his native city. He encountered Mme de Warens, a recent convert to Catholicism, who gave him harborage in the intervals between his many tramp trips, and to whom he seems to have been in turn, ward, lover and intendant. For a while he devoted himself to music and at her little farm Les Charmettes near Chambéry, spent some time in desultory study. In 1741 we find him in Paris which was to be his base during the next period of his life, 1741-1756. In 1743 for a brief and stormy interval he acted as secretary to the French Ambassador at Venice. In 1749 he wrote his famous *Discours sur les Arts et les Sciences.* At this time he had established friendly relations with a number of the Encyclopaedists, especially with Diderot, and as Secretary to Mme Dupin and to her son-in-law, M. de Francueil, had undergone a partial initiation into the life of the *beau monde* of Paris. He had already, however, conceived an attachment for Thérèse Le Vasseur, a dull and unattractive servant, by whom he had five children who were consigned to a foundlings' home. He decided to "reform" and live the simple life; and after a journey to Geneva, retired (1756) to a cottage near the forest of Montmorency. Here he broke with most of his old friends, including Diderot and his benefactress, Mme d'Épinay; and in this neighborhood in the next six years wrote or rewrote his *La Nouvelle Héloise* (1761), *Émile* (1762) and *Le Contrat Social* (1762). His misanthropy and distrust of the world at large were increased by the condemnation of the *Émile* at Paris which forced him to flee from France to escape arrest. Geneva having shown itself equally hostile to both *Émile* and the *Contrat,* he set out on a painful period of wandering (1762-1770) during which he believed that he was seeking asylum from his persecutors. Among other places, he stops at Motiers; on the Ile de Saint-Pierre in the Lake of Bienne; in England, and the South of France. To defend himself he writes *Les Confessions,* and later *Rousseau Juge de Jean-Jacques,* and the *Rêveries.* In 1770 he returns to Paris where he lived simply, and, save for his own now settled delusion, in peace, until his death at Ermenonville in 1778.

INTRODUCTION

In the latter half of the nineteenth century, a century which was inclined to seek its salvation in the development of science and scientific method (a development to which Rousseau had not contributed), there seemed to be a very general disposition both in France and England to look upon the author of the *Contrat Social* as one of those great figures whose work in the world, for good or for ill, had now been finally accomplished. Critical opinion was fairly agreed in admitting that, historically considered, his rôle had been extraordinary, and usually ended by assigning to him the foremost place as a fomenter of eighteenth century discontent, and by accepting him as the virtual leader of the intellectual and especially the sentimental revolt which brought about the French Revolution. It was admitted that he had influenced Wordsworth in England and perhaps unworthily Kant[1] in Germany. Here, however, agreement ceased, and in the further discussion on the value of Rousseau's services to civilization generally, the temperamental differences and political preconceptions of his critics became apparent. The interest in this phase of the quarrel was, however, largely academic, for it was tacitly assumed on both

[1] For later and juster estimates of Rousseau's influence on Kant cf. John Grier Hibben, *The Philosophy of the Enlightenment,* 1910, pp. 157-159; and V. Delbos, *La Philosophie Pratique de Kant,* 1905, pp. 106 *et seq.*

sides that the currents of nineteenth century thought had swept out beyond him. For reasons which it would be impossible to explain fully in a brief introduction there seems to be at present a strong revival of interest in this unhappy man of genius. The very violence of the attacks which have recently been directed against him and his disciples bears testimony to the fact that in certain quarters, at least, he is once more looked upon as a living menace.[2] It may be that this renewed interest is due in part to the wide appeal of Tolstoi,[3] one of the most earnest, or from the point of view of the opposition, perverted of his disciples, and to the appearance of a new philosophy[4] which in certain of its assumptions carries us back to Rousseau. For whatever cause, Rousseau has undoubtedly once more become a center of interest and a target of attack.

Coincident with this revival of interest in Rousseau as an active factor in contemporary thought, there has come a revival of interest in Rousseau scholarship, and it is safe to say that at present we know much more of his life and of the conditions under which his work was produced than did the critics and scholars of a half-century ago. Recent research has, however, failed to make quite clear along just what line it is

[2] Lasserre, *Le Romantisme Français,* 3ᵉ éd. 1907; Seillière, *Le Mal Romantique,* 1908; Maigron, *Le Romantisme et les Mœurs,* 1910; Babbitt, *Rousseau and Romanticism,* 1919.

[3] Benrubi, "Tolstoï continuateur de J.-J. Rousseau," *Annales J.-J. Rousseau,* 1907, Vol. III, pp. 83-118.

[4] Babbitt, "Bergson and Rousseau," *Nation,* 1912, Vol. XCV, pp. 452-455.

that we must seek for his own special contribution to the history of modern thought. The tendency has been to show that those elements which the earlier generation of scholars looked upon as peculiarly Rousseau's are to be found in the current thought and even in the published literature of his time.[5] The doctrine of *la bonté naturelle,* the idea that man is by nature good, might be found in an author as well known to English readers as Alexander Pope,[6] and in varying degrees it permeates the thought of an entire school of British philosophers.[7] So too, feeling for nature, of

[5] Mornet, *Le Sentiment de la Nature en France de J.-J. Rousseau à Bernardin de Saint-Pierre,* 1907; also *Le Romantisme en France au XVIIIe siècle,* 1912; Schinz, "Rousseau devant l'érudition modern," *Modern Philology,* 1912, Vol. X, pp. 265-288.

[6] "Nor think, in nature's state they blindly trod;
The state of nature, was the reign of God:
Self love and social at her birth began,
Union the bond of all things, and of man,
Pride then was not; nor arts, that pride to aid;
Man walk'd with beast, joint tenant of the shade,
The same his table, and the same his bed;
No murder clothed him, and no murder fed.
In the same temple, the resounding wood,
All vocal beings hymn'd their equal God:
The shrine with gore unstain'd, with gold undrest,
Unbrib'd, unbloody, stood the blameless priest:
Heav'n's attribute was universal care,
And man's prerogative, to rule, but spare.
Ah! how unlike the man of times to come!
Of half that live the butcher and the tomb;
Who, foe to nature, hears the gen'ral groan,
Murders their species, and betrays his own."

Essay on Man. III. 147-165.

[7] Cf. Leslie Stephen's chapters on the English Deists, *English Thought in the Eighteenth Century,* 1876, Vol. I, pp. 74-278.

a kind at least, had already found expression in English poetry before Rousseau's day.[8] If it is, therefore, no longer possible to look upon Rousseau as did an earlier generation as a *novus homo,* a sort of bewildered Man from Mars suddenly set down in the alien atmosphere of the eighteenth century, it is likewise as useless to deny him originality, or to attempt to nullify his importance by setting forth in detail the inconsistency of his practice and his doctrine and the many contradictions in his various works.[9] Not even Rousseau's friends can hold that his was a well balanced personality or intelligence. His temperament was abnormal, unstable and explosive. If consistency is the virtue of little minds, Rousseau may be said to have vindicated his claims to greatness by the number and the violence of his self-contradictions. Critics have been quick to seize upon this weakness of his exposition and have made somewhat too much of it. Rousseau from the first writes for what he considers a hostile audience and is forever in the position of one who is "hitting back." Passionate in his devotion to himself and his ideas, he surrenders to the impulse of the moment, and in the interest of driving home a telling blow fails to leave open for himself the avenue of retreat. Nowhere is this more evident than in the First Discourse and in his later attempts to answer the objections which were urged upon him from all sides. The general lines of his philosophy are none the less

[8] Myra Reynolds, *Treatment of Nature in English Poetry between Pope and Wordsworth,* Chicago, 1896.

[9] Lemaître, *J.-J. Rousseau,* 1907.

convergent, and most of the seeming contradictions will tend to disappear when the student remembers in the first place that Rousseau was an auto-didact who passed through a period of development which seriously modified the harshness of his first conclusions, and in the second, that with his passionate temper he sacrificed everything to emphasis and the momentary impression. It is only natural, therefore, to see a certain broadening of his views from the period of his first discourse (1749) to the *Émile* (1762). It is likewise possible to reconcile statements which in their violence seem to threaten each other, when we discount his emphasis and consider merely his logical intention. Only on such a basis will the student find his way out of this somewhat disconcerting maze and be able to accept Lanson's statement that at bottom Rousseau's work is consistent.[10]

Before discussing what may be called the convergence of Rousseau's efforts in the various fields of his endeavor, it will be well to turn for a moment to the famous *Discours sur les Arts et les Sciences.* It was this essay which first brought him into prominence, and it was doubtless written at a time when his ideas were as yet neither entirely clear nor altogether coordinated. According to Rousseau's own statement, which has sometimes been called into question but never seriously impeached, the idea of writing it occurred to him one day on the road from Paris to Vincennes. He was on his way to visit his friend Diderot who had been imprisoned there for an offending arti-

[10] *La Grande Encyclopédie,* Article "J.-J. Rousseau."

cle, and was reading a copy of the *Mercure de France*[11] when his eyes suddenly fell upon an announcement that the Academy of Dijon was offering a prize for the best discussion on the subject whether the re-establishment of the arts and sciences had contributed to improve *les mœurs,* which in this case we may translate by morals.[12] The announcement threw him, so he says, into a fever of excitement and in a kind of trance, oblivious of his surroundings, he sank down under a tree and began his impassioned answer, writing then and there his famous apostrophe to Fabricius. At this time Rousseau and Diderot were bound by ties of closest intimacy. Some years later, in 1755, their friendship began to cool, and not long after, ended in a noisy and undignified rupture which was followed by a long train of bitter recriminations. Those who follow with eagerness the *chronique scandaleuse* of literary history will find that the details of this somewhat unseemly quarrel have been quite fully recorded by scholars. We are interested in but a single phase of that dispute. The report was later scattered by

[11] Rousseau, *Œuvres,* Hachette, 1905, Vol. VIII, p. 249. (For a fuller discussion of this question cf. Note 1, on the text, and the first *Lettre à M. de Malesherbes* here printed.)

[12] It is worthy of remark that up to a certain point at least Rousseau accepted the eighteenth century ideas of progress and human perfectibility. It is interesting to note that in the *Confessions* he gives the subject of his discourse as follows: *"Si le progrès des sciences et des arts a contribué à corrompre ou à épurer les mœurs."* Human perfectibility he insists upon with special emphasis in the note on the Second Discourse, Vol. I, p. 142; cf. also Dreyfus-Brisac, *Du Contrat Social,* 1896, Introduction.

partisans of Diderot,[13] in particular by Marmontel, that on Rousseau's arrival at Vincennes he was inclined to take the affirmative side of the question proposed by the Academy, and that it was only on Diderot's instance that he was induced to answer in the negative. For various reasons that report no longer deserves very serious consideration.[14] It seems to indicate, however, that at this time and on this point Rousseau and Diderot were in entire agreement, and we shall find further testimony to this agreement when we remember that it was Diderot who later had Rousseau's discourse published, and that he was overjoyed at its success.[15] Much of the confusion on this point has been due to a fundamental misconception. It has been rather hastily assumed that there was something extraordinarily startling in Rousseau's negative, and that his attitude must therefore be explained. A moment's reflection will show that such was not the case. The theme was not of his choosing. It had been put out as a subject for discussion by one of the most famous learned societies of France and it is therefore necessary to accept the fact that in certain quarters even of the French intellectual world it was regarded as an open question. It should be remembered further that if it was possible that the question could be answered in the negative by Diderot, who was already the editor of the *Encyclopédie* and, therefore, the

[13] Diderot, *Œuvres,* 1875, Vol. III, p. 98; Marmontel, *Mémoires,* Bk. VII; Morellet, *Mémoires,* Chap. V.

[14] Ducros, *J.-J. Rousseau, de Genève à l'Hermitage,* 1908, pp. 167, 168.

[15] Rousseau, Vol. VIII, p. 258.

avowed champion of the scientific and artistic progress of his age, it was more reasonable and natural that Rousseau, from the first always more or less of an alien to the thought and especially the feeling of his time,[16] should so have answered it. In assigning to this discourse its proper place in the body of Rousseau's work two points should be carefully considered. In the first place we should note exactly the scope of the question under discussion. He himself takes pains to call our attention to this. The question is not whether the arts and sciences are in themselves desirable. Rousseau is willing to admit that *"si les intelligences célestes cultivaient les sciences il n'en résulterait que de bien; j'en dis autant des grands hommes qui sont faits pour guider les autres."*[17] Neither is it a question whether the arts and sciences are necessary to mankind at a certain stage in their history. He concedes, somewhat grudgingly to be sure, that the arts are necessary to us now as crutches are necessary for the old and decrepit.[18] The question to be discussed was whether in the ages marked by the discoveries and ever-widening applications of the arts and sciences there had not been a loss in moral fibre and individual character. Rousseau proclaimed in his first discourse, perhaps with a too evident satisfaction, that this moral deterioration had followed in the wake of the advancement of the arts. This fundamental conception provides him with the starting point of his system. In the second place we should remember that the form of

[16] Ducros, *op. cit.* 1908, pp. 149-167.

[17] *Œuvres,* "Réponse à M. Bordes," I, p. 48.

[18] *Œuvres,* "Lettre à M. Philopolis," I, p. 154.

expression in the discourse was not entirely of his choosing and that he was presenting his paper as a frankly *ex parte* statement in a competition organized by an academy. In such a competition a dispassionate essay was not to be expected, and it is a curious fact that not even critics friendly to Rousseau should have fully realized the ethics of his position. The ethics of discourse-writing, a favorite amusement of eighteenth century *lettrés,* was much the same as the ethics of present day intercollegiate debating. Having chosen his side of an open question it was the duty of the disputant to present it as strongly and convincingly as possible. The form, to be sure, suited Rousseau's essentially one-sided temperament, and his heart was doubtless in his work. *La nuance* was never his affair. Quite possibly too, a sudden celebrity turned his head and led him at times to *renchérir* upon what was already a paradox and to draw grotesquely flattering pictures of primitive man. If amusing, it was none the less premature to say of him, as did Voltaire, that he was merely vaunting *le bonheur à quatre pattes,* or to assume that he advocated that we should suddenly turn back the hands of the clock and run, content again, upon all fours. It is likewise unfair to hold that we catch Rousseau in flagrant contradiction of himself when we later find him with much expense of spirit elaborating a careful state and advocating a new system of education, neither of which institutions would be necessary if this stage of purely primitive bliss were his final aim and end.

To judge properly Rousseau's position we must consider his work as a whole. The fundamental unity of his purpose will be apparent if we look upon his philosophy, as does M. Émile Boutroux,[19] as presenting a mythical history of humanity as it passes through its three successive stages.

The first stage is the state of nature in which man lives out his individual life in the light of his instinct, following his impulses, which Rousseau believed to be fundamentally good and right, and guided only by his sentiment. His intelligence is as yet undeveloped and entirely subordinate to sentiment and conscience. This stage, however, is in its nature transitory, and once passed, cannot be recalled, and if Rousseau painted this way of life in attractive colors, it was, as we shall see from the *Émile* and the *Contrat Social,* by no means his purpose to bring it again into being. For in this state of nature the individual, though free, enjoys but a precarious existence and is soon constrained to combat the forces which threaten his life. To increase his power of resisting these hostile forces he now joins with his fellows and begins to develop his natural resources. At this point he from necessity passes over into the second stage which we may designate as the social state.

In entering upon this second state man's primary end was to defend himself and to increase his power of resistance. This he did largely through the development of the arts and sciences. But he soon came to seek power and preëminence for their own sakes, for-

[19] *Revue de Métaphysique et de Morale,* Vol. XX, pp. 265-274. To M. Boutroux's excellent study I am much indebted.

got his natural equality and lost touch altogether with the kind of life he had lived in the state of nature, and consequently with what Rousseau considered the proper and natural aims of the individual. The development of the intelligence having become an end in itself, the struggle is now carried on, not in the interest of safely achieving the natural destiny of man, but merely in the interest of establishing supremacy and individual domination over one's fellows. Sentiment and conscience which lead man to fulfil this natural destiny were forced to a subordinate position in his life. His moral nature became warped and perverted, and instead of obeying his conscience he enters upon what may be called in theological terms the state of perversion or sin. Moral deterioration, in other words, follows in the wake of the arts and sciences which beget inequality and injustice. Yet the enlarging of his horizon and the development of his faculties need not necessarily be an evil. Through consciousness of sin, as in Julie's case, for instance, man may rise to a plane higher than that of his first stage of ignorant if blissful innocence. To do this he must pass into the third, or what we may call the political state.

To reëstablish justice and equality, society must now be transformed into the State, which shall at once protect life and again render possible the full realization of the individual destiny. This State is based upon an ideal contract by which man submits himself not to an alien power with an independent interest, which tends to degrade him, but to the power which he himself has created for the purpose of completely realizing himself. This lends dignity to his new life. The State can act therefore only in accordance with the "general will," and under penalty of negating itself must not take any action which shall be hostile to the higher interest of its constituent members. In other words, the individuals, now joined by a mystic bond, merely through the exercise of certain of their rights, automatically become the State. The State "compels them to be free." It can therefore control the action of its members only up to a certain point. It guarantees equality and liberty which were lost in the social stage, and once again leaves man free to "pursue his happiness." Beyond him opens out again the free field for individual self-realization which must take place along the line of man's natural ends. For the purpose of his redemption, man must therefore, if he would enter into the highest stage of his progress, at once be educated as a citizen and again be put into touch with the great guiding natural forces. Feeling and conscience are again supreme.

> "One moment now may give us more
> Than years of toiling reason."[20]

For the purpose of this regeneration the life of comparative solitude, or simple rusticity which is preached in *Émile,* and of constant communion with nature, is best. In the interest of this newer "normal" education he would have subscribed to the lines of his English disciple:

[20] Wordsworth, *To my Sister.*

"Books! 'tis a dull and endless strife, . . .
Let Nature be your teacher."

The warping of man's moral nature which Rousseau accepted as the result of his participation in the merely social life could thus be rectified, for as Wordsworth says,

"One impulse from a vernal wood
May teach you more of man
Of moral evil and of good
Than all the sages can."

Therefore in this sense Rousseau too would have said and did say:

"Enough of Science and of Art;
Close up those barren leaves;
Come forth and bring with you a heart
That watches and receives."[21]

It should be remembered that we have been trying to expound and make plain Rousseau's system in order to make clearer the place and bearing of the first discourse in his completed work. It would be easy to show that from the point of view of a political instrument his state, as outlined in the *Contrat Social,* presents insuperable difficulties and that it would not accomplish in practice, the aim for which it was intended by this "utopian dreamer." It should, however, be borne in mind that Rousseau never intended the *Contrat* to be accepted as a constitution by any existing state. He designed it as a statement of general principles and of political ideals. There can be no ques-

[21] Wordsworth, *The Tables Turned.*

tion that as such it has exerted a highly important influence upon the development of democratic ideas. In politics Rousseau may well be regarded as the most important of the eighteenth century "radicals." On this question see the Introduction in this volume to the *Discours sur l'Inégalité* and the *Contrat Social.* With such criticism of details we are not for the present concerned. To understand his philosophy we must keep in mind, none the less, what, according to Rousseau's conception, was to be the function and end of this new State. His system as a whole is most easily open to attack because of the dualism which he sets up between the life of intellect and the life of feeling. Doubtless there is no such fundamental dichotomy in the human personality, and even if we grant that sentiment and reason may not always be in entire accord, the effects of this opposition are perhaps less baleful than he imagined and there may be other ways of bringing about a new *modus vivendi.* In the present discussion we desire, however, merely to point out the extraordinary importance to eighteenth and nineteenth century currents of thought of a philosophy so new, so striking, and so attractive.

We may conclude, then, that taken in isolation, it is possible to find parallels in earlier literature to many if not all of the ideas expressed by Rousseau. So far we may accept the conclusions of recent investigators. The belief in the goodness of man and of nature, the glorification of the simple life, the exalting of sentiment, the preaching of natural religion, all these have been abundantly shown to have existed before his day.[22] So too, many of the conclusions drawn from such premises, many of his recommendations with regard to the rearing and training of children, or with the assembling and governing of men in states were known to his predecessors. Even the conception that the State is based on a contract and that it should be governed by the *volonté générale* was not exclusively his discovery.[23] But it is not upon such details that his reputation must rest. His importance in the history of philosophy and of literature depends upon the general system which he presents and upon the peculiarly feverish earnestness with which he presents it.

The point may be readily illustrated by a brief comparison.

Perhaps from none of his predecessors did Rousseau borrow more extensively than from Montaigne. Yet their points of departure, their attitude and aims, were as diverse as they well could be. Montaigne was by habit a student and by temperament he had in him something of the fatalist. He observes the life about him, and his reflections are often not unlike Rousseau's

[22] On Rousseau's sources cf. Lanson, *Manuel Bibliographique, Origines et Sources des Œuvres de Rousseau,* Vol. III, pp. 802-803, and more especially, Delaruelle, "Les sources principales de J.-J. Rousseau dans le premier discours," *Revue d'histoire littéraire de la France,* 1912, Vol. XIX, pp. 245-271; also *ibid.,* p. 640; also Vol. XX, p. 424; Kreuger, *Fremde Gedanken in Rousseaus ersten Discours,* 1891; Morel, "Recherches sur les sources du Discours sur l'Inégalité," *Annales J.-J. Rousseau,* 1909, Vol. V, pp. 119-198; Villey, *L'Influence de Montaigne sur les Idées pédagogiques de Locke et de Rousseau,* 1911.

[23] Cf. Atger, *Essai sur l'histoire des doctrines du contrat social,* 1906.

conclusions. But he accepts the fact, even while he may regret that through such a world we must hunt our way. Far differently stands the case with Rousseau. He is neither fatalistic in temper, nor by training a student of human psychology. He is an advocate and a reformer. Essentially utopian, on the basis of what he believed to be a newer and better conception of the world he would demolish and reconstruct. His attitude was that of one who would

> "shatter the old world to bits, and then
> Remould it nearer to the heart's desire."

It is for this reason that he accepts very little and is forever in protest. The student who is about to consider Rousseau's various works will therefore do well to begin by regarding him as a man of letters of genius, who, in point of importance if not of time, was the first pleader for some of the most significant changes effected by the eighteenth century. To assist in this study the works are here arranged in chronological order with an introduction to each, dealing with the circumstances under which it was written, and its general bearing.

The *Manuel Bibliographique* of Lanson is so easily accessible and can be so readily supplemented by the critical yearly bibliographies of the *Annales J.-J. Rousseau* that it has seemed unnecessary to add any extended list of reference works here. In the Notes the more important recent contributions bearing on the immediate matter in hand have been indicated. The references to Rousseau's works in the footnotes are made to the Hachette edition of the *Œuvres*.

In addition to the text of Rousseau himself the *Programme* of the Académie de Dijon, as Rousseau read it in the *Mercure de France* on that eventful day of 1749 is printed at the head of the Discourse.[24] I have here followed the copy made by that veteran Rousseauiste, M. Ritter, for the *Zeitschrift für französische Sprache und Literatur*.[25] Although the *Programme* is of course not Rousseau's, it seemed to the editor that it might help the student to understand the situation, if he had this interesting and famous announcement before him.

[24] As Rousseau tells us at the close of his *Préface* (cf. p. 22 *infra*) he made a few additions to his manuscript after submitting it to the Academy and before its publication (1750). One of these is in all probability the passage on page 51, containing Rousseau's reference to the *Pensées philsophiques* (XXV) of Diderot, a volume which had been condemned by the Parlement shortly after it appeared in 1746. The Academy of Dijon could not formally have recognized an essay that cited with approval a volume which had been officially suppressed.

[25] Vol. XI, pp. 26-27.

PROGRAMME DE L'ACADEMIE DES SCIENCES ET BELLES LETTRES DE DIJON POUR LE PRIX DE MORALE DE 1750

L'Académie, fondée par M. Hector Bernard Poussier, Doyen du Parlement de Bourgogne, annonce à tous les Sçavans que le Prix de Morale pour l'année 1750—consistant en une Médaille d'or, de la valeur de trente pistoles,—sera adjugé à celui qui aura le mieux résolu le Problême suivant:

Si le rétablissement des Sciences et des Arts a contribué à épurer les mœurs.

Il sera libre à tous ceux qui voudront concourir d'écrire en François ou en Latin, observant que leurs Ouvrages soient lisibles, et que la lecture de chaque Mémoire remplisse et n'excède point une demie heure.

Les Mémoires francs de port (sans quoi ils ne seront pas retirés) seront addressés à M. Petit, secretaire de l'Académie, rue du Vieux Marché à Dijon—qui n'en recevra aucun après le premier Avril.

Comme on ne sçauroit prendre trop de précautions, tant pour rendre aux Sçavans la justice qu'ils méritent, que pour écarter autant qu'il est possible les brigues, et cet esprit de partialité qui n'entrainent que trop souvent les suffrages vers les objets connus, ou qui les en détournent par d'autres motifs également irréguliers, l'Académie déclare que tous ceux qui ayant travaillé sur le sujet donné seront convaincus de s'être fait connaître directement ou indirectement pour Auteurs des Mémoires, avant qu'elle ait décidé sur la distribution du Prix, seront exclus du concours.—Pour obvier à cet inconvénient, chaque Auteur sera tenu de mettre au bas de son Mémoire une Sentence ou Devise, et d'y joindre une feuille de papier cachetée, sous le dos de laquelle sera la même sentence, et sur le cachet son nom, ses qualités et sa demeure, pour y avoir recours à la distribution du Prix. Les dites Feuilles, ainsi cachetées de façon qu'on ne puisse y rien lire à travers, ne seront point ouvertes avant ce temps là, et le secretaire en tiendra un Régistre exact.—Ceux qui exigeront un Récépissé de leurs ouvrages le feront expédier sous un autre nom que le leur—et dans le cas ou celui qui auroit usé de cette précaution aurait obtenu le Prix, il sera obligé, en chargeant une personne domiciliée à Dijon de sa Procuration pardevant un Notaire et légalisée par le Juge, d'y joindre aussi le Récépissé.

Si celui à qui le Prix sera adjugé n'est pas de Dijon, il enverra pareillement sa Procuration en la forme susdite: et s'il est de cette ville, il viendra le recevoir en personne le jour de la distribution du Prix qui se fera dans une Assemblée publique de l'Académie, le Dimanche 23 Août 1750.

N. B. Throughout the volume all footnotes in French are from Rousseau's original text, the remainder in English are by the editor.

DISCOURS
SI LE RETABLISSEMENT DES SCIENCES ET DES ARTS A CONTRIBUE A EPURER LES MŒURS[1]

"Barbarus hic ego sum, quia non intelligor illis."
—Ovid., *Trist.* V, Eleg. X, v. 37.

[1] The title for the proposed discourse, as it appeared in the *Mercure de France,* reads as here stated. Rousseau quotes it incorrectly in the *Confessions* (Vol. VIII, p. 249). The account there given implies that he saw the announcement of the Academy of Dijon in the summer of 1749. This likewise is incorrect. The *"Programme de l'Académie des Sciences et Belles Lettres de Dijon pour le Prix de Morale de 1750"* appeared first in the October (1749) number of the *Mercure.* The contents prove that it could hardly have appeared earlier than October 1. Rousseau's assertion that his "illumination" occurred in the summer is further invalidated by his statements concerning Diderot. Diderot was imprisoned on July 24, 1749, and remained at Vincennes until November 3. From Rousseau's own account, the famous visit must have taken place some time, possibly months, after the beginning of Diderot's imprisonment (Vol. VIII, pp. 247-250). Diderot was already *"très affecté de sa prison."* The prize offered by the Academy was "une Médaille d'or, de la valeur de trentes pistoles." Rousseau's statements, if untrue, were not untruthful. They were, in all probability, not deliberately false, but the result of his uncertain memory. Cf. Eugène Ritter "Le programme du prix proposé par l'Académie de Dijon," *Zeitschrift für französische Sprache und Literatur,* Vol. XI, pp. 23-28; also Cru's *Diderot and English Thought,* 1913, pp. 42-43.

AVERTISSEMENT[2]

Qu'est-ce que la célébrité? Voici le malheureux ouvrage à qui je dois la mienne. Il est certain que cette pièce, qui m'a valu un prix, et qui m'a fait un nom, est tout au plus médiocre, et j'ose ajouter qu'elle est une des moindres de tout ce recueil.[3] Quel gouffre de misères n'eût point évité l'auteur, si ce premier écrit n'eût été reçu que comme il méritait de l'être! Mais il fallait qu'une faveur d'abord injuste m'attirât par degrés une rigueur qui l'est encore plus.

PRÉFACE

Voici une des plus grandes et belles questions qui aient jamais été agitées. Il ne s'agit point dans ce discours de ces subtilités métaphysiques qui ont gagné toutes les parties de la littérature, et dont les programmes d'académie ne sont pas toujours exempts; mais il s'agit d'une de ces vérités qui tiennent au bonheur du genre humain.

Je prévois qu'on me pardonnera difficilement le parti que j'ai osé prendre. Heurtant de front tout ce qui fait aujourd'hui l'admiration des hommes, je ne puis

[2] Rousseau liked to trace the beginning of his misfortunes to the celebrity which followed the publication of this Discourse. He consistently held it to be one of his poorest performances, *"le plus faible de raisonnement et le plus pauvre de nombre et d'harmonie"* (Vol. VIII, p. 250). He none the less took great pains with its preparation. The secret of his misfortunes, however, lies in his temperament (cf. the *Lettre à M. de Malesherbes,* January 12, 1762, which follows, pp. 194-199).

[3] The *recueil* of Rousseau's works at this time contained the two *Discours, La Lettre sur les Spectacles, Émile, La Nouvelle Héloïse* and *Le Contrat Social.*

m'attendre qu'à un blâme universel; et ce n'est pas pour avoir été honoré de l'approbation de quelques sages, que je dois compter sur celle du public: aussi mon parti est-il pris; je ne me soucie de plaire ni aux beaux
5 esprits ni aux gens à la mode. Il y aura dans tous les temps des hommes faits pour être subjugués par les opinions de leur siècle, de leur pays, et de leur société. Tel fait aujourd'hui l'esprit fort et le philosophe, qui, par la même raison, n'eût été qu'un fanatique du temps
10 de la Ligue.[4] Il ne faut point écrire pour de tels lecteurs, quand on veut vivre au delà de son siècle.

Un mot encore, et je finis. Comptant peu sur l'honneur que j'ai reçu, j'avais, depuis l'envoi, refondu et augmenté ce discours, au point d'en faire, en quelque
15 manière, un autre ouvrage. Aujourd'hui je me suis cru obligé de le rétablir dans l'état où il a été couronné. J'y ai seulement jeté quelques notes, et laissé deux additions faciles à reconnaître, et que l'Académie n'aurait peut-être pas approuvées. J'ai pensé que
20 l'équité, le respect et la reconnaissance exigeaient de moi cet avertissement.

DISCOURS

"Decipimur specie recti."
—Hor., *de Art. poet.*, v. 25.

25 Le rétablissement des sciences et des arts a-t-il contribué à épurer ou à corrompre les mœurs? Voilà ce qu'il s'agit d'examiner. Quel parti dois-je prendre dans cette question? Celui, messieurs, qui convient à

[4] The *Ligue* was the union of catholics formed in France at the close of the sixteenth century to combat protestantism.

un honnête homme qui ne sait rien, et qui ne s'en estime pas moins.

Il sera difficile, je le sens, d'approprier ce que j'ai à dire au tribunal où je comparais. Comment oser blâmer les sciences devant une des plus savantes compagnies de l'Europe, louer l'ignorance dans une célèbre Académie, et concilier le mépris pour l'étude avec le respect pour les vrais savants? J'ai vu ces contrariétés, et elles ne m'ont point rebuté. Ce n'est point la science que je maltraite, me suis-je dit, c'est la vertu que je défends devant des hommes vertueux. La probité est encore plus chère aux gens de bien que l'érudition aux doctes. Qu'ai-je donc à redouter? Les lumières de l'assemblée qui m'écoute? Je l'avoue; mais c'est pour la constitution du discours, et non pour le sentiment de l'orateur. Les souverains équitables n'ont jamais balancé à se condamner eux-mêmes dans les discussions douteuses; et la position la plus avantageuse au bon droit est d'avoir à se défendre contre une partie intègre et éclairée, juge en sa propre cause.

A ce motif qui m'encourage, il s'en joint un autre qui me détermine; c'est qu'après avoir soutenu, selon ma lumière naturelle, le parti de la vérité, quel que soit mon succès, il est un prix qui ne peut me manquer; je le trouverai dans le fond de mon cœur.

PREMIÈRE PARTIE

C'est un grand et beau spectacle de voir l'homme sortir en quelque manière du néant par ses propres efforts; dissiper, par les lumières de sa raison, les ténèbres dans lesquelles la nature l'avait enveloppé;

s'élever au-dessus de lui-même; s'élancer par l'esprit jusque dans les régions célestes; parcourir à pas de géant, ainsi que le soleil, la vaste étendue de l'univers; et, ce qui est encore plus grand et plus difficile, rentrer 5 en soi pour y étudier l'homme et connaître sa nature, ses devoirs et sa fin. Toutes ces merveilles se sont renouvelées depuis peu de générations.[5]

L'Europe était retombée dans la barbarie des premiers âges. Les peuples de cette partie du monde 10 aujourd'hui si éclairée vivaient, il y a quelques siècles, dans un état pire que l'ignorance. Je ne sais quel jargon scientifique, encore plus méprisable que l'ignorance, avait usurpé le nom du savoir, et opposait à son retour un obstacle presque invincible. Il fallait une 15 révolution pour ramener les hommes au sens commun; elle vint enfin du côté d'où on l'aurait le moins atten-

[5] Speculations that rested upon an idea of "evolution" and especially of human progress were very common in the eighteenth century, and the conception of development from lower to higher phases of life is thrown out and occasionally insisted upon in the works of many of the leading thinkers of that time. It can be found clearly stated in Diderot *Œuvres,* 1875, Vol. II, pp. 57-58, who received his suggestions from Maupertuis. Buffon hesitates between it and the creational view, cf. Marcel Landrieu, "Lamarck et ses précurseurs," *Revue Anthropologique,* 1906, Vol. XVI, pp. 152-169. It must of course be understood that the idea of evolution was not presented as a completely developed scientific theory but as a random hypothesis among others. Condillac's psychology rests on a theory of progressive development of the intelligence, so too, Rousseau's own history of language. The belief in progress may be said to have been one of the most common and fruitful ideas of the century. It finds its apotheosis in Condorcet's *Esquisse d'un Tableau historique des Progrès de l'Esprit humain* (1794).

due. Ce fut le stupide musulman,[6] ce fut l'éternel fléau des lettres qui les fit renaître parmi nous. La chute du trône de Constantin porta dans l'Italie les débris de l'ancienne Grèce. La France s'enrichit à son tour de ces précieuses dépouilles. Bientôt les sciences suivirent les lettres: à l'art d'écrire se joignit l'art de penser; gradation qui paraît étrange, et qui n'est peut-être que trop naturelle: et l'on commença à sentir le principal avantage du commerce des muses, celui de rendre les hommes plus sociables en leur inspirant le désir de se plaire les uns aux autres par des ouvrages dignes de leur approbation mutuelle.

L'esprit a ses besoins, ainsi que le corps. Ceux-ci sont les fondements de la société, les autres en font l'agrément. Tandis que le gouvernement et les lois pourvoient à la sûreté et au bien-être des hommes assemblés, les sciences, les lettres et les arts, moins despotiques et plus puissants peut-être, étendent des guirlandes de fleurs sur les chaînes de fer dont ils sont chargés, étouffent en eux le sentiment de cette liberté originelle pour laquelle ils semblaient être nés, leur font aimer leur esclavage, et en forment ce qu'on appelle des peuples policés. Le besoin éleva les trônes, les sciences et les arts les ont affermis. Puissances de la terre, aimez les talents, et protégez ceux qui les culti-

[6] If Rousseau's allusion here is unflattering, the Musulman, the Chinese, and the American Indian were often held up to eighteenth century readers as examples of virtue that might well be emulated. Such exoticism was *à la mode*. Cf. Du Fresny, *Les amusements sérieux et comiques d'un Siamois,* 1707; Montesquieu's *Les Lettres persanes,* and Voltaire's *Zaïre;* and Chinard's *L'Exotisme américain dans la littérature française,* 1911.

vent.[a] Peuples policés, cultivez-les: heureux esclaves, vous leur devez ce goût délicat et fin dont vous vous piquez; cette douceur de caractère et cette urbanité de mœurs qui rendent parmi vous le commerce si liant et 5 si facile; en un mot, les apparences de toutes les vertus sans en avoir aucune.

C'est par cette sorte de politesse, d'autant plus aimable qu'elle affecte moins de se montrer, que se distinguèrent autrefois Athènes et Rome dans les jours si 10 vantés de leur magnificence et de leur éclat, c'est par elle, sans doute, que notre siècle et notre nation l'emporteront sur tous les temps et sur tous les peuples. Un ton philosophe sans pédanterie, des manières naturelles et pourtant prévenantes, également éloignées de 15 la rusticité tudesque et de la pantomime ultramontaine: voilà les fruits du goût acquis par de bonnes études et perfectionné dans le commerce du monde.

Qu'il serait doux de vivre parmi nous si la conten-

[a] Les princes voient toujours avec plaisir le goût des arts agréables et des superfluités, dont l'exportation de l'argent ne résulte pas, s'étendre parmi leurs sujets: car, outre qu'ils les nourrissent ainsi dans cette petitesse d'âme si propre à la servitude, ils savent très bien que tous les besoins que le peuple se donne sont autant de chaînes dont il se charge. Alexandre, voulant maintenir les Ichthyophages dans sa dépendance, les contraignit de renoncer à la pêche, et de se nourrir des aliments communs aux autres peuples; et les sauvages de l'Amérique, qui vont tout nus, et qui ne vivent que du produit de leur chasse, n'ont jamais pu être domptés: en effet, quel joug imposerait-on à des hommes qui n'ont besoin de rien*?

*Ce qui est rapporté ici d'Alexandre n'a d'autre fondement qu'un passage de Pline l'Ancien, copié depuis par Solin (chap. LIV): "Ichthyophages omnes Alexander vetuit piscibus vivere." (*Hist. nat.*, lib. VI, cap. XXV.)

ance extérieure était toujours l'image des dispositions du cœur, si la décence était la vertu,[7] si nos maximes nous servaient de règle, si la véritable philosophie était inséparable du titre de philosophe! Mais tant de qualitées vont trop rarement ensemble, et la vertu ne 5 marche guère en si grande pompe. La richesse de la parure peut annoncer un homme opulent, et son élégance un homme de goût: l'homme sain et robuste se reconnaît à d'autres marques; c'est sous l'habit rustique d'un laboureur, et non sous la dorure d'un courtisan, 10 qu'on trouvera la force et la vigueur du corps. La parure n'est pas moins étrangère à la vertu, qui est la force et la vigueur de l'âme. L'homme de bien est un athlète qui se plaît à combattre nu; il méprise tous ces vils ornements qui gêneraient l'usage de ses forces, et 15 dont la plupart n'ont été inventés que pour cacher quelque difformité.

Avant que l'art eût façonné nos manières et appris à nos passions à parler un langage apprêté, nos mœurs étaient rustiques, mais naturelles; et la différence des 20 procédés annonçait, au premier coup d'œil, celle des caractères. La nature humaine, au fond, n'était pas meilleure; mais les hommes trouvaient leur sécurité dans la facilité de se pénétrer réciproquement; et cet

[7] From the beginning of his career, *vertu* was a favorite word with Rousseau. It occurs already in his *Le Verger des Charmettes*. In this *Discours* it appears over forty times, and as Professor Schinz has shown, in three different senses (*Mercure de France,* June 1912, Vol. XCII, pp. 532-555). If Rousseau did not always practice virtue, he at least always talked about it with a seriousness, which, if not new in France, may at least be said to have become old-fashioned in the age of Voltaire.

avantage, dont nous ne sentons plus le prix, leur épargnait bien des vices.

Aujourd'hui que des recherches plus subtiles et un goût plus fin ont réduit l'art de plaire en principes, il règne dans nos mœurs une vile et trompeuse uniformité, et tous les esprits semblent avoir été jetés dans un même moule : sans cesse la politesse exige, la bienséance ordonne ; sans cesse on suit des usages, jamais son propre génie. On n'ose plus paraître ce qu'on est ; et, dans cette contrainte perpétuelle, les hommes qui forment ce troupeau qu'on appelle société, placés dans les mêmes circonstances, feront tous les mêmes choses si des motifs plus puissants ne les en détournent. On ne saura donc jamais bien à qui l'on a affaire : il faudra donc, pour connaître son ami, attendre les grandes occasions, c'est-à-dire attendre qu'il n'en soit plus temps, puisque c'est pour ces occasions mêmes qu'il eût été essentiel de le connaître.

Quel cortège de vices n'accompagnera point cette incertitude ! Plus d'amitiés sincères ; plus d'estime réelle ; plus de confiance fondée. Les soupçons, les ombrages, les craintes, la froideur, la réserve, la haine, la trahison, se cacheront sans cesse sous ce voile uniforme et perfide de politesse, sous cette urbanité si vantée que nous devons aux lumières de notre siècle. On ne profanera plus par des jurements le nom du maître de l'univers ; mais on l'insultera par des blasphèmes, sans que nos oreilles scrupuleuses en soient offensées. On ne vantera pas son propre mérite, mais on rabaissera celui d'autrui. On n'outragera point grossièrement son ennemi, mais on le calomniera avec adresse. Les haines nationales s'éteindront, mais ce sera avec l'amour de la patrie. A l'ignorance méprisée on substituera un dangereux pyrrhonisme. Il y aura des excès proscrits, des vices déshonorés; mais d'autres seront décorés du nom de vertus; il faudra ou les avoir ou les affecter. Vantera qui voudra la sobriété des sages du temps; je n'y vois, pour moi, qu'un raffinement d'intempérance autant indigne de mon éloge que leur artificieuse simplicité.[b]

Telle est la pureté que nos mœurs out acquise; c'est ainsi que nous sommes devenus gens de bien. C'est aux lettres, aux sciences et aux arts, à revendiquer ce qui leur appartient dans un si salutaire ouvrage. J'ajouterai seulement une réflexion, c'est qu'un habitant de quelques contrées éloignées qui chercherait à se former une idée des mœurs européennes sur l'état des sciences parmi nous, sur la perfection de nos arts, sur la bienséance de nos spectables, sur la politesse de nos manières, sur l'affabilité de nos discours, sur nos démonstrations perpétuelles de bienveillance, et sur ce concours tumultueux d'hommes de tout âge et de tout état qui semblent empressés depuis le lever de l'aurore jusqu'au coucher du soleil à s'obliger réciproquement; c'est que cet étranger, dis-je, devinerait exactement de nos mœurs le contraire de ce qu'elles sont.

[b] "J'aime, dit Montaigne, à contester et à discourir, mais c'est avecques peu d'hommes, et pour moy. Car de servir de spectacle aux grands, et faire à l'envy parade de son esprit et de son caquet, je treuve que c'est un mestier tresmesséant à un homme d'honneur." (Liv. III, chap. viii.) C'est celui de tous nos beaux esprits, hors un.*

* On pense que cette exception unique ne peut regarder que Diderot.

Où il n'y a nul effet, il n'y a point de cause à chercher: mais ici l'effet est certain, la dépravation réelle; et nos âmes se sont corrompues à mesure que nos sciences et nos arts se sont avancés à la perfection. Dira-t-on que c'est un malheur particulier à notre âge? Non, messieurs; les maux causés par notre vaine curiosité sont aussi vieux que le monde. L'élévation et l'abaissement journaliers des eaux de l'Océan n'ont pas été plus régulièrement assujettis au cours de l'astre qui nous éclaire durant la nuit, que le sort des mœurs et de la probité au progrès des sciences et des arts. On a vu la vertu s'enfuir à mesure que leur lumière s'élevait sur notre horizon, et le même phénomène s'est observé dans tous les temps et dans tous les lieux.

Voyez l'Égypte, cette première école de l'univers, ce climat si fertile sous un ciel d'airain, cette contrée célèbre d'où Sésostris partit autrefois pour conquérir le monde. Elle devient la mère de la philosophie et des beaux-arts, et, bientôt après, la conquête de Cambyse, puis celle des Grecs, des Romains, des Arabes, et enfin des Turcs.[8]

Voyez la Grèce, jadis peuplée de héros qui vainquirent deux fois l'Asie, l'une devant Troie, et l'autre dans leurs propres foyers. Les lettres naissantes n'avaient point porté encore la corruption dans les cœurs de ses habitants; mais le progrès des arts, la dissolution des mœurs, et le joug du Macédonien, se suivirent de près; et la Grèce, toujours savante, toujours voluptueuse, et

[8] The weakness of Rousseau's historical argument need hardly be dwelt upon. For Rousseau, as for many of his contemporaries, history was too often a repository of "horrible examples." Even his isolated cases here contradict one another.

toujours esclave, n'éprouva plus dans ses révolutions que des changements de maîtres. Toute l'éloquence de Démosthène ne put jamais ranimer un corps que le luxe et les arts avaient énervé.

C'est au temps des Ennius et des Térence que Rome, fondée par un pâtre et illustrée par des laboureurs, commence à dégénérer. Mais après les Ovide, les Catulle, les Martial, et cette foule d'auteurs obscènes dont les noms seuls alarment la pudeur, Rome, jadis le temple de la vertu, devient le théâtre du crime, l'opprobre des nations, et le jouet des barbares. Cette capitale du monde tombe enfin sous le joug qu'elle avait imposé à tant de peuples, et le jour de sa chute fut la veille de celui où l'on donna à l'un de ses citoyens le titre d'arbitre du bon goût![8a]

Que dirai-je de cette métropole de l'empire d'Orient, qui par sa position semblait devoir l'être du monde entier, de cet asile des sciences et des arts proscrits du reste de l'Europe, plus peut-être par sagesse que par barbarie? Tout ce que la débauche et la corruption ont de plus honteux; les trahisons, les assassinats et les poisons de plus noir; le concours de tous les crimes de plus atroce: voilà ce qui forme le tissu de l'histoire de Constantinople; voilà la source pure d'où nous sont émanées les lumières dont notre siècle se glorifie.

Mais pourquoi chercher dans des temps reculés des preuves d'une vérité dont nous avons sous nos yeux des témoignages subsistants? Il est en Asie une contrée immense où les lettres honorées conduisent aux

[8a] This title, *arbiter elegantiarum,* was bestowed upon Petronius in the reign of Nero.

Chine

premières dignités de l'État. Si les sciences épuraient les mœurs, si elles apprenaient aux hommes à verser leur sang pour la patrie, si elles animaient le courage, les peuples de la Chine devraient être sages, libres et 5 invincibles. Mais s'il n'y a point de vice qui ne les domine, point de crime qui ne leur soit familier; si les lumières des ministres, ni la prétendue sagesse des lois, ni la multitude des habitants de ce vaste empire, n'ont pu le garantir du joug du Tartare ignorant et grossier; 10 de quoi lui ont servi tous ses savants? Quel fruit a-t-il retiré des honneurs dont ils sont comblés? serait-ce d'être peuplé d'esclaves et de méchants?

Perses

Scythes

Germains

Opposons à ces tableaux celui des mœurs du petit nombre de peuples qui, préserves de cette contagion des 15 vaines connaissances, ont par leurs vertus fait leur propre bonheur et l'exemple des autres nations. Tels furent les premiers Perses: nation singulière, chez laquelle on apprenait la vertu comme chez nous on apprend la science; qui subjugua l'Asie avec tant de 20 facilité, et qui seule a eu cette gloire, que l'histoire de ses institutions ait passé pour un roman de philosophie. Tels furent les Scythes, dont on nous a laissé de si magnifiques éloges. Tels les Germains, dont une plume,[9] lasse de tracer les crimes et les noirceurs d'un 25 peuple instruit, opulent et voluptueux, se soulageait à peindre la simplicité, l'innocence et les vertus. Telle avait été Rome même, dans les temps de sa pauvreté et de son ignorance. Telle enfin s'est montrée jusqu'à

[9] It is hardly necessary to say that in the light of modern scholarship the motives of Tacitus were possibly not those here given by Rousseau. Political passion and prejudice seem to have had their part in coloring his famous narrative.

nos jours cette nation rustique si vantée pour son courage que l'adversité n'a pu abattre, et pour sa fidélité que l'exemple n'a pu corrompre.[c]

Ce n'est point par stupidité que ceux-ci ont préféré d'autres exercices à ceux de l'esprit. Ils n'ignoraient 5 pas que dans d'autres contrées des hommes oisifs passaient leur vie à disputer sur le souverain bien, sur le vice et sur la vertu, et que d'orgueilleux raisonneurs, se donnant à eux-mêmes les plus grands éloges, confondaient les autres peuples sous le nom méprisant de 10 barbares;[10] mais ils ont considéré leurs mœurs et appris à dédaigner leur doctrine.[d]

[c] Je n'ose parler de ces nations heureuses qui ne connaissent pas même de nom les vices que nous avons tant de peine à réprimer; de ces sauvages de l'Amérique dont Montaigne ne balance point à préférer la simple et naturelle police, non seulement aux lois de Platon, mais même à tout ce que la philosophie pourra jamais imaginer de plus parfait pour le gouvernement des peuples. Il en cite quantité d'exemples frappants pour qui les saurait admirer: "Mais quoy! dit-il, ils ne portent point de hault-de-chausses." (Liv. I, chap. xxx.)

[10] On Rousseau's fondness for the *barbare* and glorification of the primitive life, see more particularly the *Discours sur l'origine de l'inégalité* and Morel's study on the sources of this discourse, *Annales J.-J. Rousseau*, Vol. V, pp. 119-198.

[d] De bonne foi, qu'on me dise quelle opinion les Athéniens mêmes devaient avoir de l'éloquence, quand ils l'écartèrent avec tant de soin de ce tribunal intègre des jugements duquel les dieux mêmes n'appelaient pas. Que pensaient les Romains de la médecine, quand ils la bannirent de leur république? Et quand un reste d'humanité porta les Espagnols à interdire à leurs gens de loi l'entrée de l'Amérique, quelle idée fallait-il qu'ils eussent de la jurisprudence? Ne dirait-on pas qu'ils ont cru réparer par ce seul acte tous les maux qu'ils avaient faits à ces malheureux Indiens*?

* Le roy Ferdinand, envoyant des colonies aux Indes, pour-

Oublierais-je que ce fut dans le sein même de la Grèce qu'on vit s'élever cette cité aussi célèbre par son heureuse ignorance que par la sagesse de ses lois, cette république de demi-dieux plutôt que d'hommes, tant leurs vertus semblaient supérieures à l'humanité? O Sparte, opprobre éternel d'une vaine doctrine! tandis que les vices conduits par les beaux-arts s'introduisaient ensemble dans Athènes, tandis qu'un tyran[11] y rassemblait avec tant de soin les ouvrages du prince des poëtes, tu chassais de tes murs les arts et les artistes, les sciences et les savants!

L'événement marqua cette différence. Athènes devint le séjour de la politesse et du bon goût, le pays des orateurs et des philosophes: l'élégance des bâtiments y répondait à celle du langage: on y voyait de toutes parts le marbre et la toile animés par les mains des maîtres les plus habiles. C'est d'Athènes que sont sortis ces ouvrages surprenants qui serviront de modèles dans tous les âges corrompus. Le tableau de Lacédémone est moins brillant. Là, disaient les autres peuples, les hommes naissent vertueux, et l'air même du pays semble inspirer la vertu. Il ne nous reste de ses habitants que la mémoire de leurs actions héroïques. De tels monuments vaudraient-ils moins pour nous que les marbres curieux qu'Athènes nous a laissés?

veut sagement qu'on n'y menast aulcuns escoliers de la iurisprudence . . .iugeant avecques Platon *que c'est une mauvaise provision de pais, que iurisconsultes et médecins.*" (Montaigne, liv. III, chap. xiii.)

[11] Peisistratus (605?-527 B.C.), tyrant of Athens. According to a tradition universally accepted in Rousseau's day, he first collected the poems of Homer. This tradition arose so late, however, that many modern scholars are inclined to doubt it.

Quelques sages, il est vrai, ont résisté au torrent général, et se sont garantis du vice dans le séjour des Muses. Mais qu'on écoute le jugement que le premier et le plus malheureux d'entre eux portait des savants et des artistes de son temps.

"J'ai examiné, dit-il, les poètes, et je les regarde comme des gens dont le talent en impose à eux-mêmes et aux autres, qui se donnent pour sages, qu'on prend pour tels, et qui ne sont rien moins.

"Des poètes, continue Socrate, j'ai passé aux artistes. Personne n'ignorait plus les arts que moi; personne n'était plus convaincu que les artistes possédaient de fort beaux secrets. Cependant je me suis aperçu que leur condition n'est pas meilleure que celle des poètes, et qu'ils sont, les uns et les autres, dans le même préjugé. Parce que les plus habiles d'entre eux excellent dans leur partie, ils se regardent comme les plus sages des hommes. Cette présomption a terni tout à fait leur savoir à mes yeux: de sorte que, me mettant à la place de l'oracle, et me demandant ce que j'aimerais le mieux être, ce que je suis ou ce qu'ils sont, savoir ce qu'ils ont appris ou savoir que je ne sais rien, j'ai répondu à moi-même et au dieu: "Je veux rester ce que je suis."

"Nous ne savons, ni les sophistes, ni les poètes, ni les orateurs, ni les artistes, ni moi, ce que c'est que le vrai, le bon et le beau. Mais il y a entre nous cette différence, que, quoique ces gens ne sachent rien, tous croient savoir quelque chose: au lieu que moi si je ne sais rien, au moins je n'en suis pas en doute. De sorte que toute cette supériorité de sagesse qui m'est accordée par l'oracle se réduit seulement à être bien convaincu que j'ignore ce que je ne sais pas."[12]

Voilà donc le plus sage des hommes au jugement des dieux, et le plus savant des Athéniens au sentiment 5 de la Grèce entière, Socrate, faisant l'éloge de l'ignorance! Croit-on que, s'il ressuscitait parmi nous, nos savants et nos artistes lui feraient changer d'avis? Non, messieurs: cet homme juste continuerait de mépriser nos vaines sciences; il n'aiderait point à grossir 10 cette foule de livres dont on nous inonde de toutes parts, et ne laisserait, comme il a fait, pour tout précepte à ses disciples et à nos neveux, que l'exemple et la mémoire de sa vertu. C'est ainsi qu'il est beau d'instruire les hommes.

15 Socrate avait commencé dans Athènes, le vieux Caton continua dans Rome, de se déchaîner contre ces Grecs artificieux et subtils qui séduisaient la vertu et amollissaient le courage de ses concitoyens. Mais les sciences, les arts et la dialectique prévalurent encore: 20 Rome se remplit de philosophes et d'orateurs; on négligea la discipline militaire, on méprisa l'agriculture, on embrassa des sectes, et l'on oublia la patrie. Aux noms sacrés de liberté, de désintéressement, d'obéissance aux lois, succédèrent les noms d'Épicure, de Zénon, d'Arcé- 25 silas.[13] *Depuis que les savants ont commencé à paraî-*

[12] The passage is a synopsis of a portion of Plato's *Apology* (cf. Jowett's translation, 1875, Vol. I, pp. 352-355). Rousseau frequently drew on Plato whom he seems to have read in a Latin version. He cites him in Latin in the *Lettre à d'Alembert*. The reference at the opening of the *Seconde Partie* is likewise to Plato.

[13] Arcesilas (316-241 B.C.) like Zeno and Epicurus, a Greek

tre parmi nous, disaient leurs propres philosophes, *les gens de bien se sont éclipsés.*[14] Jusqu'alors les Romains s'étaient contentés de pratiquer la vertu; tout fut perdu quand ils commencèrent à l'étudier.

O Fabricius![15] qu'eût pensé votre grande âme, si, 5 pour votre malheur, rappelé à la vie, vous eussiez vu la face pompeuse de cette Rome sauvée par votre bras, et que votre nom respectable avait plus illustrée que toutes ses conquêtes? "Dieux! eussiez-vous dit, que sont devenus ces toits de chaume et ces foyers rustiques 10 qu'habitaient jadis la modération et la vertu? Quelle splendeur funeste a succédé à la simplicité romaine? quel est ce langage étranger? quelles sont ces mœurs efféminées? que signifient ces statues, ces tableaux, ces édifices? Insensés, qu'avez-vous fait? Vous, les 15 maîtres des nations, vous vous êtes rendus les esclaves des hommes frivoles que vous avez vaincus! Ce sont des rhéteurs qui vous gouvernent! C'est pour enrichir des architectes, des peintres, des statuaires et des histrions, que vous avez arrosé de votre sang la Grèce et 20

philosopher and one of somewhat similar tendencies. We know him only from the writings of others. He held that because of the uncertainty of sensible data man must be content with probability; Diogenes Laertius says that he died of drink, but this is most probably a slander like those on Epicurus.

[14] This phrase, rendered famous by Rousseau is taken from Seneca, "Postquam docti prodierunt, boni desunt." Like many another of his classical allusions, it probably came to him via Montaigne (cf. *Essais,* Bk. I, Chap. XXIV).

[15] The Roman general of the third century B.C. model of simplicity and incorruptible integrity. This is the portion of the discourse which Rousseau wrote in his first "illumination" on the road to Vincennes.

l'Asie! Les dépouilles de Carthage sont la proie d'un joueur de flûte! Romains, hâtez-vous de renverser ces amphithéâtres; brisez ces marbres, brûlez ces tableaux, chassez ces esclaves qui vous subjuguent, et dont
5 les funestes arts vous corrompent. Que d'autres mains s'illustrent par de vains talents; le seul talent digne de Rome est celui de conquérir le monde, et d'y faire régner la vertu. Quand Cynéas[16] prit notre sénat pour une assemblée de rois, il ne fut ébloui ni par une pompe
10 vaine, ni par une élégance recherchée; il n'y entendit point cette éloquence frivole, l'étude et le charme des hommes futiles. Que vit donc Cynéas de si majestueux? O citoyens! il vit un spectacle que ne donneront jamais vos richesses ni tous vos arts, le plus
15 beau spectacle qui ait jamais paru sous le ciel: l'assemblée de deux cents hommes vertueux, dignes de commander à Rome, et de gouverner la terre."

Mais franchissons la distance des lieux et des temps, et voyons ce qui s'est passé dans nos contrées et sous
20 nos yeux; ou plutôt, écartons des peintures odieuses qui blesseraient notre délicatesse, et épargnons-nous la peine de répéter les mêmes choses sous d'autres noms. Ce n'est point en vain que j'évoquais les mânes de Fabricius; et qu'ai-je fait dire à ce grand homme,
25 que je n'eusse pu mettre dans la bouche de Louis XII ou de Henri IV? Parmi nous, il est vrai, Socrate n'eût point bu la ciguë; mais il eût bu dans une coupe encore plus amère la raillerie insultante, et le mépris pire cent fois que la mort.

[16] Cineas, physician and friend of Pyrrhus, an ambassador who came to Rome in the time of Fabricius. The incident is taken from Plutarch's *Life of Pyrrhus,* 14-22.

Voilà comment le luxe, la dissolution et l'esclavage ont été de tout temps le châtiment des efforts orgueilleux que nous avons faits pour sortir de l'heureuse ignorance où la sagesse éternelle nous avait placés. Le voile épais dont elle a couvert toutes ses opérations 5 semblait nous avertir assez qu'elle ne nous a point destinés à de vaines recherches. Mais est-il quelqu'une de ses leçons dont nous ayons su profiter, ou que nous ayons négligée impunément? Peuples, sachez donc une fois que la nature a voulu vous préserver de la 10 science, comme une mère arrache une arme dangereuse des mains de son enfant; que tous les secrets qu'elle vous cache sont autant de maux dont elle vous garantit, et que la peine que vous trouvez à vous instruire n'est pas le moindre de ses bienfaits. Les hommes sont 15 pervers; ils seraient pires encore, s'ils avaient eu le malheur de naître savants.

Que ces réflexions sont humiliantes pour l'humanité! que notre orgueil en doit être mortifié! Quoi! la probité serait fille de l'ignorance? la science et la vertu 20 seraient incompatibles? Quelles conséquences ne tirerait-on point de ces préjugés? Mais, pour concilier ces contrariétés apparentes, il ne faut qu'examiner de près la vanité et le néant de ces titres orgueilleux qui nous éblouissent, et que nous donnons si gratuitement 25 aux connaissances humaines. Considérons donc les sciences et les arts en eux-mêmes. Voyons ce qui doit résulter de leur progrès: et ne balançons plus à convenir de tous les points où nos raisonnements se trouveront d'accord avec les inductions historiques. 30

SECONDE PARTIE

C'était une ancienne tradition passée de l'Égypte en Grèce, qu'un dieu ennemi du repos des hommes était l'inventeur des sciences.[e] Quelle opinion fallait-il donc
5 qu'eussent d'elles les Égyptiens mêmes, chez qui elles étaient nées. C'est qu'ils voyaient de près les sources qui les avaient produites. En effet, soit qu'on feuillette les annales du monde, soit qu'on supplée à des chroniques incertaines par des recherches philosophiques,[17]
10 on ne trouvera pas aux connaissances humaines une origine qui réponde à l'idée qu'on aime à s'en former. L'astronomie est née de la superstition; l'éloquence, de l'ambition, de la haine, de la flatterie, du mensonge; la géométrie, de l'avarice; la physique, d'une vaine curi-
15 osité; toutes, et la morale même, de l'orgueil humain. Les sciences et les arts doivent donc leur naissance à nos vices; nous serions moins en doute sur leurs avantages, s'ils la devaient à nos vertus.

Le défaut de leur origine ne nous est que trop re-
20 tracé dans leurs objets. Que ferions-nous des arts,

[e] On voit aisément l'allégorie de la fable de Prométhée, et il ne paraît pas que les Grecs, qui l'ont cloué sur le Caucase, en pensassent guère plus favorablement que les Égyptiens de leur dieu Teuthus. Le satyre, dit une ancienne fable, voulut baiser et embrasser le feu, la première fois qu'il le vit; mais Prométhée lui cria: "Satyre, tu pleureras la barbe de ton menton, car il brûle quand on y touche."

[17] In the eighteenth century historical studies may be said to have been in their infancy. To supplement history by *recherches philosophiques* was a favorite and often unfortunate tendency which resulted in forcing the facts and building up magnificently logical structures on insufficient data; this is perhaps the commonest vice of eighteenth century thinking.

sans le luxe qui les nourrit? Sans les injustices des hommes, à quoi servirait la jurisprudence? Que deviendrait l'histoire, s'il n'y avait ni tyrans, ni guerres, ni conspirateurs? Qui voudrait, en un mot, passer sa vie à de stériles contemplations, si chacun, ne consultant que les devoirs de l'homme et les besoins de la nature, n'avait de temps que pour la patrie, pour les malheureux, et pour ses amis? Sommes-nous donc faits pour mourir attachés sur les bords du puits où la vérité s'est retirée? Cette seule réflexion devrait rebuter dès les premiers pas tout homme qui chercherait sérieusement à s'instruire par l'étude de la philosophie.

Que de dangers, que de fausses routes dans l'investigation des sciences! Par combien d'erreurs, mille fois plus dangereuses que la vérité n'est utile, ne faut-il point passer pour arriver à elle! Le désavantage est visible: car le faux est susceptible d'une infinité de combinaisons: mais la vérité n'a qu'une manière d'être. Qui est-ce d'ailleurs qui la cherche bien sincèrement? Même avec la meilleure volonté, à quelles marques eston sûr de la reconnaître? Dans cette foule de sentiments différents, quel sera notre *criterium* pour en bien juger?[1] Et, ce qui est le plus difficile, si par bonheur nous le trouvons à la fin, qui de nous en saura faire un bon usage?

Si nos sciences sont vaines dans l'objet qu'elles se

[1] Moins on sait, plus on croit savoir. Les péripatéticiens doutaient-ils de rien? Descartes n'a-t-il pas construit l'univers avec des cubes et des tourbillons? Et y a-t-il aujourd'hui même en Europe si mince physicien qui n'explique hardiment ce profond mystère de l'électricité qui fera peut-être à jamais le désespoir des vrais philosophes?

proposent, elles sont encore plus dangereuses par les effets qu'elles produisent. Nées dans l'oisiveté, elles la nourrissent à leur tour; et la perte irréparable du temps est le premier préjudice qu'elles causent néces-
5 sairement à la société. En politique comme en morale, c'est un grand mal que de ne point faire de bien; et tout citoyen inutile peut être regardé comme un homme pernicieux. Répondez-moi donc, philosophes illustres,[18] vous par qui nous savons en quelles raisons les
10 corps s'attirent dans le vide; quels sont, dans les révolutions des planètes, les rapports des aires parcourues en temps égaux; quelles courbes ont des points conjugués, des points d'inflexion et de rebroussement: comment l'homme voit tout en Dieu; comment l'âme
15 et le corps se correspondent sans communication, ainsi que feraient deux horloges; quels astres peuvent être habités; quels insectes se reproduisent d'une manière

[18] The eighteenth century was very generally and very keenly interested in the mathematical and later in the natural sciences. Lectures with experiments in physics and chemistry by "natural philosophers" were immensely popular. (Cf. Mornet, *Les Sciences de la Nature en France au XVIIIe siècle*, 1911.) Rousseau had attended the courses of the elder Rouelle, who is counted as one of the founders of chemistry. He had as classmates Diderot, and possibly Lavoisier. He himself had written a treatise on this subject. The first part of the passage refers to definite discoveries, the second to more general problems of his time. It may be translated as follows: "Tell me then, illustrious philosophers, you through whom we know according to what law bodies attract one another in empty space (Newton's Law of Gravitation): what are, in the revolutions of the planets, the ratios of the areas described in equal times (Kepler's Second Law); what curves possess conjugate points, points of inflexion, and cusps (Theory of Singular Points of Curves)."

extraordinaire: répondez-moi, dis-je, vous de qui nous avons reçu tant de sublimes connaissances: quand vous ne nous auriez jamais rien appris de ces choses, en serions nous moins nombreux, moins bien gouvernés, moins redoutables, moins florissants, ou plus pervers? 5
Revenez donc sur l'importance de vos productions; et si les travaux des plus éclairés de nos savants et de nos meilleurs citoyens nous procurent si peu d'utilité, dites-nous ce que nous devons penser de cette foule d'écrivains obscurs et de lettrés oisifs qui dévorent en pure 10
perte la substance de l'État.

Que dis-je, oisifs? et plût à Dieu qu'ils le fussent en effet! Les mœurs en seraient plus saines et la société plus paisible. Mais ces vains et futiles déclamateurs vont de tous côtés, armés de leurs funestes paradoxes, 15
sapant les fondements de la foi, et anéantissant la vertu. Ils sourient dédaigneusement à ces vieux mots de patrie et de religion, et consacrent leurs talents et leur philosophie à détruire et avilir tout ce qu'il y a de sacré parmi les hommes. Non qu'au fond ils haïs- 20
sent ni la vertu ni nos dogmes; c'est de l'opinion publique qu'ils sont ennemis; et, pour les ramener au pied des autels, il suffirait de les reléguer parmi les athées. O fureur de se distinguer, que ne pouvez-vous point!

C'est un grand mal que l'abus du temps. D'autres 25
maux pires encore suivent les lettres et les arts. Tel est le luxe, né comme eux de l'oisiveté et de la vanité des hommes. Le luxe va rarement sans les sciences et les arts, et jamais ils ne vont sans lui. Je sais que notre philosophie, toujours féconde en maximes sin- 30
gulières, prétend, contre l'expérience de tous les siècles,

que le luxe fait la splendeur des États: mais, après avoir oublié la nécessité des lois somptuaires,[19] osera-t-elle nier encore que les bonnes mœurs ne soient essentielles à la durée des empires, et que le
5 luxe ne soit diamétralement opposé aux bonnes mœurs? Que le luxe soit un signe certain des richesses: qu'il serve même si l'on veut à les multiplier: que faudra-t-il conclure de ce paradoxe si digne d'être né de nos jours? et que deviendra la vertu, quand il faudra
10 s'enrichir à quelque prix que ce soit? Les anciens politiques parlaient sans cesse de mœurs et de vertu; les nôtres ne parlent que de commerce et d'argent.[20] L'un vous dira qu'un homme vaut en telle contrée la somme qu'on le vendrait à Alger; un autre, en suivant
15 ce calcul, trouvera des pays où un homme ne vaut rien, et d'autres où il vaut moins que rien. Ils évaluent les hommes comme des troupeaux de bétail. Selon eux, un homme ne vaut à l'État que la consommation qu'il y fait; ainsi un Sybarite[20a] aurait bien valu trente
20 Lacédémoniens. Qu'on devine donc laquelle de ces deux républiques, de Sparte ou de Sybaris, fut subju-

[19] Sumptuary laws were laws designed to curb excessive expenditure and luxurious living on the part of citizens. Some of the most famous were those established at Rome by Augustus. Montesquieu favored something of the sort as did Rousseau in his *Discours sur l'économie politique.* He was consistently opposed to luxurious living.

[20] The modern science of economics arose in the eighteenth century, at that time it was far from "dismal" and speculations on this subject were dazzlingly attractive.

[20a] Sybarite, one of the inhabitants of ancient Sybaris, a Greek city of southern Italy, noted for its love of luxury and pleasure; hence a person devoted to ease and luxury.

guée par une poignée de paysans, et laquelle fit trembler l'Asie.

La monarchie de Cyrus a été conquise avec trente mille hommes par un prince plus pauvre que le moindre des satrapes de Perse; et les Scythes, le plus misérable de tous les peuples, ont résisté aux plus puissants monarques de l'univers. Deux fameuses républiques se disputèrent l'empire du monde; l'une était très riche, l'autre n'avait rien, et ce fut celle-ci qui détruisit l'autre. L'empire romain, à son tour, après avoir englouti toutes les richesses de l'univers, fut la proie des gens qui ne savaient pas même ce que c'était que richesse. Les Francs conquirent les Gaules, les Saxons l'Angleterre, sans autres trésors que leur bravoure et leur pauvreté. Une troupe de pauvres montagnards[20b] dont toute l'avidité se bornait à quelques peaux de moutons, après avoir dompté la fierté autrichienne, écrasa cette opulente et redoutable maison de Bourgogne qui faisait trembler les potentats de l'Europe. Enfin toute la puissance et toute la sagesse de l'héritier de Charles-Quint, soutenues de tous les trésors des Indes, vinrent se briser contre une poignée de pêcheurs de harengs.[20c] Que nos politiques daignent suspendre leurs calculs pour réfléchir à ces exemples, et qu'ils apprennent une fois qu'on a de tout avec de l'argent, hormis des mœurs et des citoyens.

De quoi s'agit-il donc précisément dans cette question du luxe? De savoir lequel importe le plus aux empires, d'être brillants et momentanés ou vertueux et

[20b] The Swiss.
[20c] The Dutch.

durables. Je dis brillants, mais de quel éclat? Le goût du faste ne s'associe guère dans les mêmes âmes avec celui de l'honnête. Non, il n'est pas possible que des esprits dégradés par une multitude de soins futils
5 s'élèvent jamais à rien de grand; et, quand ils en auraient la force, le courage leur manquerait.

Tout artiste veut être applaudi. Les éloges de ses contemporains sont la partie la plus précieuse de sa récompense. Que fera-t-il donc pour les obtenir, s'il
10 a le malheur d'être chez un peuple et dans des temps où les savants devenus à la mode ont mis une jeunesse frivole en état de donner le ton; où les hommes ont sacrifié leur goût aux tyrans de leur liberté;[g] où, l'un des sexes n'osant approuver que ce qui est proportion-
15 né à la pusillanimité de l'autre, on laisse tomber des chefs-d'œuvre de poésie dramatique, et des prodiges d'harmonie sont rebutés? Ce qu'il fera, messieurs? Il rabaissera son génie au niveau de son siècle, et aimera mieux composer des ouvrages communs qu'on
20 admire pendant sa vie, que des merveilles qu'on n'ad-

[g] Je suis bien éloigné de penser que cet ascendant des femmes soit un mal en soi. C'est un présent que leur a fait la nature, pour le bonheur du genre humain; mieux dirigé, il pourrait produire autant de bien qu'il fait de mal aujourd'hui. On ne sent point assez quels avantages naîtraient dans la société d'une meilleure éducation donnée à cette moitié du genre humain qui gouverne l'autre. Les hommes seront toujours ce qu'il plaira aux femmes; si vous voulez donc qu'ils deviennent grands et vertueux, apprenez aux femmes ce que c'est que grandeur d'âme et vertu. Les réflexions que ce sujet fournit, et que Platon a faites autrefois, mériteraient fort d'être mieux développés par une plume digne d'écrire d'après un tel maître, et de défendre une si grande cause.

mirerait que longtemps après sa mort. Dites-nous, célèbre Arouet,[21] combien vous avez sacrifié de beautés mâles et fortes à notre fausse délicatesse! et combien l'esprit de la galanterie, si fertile en petites choses, vous en a coûté de grandes! 5

C'est ainsi que la dissolution des mœurs, suite nécessaire du luxe, entraîne à son tour la corruption du goût. Que si par hasard, entre les hommes extraordinaires par leurs talents, il s'en trouve quelqu'un qui ait de la fermeté dans l'âme et qui refuse de se prêter au génie 10 de son siècle et de s'avilir par des productions puériles, malheur à lui! il mourra dans l'indigence et dans l'oubli. Que n'est-ce ici un pronostic que je fais, et non une expérience que je rapporte! Carle, Pierre,[22]

[21] François Arouet de Voltaire (1694-1778). In one of his early poems, *Le Verger des Charmettes* (1739), Rousseau wrote of him,

"touchant Voltaire
Ta lecture à mon cœur restera toujours chère."

It is interesting to contrast this modest admiration with the assurance, let us not say the *forfanterie* of the *Discours.* The acquaintance so pleasantly begun ended in denunciations on both sides.

[22] The editor of the Hachette edition explains this passage as referring to Carle (1705-1765), and Pierre Vanloo. The reference to "Carle" (Charles-André) is undoubted. He was painter to the King in Rousseau's time and handled with equal dexterity subjects sacred and profane. There is however no Pierre Vanloo, to whom Rousseau's reference could be appropriately attributed. Rousseau doubtless had in mind Jean-Baptiste-Marie Pierre (1713-1789), a French painter who likewise had the same range of subject. Religious paintings of his may still be seen in the Paris churches at Saint-Roche, Saint-Sulpice, and Saint-Germain des Près. He was professor at the *Académie des beaux-arts* in 1748 and later (1770) became first painter to the King. Cf. Diderot, *Salons, Œuvres,* Vol. X, pp. 113-175.

le moment est venu où ce pinceau destiné à augmenter la majesté de nos temples par des images sublimes et saintes, tombera de vos mains, ou sera prostitué à orner de peintures lascives les panneaux d'un vis-à-vis. Et toi, rival des Praxitèle et des Phidias; toi, dont les anciens auraient employé le ciseau à leur faire des dieux capables d'excuser à nos yeux leur idolâtrie; inimitable Pigal,[23] ta main se résoudra à ravaler le ventre d'un magot, ou il faudra qu'elle demeure oisive.

On ne peut réfléchir sur les mœurs, qu'on ne se plaise à se rappeler l'image de la simplicité des premiers temps. C'est un beau rivage, paré des seules mains de la nature, vers lequel on tourne incessamment les yeux, et dont on se sent éloigner à regret. Quand les hommes innocents et vertueux aimaient à avoir les dieux pour témoins de leurs actions, ils habitaient ensemble sous les mêmes cabanes, mais, bientôt devenus méchants, ils se lassèrent de ces incommodes spectateurs, et les reléguèrent dans des temples magnifiques. Ils les en chassèrent enfin pour s'y établir eux-mêmes, ou du moins les temples des dieux ne se distinguèrent plus des maisons des citoyens. Ce fut alors le comble de la dépravation, et les vices ne furent jamais poussés plus loin que quand on les vit pour ainsi dire soutenus à l'entrée des palais des grands, sur des colonnes de marbre, et gravés sur des chapiteaux corinthiens.

Tandis que les commodités de la vie se multiplient, que les arts se perfectionnent, et que le luxe s'étend, le vrai courage s'énerve, les vertus militaires s'évanouissent; et c'est encore l'ouvrage des sciences et de

[23] Pigalle (1714-1785), eminent French sculptor.

tous ces arts qui s'exercent dans l'ombre du cabinet. Quand les Goths ravagèrent la Grèce, toutes les bibliothèques ne furent sauvées du feu que par cette opinion semée par l'un d'entre eux, qu'il fallait laisser aux ennemies des meubles si propres à les détourner de 5 l'exercice militaire, et à les amuser à des occupations oisives et sédentaires. Charles VIII se vit maître de la Toscane et du royaume de Naples sans avoir presque tiré l'épée, et toute sa cour attribua cette facilité inespérée à ce que les princes et la noblesse d'Italie s'a- 10 musaient plus à se rendre ingénieux et savants, qu'ils ne s'exerçaient à devenir vigoureux et guerriers. En effet, dit l'homme de sens qui rapporte ces deux traits,[24] tous les exemples nous apprennent qu'en cette martiale police, et en toutes celles qui lui sont semb- 15 lables, l'étude des sciences est bien plus propre à amollir et efféminer les courages, qu'à les affermir et les animer.

Les Romains ont avoué que la vertu militaire s'était éteinte parmi eux à mesure qu'ils avaient commencé à 20 se connaître en tableaux, en gravures, en vases d'orfévrerie, et à cultiver les beaux-arts; et comme si cette contrée fameuse était destinée à servir sans cesse d'exemple aux autres peuples, l'élévation des Médicis et le rétablissement des lettres ont fait tomber derechef, 25 et peut-être pour toujours, cette réputation guerrière que l'Italie semblait avoir recouvrée il y a quelques siècles.

Les anciennes républiques de la Grèce, avec cette sagesse qui brillait dans la plupart de leurs institutions, 30

[24] Montaigne, *Essais,* Bk. I, Chap. XXIV.

avaient interdit à leurs citoyens tous ces métiers tranquilles et sédentaires qui, en affaissant et corrompant le corps, énervent sitôt la vigueur de l'âme. De quel œil, en effet, pense-t-on que puissent envisager la faim, la soif, les fatigues, les dangers et la mort, des hommes que le moindre besoin accable, et que la moindre peine rebute? Avec quelle courage les soldats suppoteront-ils des travaux excessifs dont ils n'ont aucune habitude? Avec quelle ardeur feront-ils des marches forcés sous des officiers qui n'ont pas même la force de voyager à cheval? Qu'on ne m'objecte point la valeur renommée de tous ces modernes guerriers si savamment disciplinés. On me vante bien leur bravoure en un jour de bataille; mais on ne me dit point comment ils supportent l'excès du travail, comment ils résistent à la rigueur des saisons et aux intempéries de l'air. Il ne faut qu'un peu de soleil ou de neige, il ne faut que la privation de quelques superfluités, pour fondre et détruire en peu de jours la meilleure de nos armées. Guerriers intrépides, souffrez une fois la vérité qu'il vous est si rare d'entendre. Vous êtes braves, je le sais; vous eussiez triomphé avec Annibal à Cannes et à Trasymène; César avec vous eût passé le Rubicon et asservi son pays: mais ce n'est point avec vous que le premier eût traversé les Alpes, et que l'autre eût vaincu vos aïeux.

Les combats ne font pas toujours le succès de la guerre, et il est pour les généraux un art supérieur à celui de gagner des batailles. Tel court au feu avec intrépidité, qui ne laisse pas d'être un très mauvais officier: dans le soldat même, un peu plus de force et de vigueur serait peut-être plus nécessaire que tant de bravoure, qui ne le garantit pas de la mort. Et qu'importe à l'État que ses troupes périssent par la fièvre et le froid, ou par le fer de l'ennemi?

Si la culture des sciences est nuisible aux qualités 5 guerrières, elle l'est encore plus aux qualités morales. C'est dès nos premières années qu'une éducation insensée orne notre esprit et corrompt notre jugement. Je vois de toutes parts des établissements immenses, où l'on élève à grands frais la jeunesse pour lui apprendre 10 toutes choses, excepté ses devoirs. Vos enfants ignoreront leur propre langue, mais ils en parleront d'autres qui ne sont en usage nulle part; ils sauront composer des vers qu'à peine ils pourront comprendre; sans savoir démêler l'erreur de la vérité, ils posséderont l'art 15 de les rendre méconnaissables aux autres par des arguments spécieux: mais ces mots de magnanimité, d'équité, de tempérance, d'humanité, de courage, ils ne sauront ce que c'est; ce doux nom de patrie ne frappera jamais leur oreille; et s'ils entendent parler de 20 Dieu, ce sera moins pour le craindre que pour en avoir peur.[h] J'aimerais autant, disait un sage, que mon écolier eût passé le temps dans un jeu de paume, au moins le corps en serait plus dispos. Je sais qu'il faut occuper les enfants, et que l'oisiveté est pour eux le danger 25 le plus à craindre. Que faut-il donc qu'ils apprennent? Voilà certes une belle question? Qu'ils apprennent ce qu'ils doivent faire étant hommes,[1] et non ce qu'ils doivent oublier.

[h] *Pensées phisophiques.* (Cf. *supra* p. 17, Note.)

[1] Telle était l'éducation des Spartiates, au rapport du plus

Nos jardins sont ornés de statues et nos galeries de tableaux. Que penseriez-vous que représentent ces

grand de leurs rois. "C'est, dit Montaigne, chose digne de très-grande considération, qu'en cette excellente police de Lycurgus, et à la vérité monstrueuse par sa perfection si soingneuse pourtant de la nourriture des enfans, comme de sa principale charge, et au giste mesme des muses, il s'y face si peu mention de la doctrine: comme si cette généreuse jeunesse, dédaignant tout aultre joug, on luy ayt deu fournir, au lieu de nos maistres de science, seulement des maistres de vaillance, prudence et justice."

Voyons maintenant comment le même auteur parle des anciens Perses: Platon, di-il, raconte "que le fils aisné de leur succession royale estoit ainsi nourry. Aprez sa naissance, on le donnoit, non à des femmes, mais à des eunuches de la premiere auctorité autour des roys à cause de leur vertu. Ceulx-cy prenoient charge de lui rendre le corps beau et sain, et aprez sept ans, le duisoient à monter à cheval et aller à la chasse. Quand il estoit arrivé au quatorsiesme, ils le déposoient entre les mains de quatre: le plus sage, le plus juste, le plus tempérant, le plus vaillant de la nation. Le premier lui apprenoit la religion; le second, à estre tousiours véritable; le tiers, à se rendre maistre des cupiditez; le quart, à ne rien craindre;" tous, ajouterais-je, à le rendre bon, aucun à le rendre savant.

" Astyages, en Xénophon, demande à Cyrus compte de sa
" dernière leçon: C'est, dict-il, qu'en nostre eschole un grand
" garçon ayant un petit saye le donna à l'un de ses compaignons
" de plus petite taille, et lui osta son saye qui estoit plus grand.
" Nostre précepteur m'ayant faict juge de ce différend, je jugeay
" qu'il falloit laisser les choses en cet estat, et que l'un et l'aultre
" sembloit estre mieulx accommodé en ce poinct. Sur quoy il
" me remontra que j'avois mal faict; car je m'estois arresté à
" considérer la bienséance, et il falloit premierement avoir pour-
" veu à la justice, qui vouloit que nul ne fust forcé en ce qui luy
" appartenoit; et dict qu'il en fut foueté, tout ainsi que nous
" sommes en nos villages pour avoir oublié le premier aoriste
" de ὑπτω. Mon regent me feroit une belle harangue, *in genere*
" *demonstrativo,* avant qu'il me persuadast que son eschole vault
" cette-là." (Liv. I, chap. xxiv.)

chefs-d'œuvre de l'art exposés à l'admiration publique? les défenseurs de la patrie? ou ces hommes plus grands encore qui l'ont enrichie par leurs vertus? Non. Ce sont des images de tous les égarements du cœur et de la raison, tirés soigneusement de l'ancienne mythologie, et présentés de bonne heure à la curiosité de nos enfants; sans doute afin qu'ils aient sous leurs yeux des modèles de mauvaises actions, avant même que de savoir lire.

D'où naissent tous ces abus, si ce n'est de l'inégalité funeste introduite entre les hommes par la distinction des talents et par l'avilissement des vertus? Voilà l'effet le plus évident de toutes nos études, et la plus dangereuse de toutes leurs conséquences. On ne demande plus d'un homme s'il a de la probité, mais s'il a des talents; ni d'un livre s'il est utile, mais s'il est bien écrit. Les récompenses sont prodigués au bel esprit, et la vertu reste sans honneurs. Il y a mille prix pour les beaux discours, aucun pour les belles actions. Qu'on me dise cependant si la gloire attachée au meilleur des discours qui seront couronnés dans cette Académie est comparable au mérite d'en avoir fondé le prix.

Le sage ne court point après la fortune; mais il n'est pas insensible à la gloire; et quand il la voit si mal distribuée, sa vertu, qu'un peu d'émulation aurait animée et rendue avantageuse à la société, tombe en langueur, et s'éteint dans la misère et dans l'oubli. Voilà ce qu'à la longue doit produire partout la préférence des talents agréables sur les talents utiles, et ce que l'expérience n'a que trop confirmé depuis le renouvellement des sciences et des arts. Nous avons des physiciens, des géomètres, des chimistes, des astronomes, des poètes, des musiciens, des peintres: nous n'avons plus de citoyens; ou, s'il nous en reste encore, dispersés dans nos campagnes abandonnées, ils y périssent indigents 5 et méprisés. Tel est l'état où sont réduits, tels sont les sentiments qu'obtiennent de nous, ceux qui nous donnent du pain, et qui donnent du lait à nos enfants.

Je l'avoue cependant, le mal n'est pas aussi grand qu'il aurait pu le devenir. La prévoyance éternelle, 10 en plaçant à côté de diverses plantes nuisibles des simples salutaires, et dans la substance de plusieurs animaux malfaisants le remède à leurs blessures, a enseigné aux souverains, qui sont ses ministres, à imiter sa sagesse. C'est à son exemple que du sein 15 même des sciences et des arts, sources de mille déréglements, ce grand monarque,[25] dont la gloire ne fera qu'acquérir d'âge en âge un nouvel éclat, tira ces sociétés célèbres chargées à la fois du dangereux dépôt des connaissances humaines et du dépôt sacré des mœurs, 20 par l'attention qu'elles ont d'en maintenir chez elles toute la pureté, et de l'exiger dans les membres qu'elles reçoivent.

Ces sages institutions, affermies par son auguste successeur, et imitées par tous les rois de l'Europe, ser- 25 viront du moins de frein aux gens de lettres, qui tous, aspirant à l'honneur d'être admis dans les académies, veilleront sur eux-mêmes, et tâcheront de s'en rendre dignes par des ouvrages utiles et des mœurs irréprochables. Celles de ces compagnies qui pour les

[25] Louis XIV. The French Academy, founded before his day, acquired privileges, and a residence in the King's Palace in his time.

prix dont elles honorent le mérite littéraire feront un choix de sujets propres à ranimer l'amour de la vertu dans les cœurs des citoyens, montreront que cet amour règne parmi elles, et donneront aux peuples ce plaisir si rare et si doux de voir des sociétés savantes se dé- 5 vouer à verser sur le genre humain non seulement des lumières agréables, mais aussi des instructions salutaires.

Qu'on ne m'oppose donc point une objection qui n'est pour moi qu'une nouvelle preuve. Tant de soins 10 ne montrent que trop la nécessité de les prendre, et l'on ne cherche point des remèdes à des maux qui n'existent pas. Pourquoi faut-il que ceux-ci portent encore par leur insuffisance le caractère des remèdes ordinaires? Tant d'établissements faits à l'avantage des savants 15 n'en sont que plus capables d'en imposer sur les objets des sciences, et de tourner les esprits à leur culture. Il semble, aux précautions qu'on prend, qu'on ait trop de laboureurs et qu'on craigne de manquer de philosophes. Je ne veux point hasarder ici une comparaison de 20 l'agriculture et de la philosophie: on ne la supporterait pas. Je demanderai seulement: Qu'est-ce que la philosophie? que contiennent les écrits des philosophes les plus connus? quelles sont les leçons de ces amis de la sagesse? A les entendre, ne les prendrait-on pas pour 25 une troupe de charlatans criant chacun de son côté sur une place publique: Venez à moi, c'est moi seul qui ne trompe point? L'un prétend qu'il n'y a point de corps, et que tout est en représentation; l'autre, qu'il n'y a d'autre substance que la matière, ni d'autre dieu que le 30 monde. Celui-ci avance qu'il n'y a ni vertus, ni vices,

et que le bien et le mal moral sont des chimères; celui-là, que les hommes sont des loups et peuvent se dévorer en sûreté de conscience.[26] O grands philosophes! que ne réservez-vous pour vos amis et pour vos enfants ces
5 leçons profitables? vous en recevriez bientôt le prix, et nous ne craindrions pas de trouver dans les nôtres quelqu'un de vos sectateurs.

Voilà donc les hommes merveilleux à qui l'estime de leurs contemporains a été prodiguée pendant leur vie,
10 et l'immortalité réservée après leur trépas! Voilà les sages maximes que nous avons reçues d'eux et que nous transmettons d'âge en âge à nos descendants! Le paganisme, livré à tous les égarements de la raison humaine, a-t-il laissé à la postérité rien qu'on puisse
15 comparer aux monuments honteux que lui a préparés l'imprimerie, sous le règne de l'Évangile? Les écrits impies des Leucippe et des Diagoras[27] sont péris avec eux; on n'avait point encore inventé l'art d'éterniser les extravagances de l'esprit humain; mais, grâce aux
20 caractères typographiques[J] et à l'usage que nous en

[26] Rousseau is referring to various philosophers; more particularly he seems to have in mind Berkeley, and possibly Locke, the French materialists, Spinoza, and Hobbes, the two latter he mentions below. The form of the argument, the attempt to invalidate philosophy by merely enumerating contradictory systems and showing this *"tintamarre de ceruelles philosophiques"* was taken from Montaigne's *Apologie de Raimond Sebond.*

[27] Leucippus and Diagoras are both mentioned by Montaigne in the *Apologie.* Diagoras (of the fifth century B.C.) was surnamed the Atheist. Leucippus is little known except as founder of the atomic theory of the universe.

[J] A considérer les désordres affreux que l'imprimerie a déjà causés en Europe, à juger de l'avenir par le progrès que le mal fait d'un jour à l'autre, on peut prévoir aisément que les souve-

faisons, les dangereuses rêveries des Hobbes et des Spinosa resteront à jamais. Allez, écrits célèbres dont l'ignorance et la rusticité de nos pères n'auraient point été capables; accompagnez chez nos descendants ces ouvrages plus dangereux encore d'où s'exhale la corruption des mœurs de notre siècle, et portez ensemble aux siècles à venir une histoire fidèle du progrès et des avantages de nos sciences et de nos arts. S'ils vous lisent, vous ne leur laisserez aucune perplexité sur la question que nous agitons aujourd'hui; et, à moins qu'ils ne soient plus insensés que nous, ils lèveront leurs mains au ciel, et diront dans l'amertume de leur cœur: "Dieu tout-puissant, toi qui tiens dans tes mains les esprits, délivre-nous des lumières et des funestes arts de nos pères, et rends-nous l'ignorance, l'innocence et la pauvreté, les seuls biens qui puissent faire notre bonheur et qui soient précieux devant toi."

Mais si le progrès des sciences et des arts n'a rien

rains ne tarderont pas à se donner autant de soins pour bannir cet art terrible de leurs États, qu'ils en ont pris pour l'y introduire. Le sultan Achmet, cédant aux importunités de quelques prétendus gens de goût, avait consenti d'établir une imprimerie à Constantinople; mais à peine la presse fut-elle en train, qu'on fut contraint de la détruire, et d'en jeter les instruments dans un puits. On dit que le calife Omar, consulté sur ce qu'il fallait faire de la bibliothèque d'Alexandrie, répondit en ces termes: "Si les livres de cette bibliothèque contiennent des choses opposées à l'Alcoran, ils sont mauvais, et il faut les brûler; s'ils ne contiennent que la doctrine de l'Alcoran, brûlez-les encore; ils sont superflus." Nos savants ont cité ce raisonnement comme le comble de l'absurdité. Cependant, supposez Grégoire le Grand à la place d'Omar, et l'Évangile à la place de l'Alcoran, la bibliothèque aurait encore été brûlée, et ce serait peut-être le plus beau trait de la vie de cet illustre pontife.

ajouté à notre véritable félicité; s'il a corrompu nos mœurs, et si la corruption des mœurs a porté atteinte à la pureté du goût, que penserons-nous de cette foule d'auteurs élémentaires qui ont écarté du temple des
5 Muses les difficultés qui défendaient son abord, et que la nature y avait répandues comme une épreuve des forces de ceux qui seraient tentés de savoir? Que penserons-nous de ces compilateurs d'ouvrages qui ont indiscrètement brisé la porte des sciences et introduit
10 dans leur sanctuaire une populace indigne d'en approcher, tandis qu'il serait à souhaiter que tous ceux qui ne pouvaient avancer loin dans la carrière des lettres eussent été rebutés dès l'entrée, et se fussent jetés dans des arts utiles à la société?[28] tel qui sera toute sa
15 vie un mauvais versificateur, un géomètre subalterne, serait peut-être devenu un grand fabricateur d'étoffes. Il n'a point fallu de maîtres à ceux que la nature destinait à faire des disciples. Les Verulam,[29] les Descartes et les Newton, ces précepteurs du genre humain,
20 n'en ont point eu eux-mêmes; et quels guides les eussent conduits jusqu'où leur vaste génie les a portés? Des maîtres ordinaires n'auraient pu que rétrécir leur entendement en le resserrant dans l'étroite capacité du leur. C'est par les premiers obstacles qu'ils ont appris

[28] The idea in this and the following sentence is again Montaigne's. *"C'est pourquoy on voit tant d'ineptes ames entre les sçavantes, et plus d'autres: il s'en fust faict des bons hommes de mesnage, bons marchans, bons artisans."*

[29] Francis Bacon, Lord Verulam, was especially admired by Diderot. Diderot was inclined to look back to him, rather than to Descartes as the founder of modern science and philosophy. Cf. Diderot, *Œuvres* (1875-7) Vol. XIII, pp. 133-4.

à faire des efforts, et qu'ils se sont exercés à franchir l'espace immense qu'ils ont parcouru. S'il faut permettre à quelques hommes de se livrer à l'étude des sciences et des arts, ce n'est qu'à ceux qui se sentiront la force de marcher seuls sur leurs traces, et de les devancer; c'est à ce petit nombre qu'il appartient d'élever des monuments à la gloire de l'esprit humain. Mais si l'on veut que rien ne soit au-dessus de leur génie, il faut que rien ne soit au-dessus de leurs espérances; voilà l'unique encouragement dont ils ont besoin. L'âme se proportionne insensiblement aux objets qui l'occupent, et ce sont les grandes occasions qui font les grands hommes. Le prince de l'éloquence fut consul de Rome, et le plus grand peut-être des philosophes, chancelier d'Angleterre. Croit-on que si l'un n'eût occupé qu'une chaire dans quelque université, et que l'autre n'eût obtenu qu'une modique pension d'Académie; croit-on, dis-je, que leurs ouvrages ne se sentiraient pas de leur état? Que les rois ne dédaignent donc pas d'admettre dans leurs conseils les gens les plus capables de les bien conseiller; qu'ils renoncent à ce vieux préjugé inventé par l'orgueil des grands, que l'art de conduire les peuples est plus difficile que celui de les éclairer; comme s'il était plus aisé d'engager les hommes à bien faire de leur bon gré, que de les y contraindre par la force: que les savants du premier ordre trouvent dans leurs cours d'honorables asiles; qu'ils y obtiennent la seule récompense digne d'eux, celle de contribuer par leur crédit au bonheur des peuples à qui ils auront enseigné la sagesse: c'est alors seulement qu'on verra ce que peuvent la vertu, la science et l'autorité animées d'une noble émulation, et travaillant de concert à la félicité du genre humain. Mais tant que la puissance sera seule d'un côté, les lumières et la sagesse seules d'un autre, les savants penseront rarement de grandes choses, les princes en feront plus rarement de belles, et les peuples continueront d'être vils, corrompus et malheureux.

Pour nous, hommes vulgaires, à qui le ciel n'a point départi de si grands talents et qu'il ne destine pas à tant de gloire, restons dans notre obscurité. Ne courons point après une réputation qui nous échapperait, et qui dans l'état présent des choses, ne nous rendrait jamais ce qu'elle nous aurait coûté, quand nous aurions tous les titres pour l'obtenir. A quoi bon chercher notre bonheur dans l'opinion d'autrui, si nous pouvons le trouver en nous-mêmes? Laissons à d'autres le soin d'instruire les peuples de leurs devoirs, et bornons-nous à bien remplir les nôtres; nous n'avons pas besoin d'en savoir davantage.

O vertu! science sublime des âmes simples, faut-il donc tant de peines et d'appareil pour te connaître? Tes principes ne sont-ils pas gravés dans tous les cœurs? et ne suffit-il pas pour apprendre tes lois de rentrer en soi-même et d'écouter la voix de sa conscience dans le silence des passions? Voilà la véritable philosophie, sachons nous en contenter; et, sans envier la gloire de ces hommes célèbres qui s'immortalisent dans la république des lettres, tâchons de mettre entre eux et nous cette distinction glorieuse qu'on remarquait jadis entre deux grands peuples; que l'un savait bien dire, et l'autre bien faire.

DISCOURS SUR L'ORIGINE ET LES FONDEMENTS DE L'INEGALITE PARMI LES HOMMES

The *Discours sur l'Origine de l'inégalité* was written for the prize offered by the Academy of Dijon in 1754. Although far abler both in thought and style than the first discourse it failed to win the prize which went to the duller but safer discussion by the Abbé Talbert. Rousseau dedicated it to the Republic of Geneva which he had revisited in 1754 and which had conferred citizenship upon him.

The discourse proper begins with a distinction between natural inequality and civil or social inequality which superficial critics have frequently overlooked. Rousseau held that natural inequality was inevitable, indeed, good and necessary; some men having been born stronger and abler than others. In a civilized state he finds that inequality is likewise inevitable because of the necessity of what might today be called the "division of labor," the coördinating and subordinating of functions of what he assumes were once entirely self-sufficient and free individuals. Necessary though this subordination may seem to be in our present state, the tenor of the discourse is such that it implies that the state of nature was preferable and richer in individual happiness and of course in liberty. Rousseau here gives us his most glowing and enthusiastic picture of man in the pre-social state. His test of an acceptable social state would be one in which natural and social inequalities correspond, that is in which the individuals most highly endowed by nature occupy the most important and responsible positions. Such a correspondence he does not find in the Society about him.

He then gives us his version of the origin of inequality which he finds in the institution of property.

In essence and in effect this Discourse may well be considered the most revolutionary of Rousseau's writings, and Vaughan has said of it:

> It was, and still remains, the most complete expression of the craving for a return to simpler and freer conditions, for a renewal of man's communion with God and nature—which was to breathe a new life into the thought, the imagination, the social ideals of the civilised world. In this sense, it stands at the fountain head of the influences which largely went to remould the philosophy, the literature, the practical energies of Europe during the next two generations, and which, even now, have not wholly spent their force.[30]

The first edition of the Discourse was published in 1755 by Rey at Amsterdam. The best edition for the student is at present to be found in Vol. I of Vaughan's *The Political Writings of Jean-Jacques Rousseau,* Cambridge University Press, 1915. For the sources of Rousseau's ideas see M. Morel, *Sources du Discours sur l'inégalité,* in *Annales J.-J. Rousseau,* Vol. V. (1909).

[30] Vol. I, p. 119.

INTRODUCTION

NATURAL AND UNNATURAL INEQUALITY

C'est de l'homme que j'ai à parler; et la question que j'examine m'apprend que je vais parler à des hommes; car on n'en propose point de semblables quand on craint d'honorer la vérité. Je défendrai donc avec confiance la cause de l'humanité devant les sages qui m'y invitent, et je ne serai pas mécontent de moi-même si je me rends digne de mon sujet et de mes juges.

Je conçois dans l'espèce humaine deux sortes d'inégalités: l'une, que j'appelle naturelle ou physique, parce qu'elle est établie par la nature, et qui consiste dans la différence des âges, de la santé, des forces du corps et des qualités de l'esprit ou de l'âme; l'autre, qu'on peut appeler inégalité morale ou politique, parce qu'elle dépend d'une sorte de convention, et qu'elle est établie ou du moins autorisée par le consentement des hommes. Celle-ci consiste dans les différents privilèges dont quelques-uns jouissent au préjudice des autres, comme d'être plus riches, plus honorés, plus puissants qu'eux, ou même de s'en faire obéir.

On ne peut pas demander quelle est la source de l'inégalité naturelle, parce que la réponse se trouverait énoncée dans la simple définition du mot. On peut encore moins chercher s'il n'y aurait point quelque liaison essentielle entre les deux inégalités, car ce serait demander, en d'autres termes, si ceux qui commandent valent nécessairement mieux que ceux qui obéissent, et si la force du corps ou de l'esprit, la sagesse ou la vertu, se trouvent toujours dans les mêmes individus en proportion de la puissance ou de la richesse: question bonne peut-être à agiter entre des hommes raisonnables et libres, qui cherchent la vérité.

5 De quoi s'agit-il donc précisément dans ce Discours? De marquer dans le progrès des choses le moment où, le droit succédant à la violence, la nature fut soumise à la loi; d'expliquer par quel enchaînement de prodiges le fort put se résoudre à servir le faible, et le peuple 10 à acheter un repos en idée au prix d'une félicité réelle.

Les philosophes qui ont examiné les fondements de la société ont tous senti la nécessité de remonter jusqu'à l'état de nature,[31] mais aucun d'eux n'y est arrivé. Les uns n'ont point balancé à supposer à l'homme dans cet 15 état la notion du juste et de l'injuste, sans se soucier de montrer qu'il dût avoir cette notion, ni même qu'elle lui fût utile. D'autres ont parlé du droit naturel que chacun a de conserver ce qui lui appartient, sans expliquer ce qu'ils entendaient par appartenir. D'autres, 20 donnant d'abord au plus fort l'autorité sur le plus faible, ont aussitôt fait naître le Gouvernement, sans

[31] Philosophers, especially political philosophers, of the seventeenth and eighteenth century were in the habit of assuming "the state of nature" and of finding in it the origin of human rights, "natural rights" as they were generally called. (Cf. *Natural Rights* by David George Ritchie, London, 2nd edition, 1903, pp. 3-77). Descriptions of this state varied from pictures of a golden age or of paradisiac felicity, as in Pope (see note [6], p. 3) to the state of war (what we should today call the unmitigated "struggle for existence") of Hobbes. Though the theory of natural rights is now much less generally accepted it was stoutly defended by Herbert Spencer in *Man Versus the State,* and in his *Ethics.*

songer au temps qui dut s'écouler avant que le sens des mots d'autorité et de Gouvernement pût exister parmi les hommes. Enfin tous, parlant sans cesse de besoin, d'avidité, d'oppression, de désirs et d'orgueil, ont transporté à l'état de nature des idées qu'ils avaient 5
prises dans la société : ils parlaient de l'homme sauvage, et ils peignaient l'homme civil. Il n'est pas même venu dans l'esprit de la plupart des nôtres de douter que l'état de nature eût existé, tandis qu'il est évident, par la lecture des livres sacrés, que le premier homme, 10
ayant reçu immédiatement de Dieu des lumières et des préceptes, n'était point lui-même dans cet état, et qu'en ajoutant aux écrits de Moïse la foi que leur doit tout philosophe chrétien, il faut nier que, même avant le déluge, les hommes se soient jamais trouvés dans le 15
pur état de nature, à moins qu'ils n'y soient retombés par quelque événement extraordinaire : paradoxe fort embarrassant à défendre, et tout à fait impossible à prouver.

Commençons donc par écarter tous les faits, car ils 20
ne touchent point à la question. Il ne faut pas prendre les recherches, dans lesquelles on peut entrer sur ce sujet pour des vérités historiques, mais seulement pour des raisonnements hypothétiques et conditionnels, plus propres à éclaircir la nature des choses qu'à en montrer 25
la véritable origine, et semblables à ceux que font tous les jours nos physiciens sur la formation du monde. La religion nous ordonne de croire que Dieu lui-même ayant tiré les hommes de l'état de nature immédiatement après la création, ils sont inégaux parce qu'il a 30
voulu qu'ils le fussent ; mais elle ne nous défend pas

de former des conjectures tirées de la seule nature de l'homme et des êtres qui l'environnent, sur ce qu'aurait pu devenir le genre humain s'il fût resté abandonné à lui-même. Voilà ce qu'on me demande, et ce que je me
5 propose d'examiner dans ce Discours. Mon sujet intéressant l'homme en général, je tâcherai de prendre un langage qui convienne à toutes les nations; ou plutôt oubliant les temps et les lieux pour ne songer qu'aux hommes à qui je parle, je me supposerai dans le lycée
10 d'Athènes, répétant les leçons de mes maîtres, ayant les Platon et les Xénocrate[32] pour juges, et le genre humain pour auditeur.

O homme, de quelque contrée que tu sois, quelles que soient tes opinions, écoute; voici ton histoire, telle que
15 j'ai cru la lire, non dans les livres de tes semblables, qui sont menteurs, mais dans la nature, qui ne ment jamais. Tout ce qui sera d'elle sera vrai; il n'y aura de faux que ce que j'y aurai mêlé du mien sans le vouloir. Les temps dont je vais parler sont bien éloig-
20 nés: combien tu as changé de ce que tu étais! C'est, pour ainsi dire, la vie de ton espèce que je te vais décrire d'après les qualités que tu as reçues, que ton éducation et tes habitudes ont pu dépraver, mais qu'elles n'ont pu détruire. Il y a, je le sens, un âge auquel
25 l'homme individuel voudrait s'arrêter: tu chercheras l'âge auquel tu désirerais que ton espèce se fût arrêtée. Mécontent de ton état présent par des raisons qui annoncent à ta postérité malheureuse de plus grands mécontentements encore, peut-être voudrais-tu

[32] Xenocrates, a disciple of Plato 396-314 B.C., known for his earnest and unselfish devotion to truth.

pouvoir rétrograder; et ce sentiment doit faire l'éloge de tes premiers aïeux, la critique de tes contemporains, et l'effroi de ceux qui auront le malheur de vivre après toi.[33]

The Origin of Inequality

Le premier qui ayant enclos un terrain s'avisa de dire, *Ceci est à moi,* et trouva des gens assez simples pour le croire, fut le vrai fondateur de la société civile. Que de crimes, de guerres, de meurtres, que de misères et d'horreurs n'eût point épargnés au genre humain celui qui, arrachant les pieux ou comblant le fossé, eût crié à ses semblables: "Gardez-vous d'écouter cet imposteur; vous êtes perdus si vous oubliez que les fruits sont à tous, et que la terre n'est à personne!" Mais il y a grande apparence qu'alors les choses en étaient déjà venues au point de ne pouvoir plus durer comme elles étaient: car cette idée de propriété, dépendant de beaucoup d'idées antérieures qui n'ont pu naître que successivement, ne se forma pas tout d'un coup dans l'esprit humain: il fallut faire bien des progrès, acquérir bien de l'industrie et des lumières, les transmettre et

[33] It is in feverish, eloquent passages like this that we must look for the secret of Rousseau's appeal to eighteenth century reformers. Such passages and the alluring description of the state of nature which followed make the *Discours sur l'inégalité* far more revolutionary than the *Contrat Social* where the state of nature is not vaunted and where it is presented as inferior to a tolerable civil state (cf. pp. 177-8). The whole point of Rousseau's appeal to nature in his political philosophy has often been overlooked. Its revolutionary quality was due to the fact that in the eighteenth century to appeal to nature was to make the most effective possible protest against authority.

les augmenter d'âge en âge, avant que d'arriver à ce dernier terme de l'état de nature. Reprenons donc les choses de plus haut, et tâchons de rassembler sous un seul point de vue cette lente succession d'événements et 5 de connaissances dans leur ordre le plus naturel.

Le premier sentiment de l'homme fut celui de son existence; son premier soin celui de sa conservation. Les productions de la terre lui fournissaient tous les secours nécessaires; l'instinct le porta à en faire usage. 10 Telle fut la condition de l'homme naissant; telle fut la vie d'un animal borné d'abord aux pures sensations, et profitant à peine des dons que lui offrait la nature, loin de songer à lui rien arracher. Mais il se présenta bientôt des difficultés; il fallut apprendre à les vaincre: 15 la hauteur des arbres qui l'empêchait d'atteindre à leurs fruits, la concurrence des animaux qui cherchaient à s'en nourrir, la férocité de ceux qui en voulaient à sa propre vie, tout l'obligea de s'appliquer aux exercices du corps; il fallut se rendre agile, vite à la course, 20 vigoureux au combat. Les armes naturelles, qui sont les branches d'arbres et les pierres, se trouvèrent bientôt sous sa main. Il apprit à surmonter les obstacles de la nature, à combattre au besoin les autres animaux, à disputer sa subsistance aux hommes mêmes, ou à se 25 dédommager de ce qu'il fallait céder au plus fort.

A mesure que le genre humain s'étendit, les peines se multiplièrent avec les hommes. La différence des terrains, des climats, des saisons, put les forcer à en mettre dans leurs manières de vivre. Des années 30 stériles, des hivers longs et rudes, des étés brûlants, qui consument tout, exigèrent d'eux une nouvelle industrie.

Le long de la mer et des rivières ils inventèrent la ligne et l'hameçon, et devinrent pêcheurs et ichthyophages. Dans les forêts ils se firent des arcs et des flèches, et devinrent chasseurs et guerriers. Dans les pays froids ils se couvrirent des peaux des bêtes qu'ils avaient tuées. Le tonnerre, un volcan, ou quelque heureux hasard, leur fit connaître le feu, nouvelle ressource contre la rigueur de l'hiver : ils apprirent à conserver cet élément, puis à le reproduire, et enfin à en préparer les viandes qu'auparavant ils dévoraient crues.

Cette application réitérée des êtres divers à lui-même, et des uns aux autres, dut naturellement engendrer dans l'esprit de l'homme les perceptions de certains rapports. Ces relations que nous exprimons par les mots de grand, de petit, de fort, de faible, de vite, de lent, de peureux, de hardi, et d'autres idées pareilles, comparées au besoin, et presque sans y songer, produisirent enfin chez lui quelque sorte de réflexion, ou plutôt une prudence machinale qui lui indiquait les précautions les plus nécessaires à sa sûreté.

Les nouvelles lumières qui résultèrent de ce développement augmentèrent sa supériorité sur les autres animaux en la lui faisant connaître. Il s'exerça à leur dresser des pièges, il leur donna le change en mille manières ; et quoique plusieurs le surpassassent en force au combat, ou en vitesse à la course, de ceux qui pouvaient lui servir ou lui nuire, il devint avec le temps le maître des uns et le fléau des autres. C'est ainsi que le premier regard qu'il porta sur lui-même y produisit le premier mouvement d'orgueil ; c'est ainsi que sachant encore à peine distinguer les rangs, et se contemplant au premier par son espèce, il se préparait de loin à y prétendre par son individu.

Instruit par l'expérience que l'amour du bien-être est le seul mobile des actions humaines, il se trouva en état
5 de distinguer les occasions rares où l'intérêt commun devait le faire compter sur l'assistance de ses semblables, et celles plus rares encore où la concurrence devait le faire défier d'eux. Dans le premier cas, il s'unissait avec eux en troupeau, ou tout au plus par quelque sorte
10 d'association libre qui n'obligeait personne, et qui ne durait qu'autant que le besoin passager qui l'avait formée. Dans le second, chacun cherchait à prendre ses avantages, soit à force ouverte, s'il croyait le pouvoir, soit par adresse et subtilité, s'il se sentait le plus faible.
15 Voilà comment les hommes purent insensiblement acquérir quelque idée grossière des engagements mutuels, et de l'avantage de les remplir, mais seulement autant que pouvait l'exiger l'intérêt présent et sensible; car la prévoyance n'était rien pour eux; et, loin de s'oc-
20 cuper d'un avenir éloigné, ils ne songeaient pas même au lendemain. S'agissait-il de prendre un cerf, chacun sentait bien qu'il devait pour cela garder fidèlement son poste; mais si un lièvre venait à passer à la portée de l'un d'eux, il ne faut pas douter qu'il ne le poursuivît
25 sans scrupule, et qu'ayant atteint sa proie il ne se souciât fort peu de faire manquer la leur à ses compagnons.

Je parcours comme un trait des multitudes de siècles forcé par le temps qui s'écoule, par l'abondance des
30 choses que j'ai à dire, et par le progrès presque insensible des commencements; car plus les événements

étaient lents à se succéder, plus ils sont prompts à décrire.

Ces premiers progrès mirent enfin l'homme à portée d'en faire de plus rapides. Plus l'esprit s'éclairait, et plus l'industrie se perfectionna. Bientôt, cessant de 5 s'endormir sous le premier arbre, ou de se retirer dans des cavernes, on trouva quelques sortes de haches de pierres dures et tranchantes qui servirent à couper du bois, creuser la terre, et faire des huttes de branchages qu'on s'avisa ensuite d'enduire d'argile et de boue. Ce 10 fut là l'époque d'une première révolution qui forma l'établissement et la distinction des familles, et qui introduisit une sorte de propriété, d'où peut-être naquirent déjà bien des querelles et des combats. Cependant, comme les plus forts furent vraisemblablement 15 les premiers à se faire des logements qu'ils se sentaient capables de défendre, il est à croire que les faibles trouvèrent plus court et plus sûr de les imiter que de tenter de les déloger; et quant à ceux qui avaient déjà des cabanes, chacun dut peu chercher à s'approprier 20 celle de son voisin, moins parce qu'elle ne lui appartenait pas, que parce qu'elle lui était inutile, et qu'il ne pouvait s'en emparer sans s'exposer à un combat très vif avec la famille qui l'occupait.

Les premiers développements du cœur furent l'effet 25 d'une situation nouvelle qui réunissait dans une habitation commune les maris et les femmes, les pères et les enfants. L'habitude de vivre ensemble fit naître les plus doux sentiments qui soient connus des hommes, l'amour conjugal et l'amour paternel. Chaque famille 30 devint une petite société d'autant mieux unie, que l'at-

tachement réciproque et la liberté en étaient les seuls liens; et ce fut alors que s'établit la première différence dans la manière de vivre des deux sexes, qui jusqu'ici n'en avaient eu qu'une. Les femmes devinrent plus
5 sédentaires, et s'accoutumèrent à garder la cabane et les enfants, tandis que l'homme allait chercher la subsistance commune. Les deux sexes commencèrent aussi, par une vie un peu plus molle, à perdre quelque chose de leur férocité et de leur vigueur. Mais si
10 chacun séparément devint moins propre à combattre les bêtes sauvages, en revanche il fut plus aisé de s'assembler pour leur résister en commun.

Dans ce nouvel état, avec une vie simple et solitaire, des besoins très bornés, et les instruments qu'ils avaient
15 inventés pour y pourvoir, les hommes, jouissant d'un fort grand loisir, l'employèrent à se procurer plusieurs sortes de commodités inconnues à leurs pères; et ce fut là le premier joug qu'ils s'imposèrent sans y songer, et la première source de maux qu'ils préparèrent à leur
20 descendants; car, outre qu'ils continuèrent ainsi à s'amollir le corps et l'esprit, ces commodités ayant par l'habitude perdu presque tout leur agrément, et étant en même temps dégénérées en de vrais besoins, la privation en devint beaucoup plus cruelle que la possession
25 n'en était douce; et l'on était malheureux de les perdre, sans être heureux de les posséder.

JULIE OU LA NOUVELLE HELOISE

The freest expression of Rousseau's literary genius is to be found in his novel *Julie ou la nouvelle Héloïse.* Unlike his other works it was not written under provocation but was an unhampered and unhurried presentation of his ideal of life. He had arrived at the maturity of his talent and as a man of letters with the publication of the first and second discourses had tasted the savor of success. His life had fallen in pleasant places. For a brief period he was at ease with himself. He turned to his subject naturally, and as he tells us in the *Confessions,* under no outward constraint. Impelled only by his artistic conscience, by his desire to give local habitations and names to the visions that had floated before him, and completeness to a life which he recognized as incomplete, he began this masterpiece.

In April 1756 he had with a strange, if illusory, sense of triumph and release left Paris to take up his residence in the cottage of Mme d'Épinay at the *Ermitage* near the wood of Montmorency. He had planned to work on his *Institutions Politiques* and the papers of the Abbé de Saint-Pierre, but as he walked and dreamed in those pleasant spring days the new subject imposed itself and he began his story at first without a plan and in sheer delight of creation. By a singular good fortune for his novel the passion which he sought to express in fiction came to him in reality as he wrote. He fell deeply in love with Mme d'Houdetot the friend of Saint-Lambert.[1] Here was a subject made to his hand. His story was to be the love of Saint-Preux a plebeian for Julie d'Étange in station above him. After a brief period of fiery passion Saint-Preux in the interest of Julie's honor and happiness must set out on a long exile while Julie to meet her father's wish and obligation must wed M. de Wolmar. At Wolmar's invitation Saint-Preux returns to live in a bitter-sweet friendship by the side of her whom he had loved. This incongruous and strained situation was seemingly what the author would have preferred in the Saint-Lambert, d'Houdetot, Rousseau relation. In spite of the breaks with his friends which were to supervene, little of the bitterness of those later years penetrates to the story in which Jean-Jacques was so entirely absorbed.

Completed in 1758 and published in February 1761, the novel proved to be the most popular and in point of literary influence the most important of the eighteenth century. More than fifty editions were printed in a time when successful romances counted three or four.[2] Copies could not be printed rapidly enough to satisfy the demand and lines were formed before the circulating libraries which rented them at ten sous an hour. The beauties of the mountain and lake scenery of Switzerland had as yet generally passed unrecog-

[1] On this subject see Ritter's account *Annales J.-J. R.*, Vol. II, 1906, pp. 1-136.

[2] For a list of the editions of the *Nouvelle Héloïse* see the studies by Mornet in *Annales J.-J. R.*, Vol. V (1909), pp. 1-118, Vol. IX, pp. 67-80.

nized. Rousseau's novel brought crowds of tourists to the shores of Lake Geneva, who visited Clarens and Meillerie as places of pilgrimage and followed the course of the story, book in hand.

The reasons for this success and influence were in the main three; Rousseau's treatment of sentiment, of nature, and of the rural or "simple" life.

It would be a mistake to believe that the *Nouvelle Héloïse* introduced the novel of sentiment. It had long been in vogue and its popularity had recently been increased by the translations of Richardson's *Clarissa Harlowe* and *Grandisson* with which Rousseau was familiar. It was not the subject so much as the treatment which was new. We have seen that as the result of a fortunate juncture of circumstances Rousseau wrote with an impassioned sincerity that carried with it a new accent of depth and conviction. Racine in his *Phèdre* for instance was interested in passion, but more particularly in its effects and in the psychological analysis of these troubled states of soul. Marivaux had expressed the subtleties of the affections with rare finesse. Richardson contains long passages of sentiment interspersed with much moralizing. Rousseau was not interested in passion's effects or its analysis, nor in subtleties nor moralizing. He was making passion *as such* the object of artistic expression, and it was the force and feverish sincerity of this expression which he contributed to the history of romanticism.

As to Rousseau's attitude toward nature there is likewise much confusion. Contrary to general belief he did not excel in detailed descriptions as such. He cannot be compared in this respect to Senancour or Wordsworth. Sheer description of nature furthermore was nothing new. Thomson's *Seasons* (1726-1730) for instance is almost pure description. Rousseau rarely presents a clearly outlined vista, his language is not often "picturesque" and it will be noted that he is sparing in his use of metaphor. Rousseau's contribution lay in his presenting not the outward aspect but the sense of nature, not nature as something to be *seen* but nature as something to be *felt*. With him it became one of the factors in his story, a living thing. Into the life of the characters the life of nature is, if not subtly, at least deeply "interfused." Nature is not merely a sounding board for the poet's emotions, it is a part of them. The story of Saint-Preux and Julie can no more be separated from Switzerland than Lamartine's love can be separated from *Le Lac*. This fusion of nature and personality is to be a characteristic of the great French romantic poems and will be found not only in *Le Lac* but in Hugo's *Tristesse d'Olympio* and Musset's *Souvenir*. Nature as a factor in a story, as an element of the *plot* and not the setting will of course be found again in Chateaubriand and George Sand.

The third point, the glorification of the rural or simple life calls for but little explanation. It was a part of that revolt against convention which is central to Rousseau's work, and students of English literature are familiar with its effects on Wordsworth's theory of life as well as his theory of art. Indeed this phase of Rousseau's influence was most marked outside of

France, and Wordsworth, Thoreau and Emerson have no counterparts in French literature unless Senancour is to be so considered. The romantic poets did, to be sure, make a noisy war upon literary conventions and the *style noble* and they did employ the *mot propre,* but the deeply grounded Latin tradition of eloquence persisted save perhaps in Musset, and it was to be a full century before poets like Paul Verlaine and prose artists like Anatole France and Romain Rolland, wearied of this overlong tradition of a hollow literary decorum, finally took rhetoric out behind the barn and "wrung its neck."[3]

IN THE BOSQUET DE JULIE

(Julie has fallen in love with her tutor Saint-Preux. With her friend Claire (*l'inséparable cousine*) she has discovered in her walks a grove (*le bosquet de Julie*) and Julie agreed with Claire that they were to bring Saint-Preux to the grove and on his entrance each of the cousins would greet him with a kiss.)

De Saint-Preux à Julie

Qu'as-tu fait, ah! qu'as-tu fait, ma Julie? tu voulais me récompenser, et tu m'as perdu. Je suis ivre, ou plutôt insensé. Mes sens sont altérés, toutes mes facultés sont troublées par ce baiser mortel. Tu voulais soulager mes maux! Cruelle! tu les aigris. C'est du 5
poison que j'ai cueilli sur tes lèvres; il fermente, il embrase mon sang; il me tue, et ta pitié me fait mourir.

[3] For Rousseau's description of the writing of *La Nouvelle Héloïse* the student is referred to the extract appearing under the *Confessions,* pp. 186-193. On this subject cf. Vreeland, *Étude sur les rapports littéraires entre Genève et l'Angleterre,* Geneva, 1901.

O souvenir immortel de cet instant d'illusion, de délire et d'enchantement, jamais, jamais tu ne t'effaceras de mon âme; et, tant que les charmes de Julie y seront gravés, tant que ce cœur agité me fournira des 5 sentiments et des soupirs, tu feras le supplice et le bonheur de ma vie!

Hélas! je jouissais d'une apparente tranquillité; soumis à tes volontés suprêmes, je ne murmurais plus d'un sort auquel tu daignais présider. J'avais dompté 10 les fougueuses saillies d'une imagination téméraire; j'avais couvert mes regards d'un voile et mis une entrave à mon cœur; mes désirs n'osaient plus s'échapper qu'à demi; j'étais aussi content que je pouvais l'être. Je reçois ton billet, je vole chez ta cousine; nous 15 nous rendons à Clarens, je t'aperçois, et mon sein palpite; le doux son de ta voix y porte une agitation nouvelle; je t'aborde comme transporté, et j'avais grand besoin de la diversion de ta cousine pour cacher mon trouble à ta mère. On parcourt le jardin, l'on dîne 20 tranquillement, tu me rends en secret ta lettre, que je n'ose lire devant ce redoutable témoin; le soleil commence à baisser, nous fuyons tous trois dans le bois le reste de ses rayons, et ma paisible simplicité n'imaginait pas même un état plus doux que le mien.

25 En approchant du bosquet j'aperçus, non sans une émotion secretè, vos signes d'intelligence, vos sourires mutuels, et le coloris de tes joues prendre un nouvel éclat. En y entrant, je vis avec surprise ta cousine s'approcher de moi, et, d'un air plaisamment suppliant, 30 me demander un baiser. Sans rien comprendre à ce mystère, j'embrassai cette charmante amie; et, tout

aimable, toute piquante qu'elle est, je ne connus jamais mieux que les sensations ne sont rien que ce que le cœur les fait être. Mais que devins-je un moment après, quand je sentis... la main me tremble... un doux frémissement... ta bouche de roses... la bouche de Julie... 5
se poser, se presser sur la mienne, et mon corps serré dans tes bras? Non, le feu du ciel n'est pas plus vif ni plus prompt que celui qui vint à l'instant m'embraser. Toutes les parties de moi-même se rassemblèrent sous ce toucher délicieux. Le feu s'exhalait avec nos soupirs 10
de nos lèvres brûlantes, et mon cœur se mourait sous le poids de la volupté... quand tout à coup je te vis pâlir, fermer tes beaux yeux, t'appuyer sur ta cousine, et tomber en défaillance. Ainsi la frayeur éteignit le plaisir, et mon bonheur ne fut qu'un éclair. 15

A peine sais-je ce qui m'est arrivé depuis ce fatal moment. L'impression profonde que j'ai reçue ne peut plus s'effacer. Une faveur!... c'est un tourment horrible... Non, garde tes baisers, je ne les saurais supporter.. ils sont trop âcres, trop pénétrants; ils percent; 20
ils brûlent jusqu'à la moelle... ils me rendraient furieux. Un seul, un seul m'a jeté dans un égarement dont je ne puis plus revenir. Je ne suis plus le même, et ne te vois plus la même. Je ne te vois plus comme autrefois réprimante et sévère; mais je te sens et te touche sans 25
cesse unie à mon sein comme tu fus un instant. O, Julie! quelque sort que m'annonce un transport dont je ne suis plus maître, quelque traitement que ta rigueur me destine, je ne puis plus vivre dans l'état où je suis, et je sens qu'il faut enfin que j'expire à tes pieds... ou 30
dans tes bras.

—*Première Partie Lettre XIV.*

Saint-Preux Sets out for Sion

(Julie has urged Saint-Preux to make a journey to Sion in the Valais and has sent him a purse which Saint-Preux, who believed his honor offended, returned. Julie sent the purse a second time with a letter which made acceptance imperative, and Saint-Preux accepts and departs.)

A Julie

J'ai reçu vos dons, je suis parti sans vous voir, me voici bien loin de vous; êtes-vous contente de vos tyrannies, et vous ai-je assez obéi?

Je ne puis vous parler de mon voyage; à peine sais-je
5 comment il s'est fait. J'ai mis trois jours à faire vingt lieues; chaque pas qui m'éloignait de vous séparait mon corps de mon âme, et me donnait un sentiment anticipé de la mort. Je voulais vous décrire ce que je verrais. Vain projet! Je n'ai rien vu que vous, et ne puis vous
10 peindre que Julie. Les puissantes émotions que je viens d'éprouver coup sur coup m'ont jeté dans des distractions continuelles; je me sentais toujours où je n'étais point: à peine avais-je assez de présence d'esprit pour suivre et demander mon chemin, et je suis arrivé à
15 Sion sans être parti de Vevey.

C'est ainsi que j'ai trouvé le secret d'éluder votre rigueur et de vous voir sans vous désobéir. Oui, cruelle, quoi que vous ayez su faire, vous n'avez pu me séparer de vous tout entier. Je n'ai traîné dans mon
20 exil que la moindre partie de moi-même: tout ce qu'il y a de vivant en moi demeure auprès de vous sans cesse. Il erre impunément sur vos yeux, sur vos lèvres,

sur votre sein, sur tous vos charmes; il pénètre partout comme une vapeur subtile; et je suis plus heureux en dépit de vous que je ne fus jamais de votre gré.

J'ai ici quelques personnes à voir, quelques affaires à traiter; voilà ce qui me désole. Je ne suis point à plaindre dans la solitude où je puis m'occuper de vous et me transporter aux lieux ou vous êtes. La vie active qui me rappelle à moi tout entier m'est seule insupportable. Je vais faire mal et vite pour être promptement libre, et pouvoir m'égarer à mon aise dans les lieux sauvages qui forment à mes yeux les charmes de ce pays. Il faut tout fuir et vivre seul au monde, quand on n'y peut vivre avec vous.

—Première Partie Lettre XVIII.

Saint-Preux on the Mountain Scenery of the Valais

(Saint-Preux writes an account of his journey which gives Rousseau's attitude toward mountain scenery, his power of observation and delight in what a later generation was to call "local color." His reflections on the life of the people show his love of directness and sincerity, while the next to the last paragraph is a good example of his lyricism. This passage, beginning "O ma Julie," needed only to be versified to make a romantic lyric.)

A Julie

A peine ai-je employé huit jours à parcourir un pays qui demanderait des années d'observation; mais outre que la neige me chasse, j'ai voulu revenir au-devant du courrier, qui m'apporte, j'espère, une de vos lettres.

En attendant qu'elle arrive, je commence par vous écrire celle-ci, après laquelle j'en écrirai, s'il est nécessaire, une seconde pour répondre à la vôtre.

Je ne vous ferai point ici un détail de mon voyage 5 et de mes remarques; j'en ai fait une relation que je compte vous porter. Il faut réserver notre correspondance pour les choses qui nous touchent de plus près l'un et l'autre. Je me contenterai de vous parler de la situation de mon âme; il est juste de vous rendre 10 compte de l'usage qu'on fait de votre bien.

J'étais parti, triste de mes peines et consolé de votre joie; ce qui me tenait dans un certain état de langueur qui n'est pas sans charme pour un cœur sensible. Je gravissais lentement et à pied des sentiers assez rudes, 15 conduit par un homme que j'avais pris pour être mon guide, et dans lequel, durant toute la route, j'ai trouvé plutôt un ami qu'un mercenaire. Je voulais rêver, et j'en étais toujours détourné par quelque spectacle inattendu. Tantôt d'immenses roches pendaient en ruines 20 au-dessus de ma tête. Tantôt de hautes et bruyantes cascades m'inondaient de leur épais brouillard. Tantôt un torrent éternel ouvrait à mes côtés un abîme dont les yeux n'osaient sonder la profondeur. Quelquefois je me perdais dans l'obscurité d'un bois touffu. 25 Quelquefois, en sortant d'un gouffre, une agréable prairie réjouissait tout à coup mes regards. Un mélange étonnant de la nature sauvage et de la nature cultivée montrait partout la main des hommes, où l'on eût cru qu'ils n'avaient jamais pénétré; à côté d'une caverne 30 on trouvait des maisons; on voyait des pampres secs où l'on n'eût cherché que des ronces, des vignes dans des terres éboulées, d'excellents fruits sur des rochers, et des champs dans des précipices.

Ce n'était pas seulement le travail des hommes qui rendait ces pays étranges si bizarrement contrastés; la nature semblait encore prendre plaisir à s'y mettre en 5 opposition avec elle-même, tant on la trouvait différente en un même lieu sous divers aspects. Au levant les fleurs du printemps, au midi les fruits de l'automne, au nord les glaces de l'hiver: elle réunissait toutes les saisons dans le même instant, tous les climats dans le 10 même lieu, des terrains contraires sur le même sol, et formait l'accord inconnu partout ailleurs des productions des plaines et de celles des Alpes. Ajoutez à tout cela les illusions de l'optique, les pointes des monts différemment éclairées, le clair-obscur du soleil et des 15 ombres, et tous les accidents de lumière qui en résultaient le matin et le soir, vous aurez quelque idée des scènes continuelles qui ne cessèrent d'attirer mon admiration, et qui semblaient m'être offertes en un vrai théâtre: car la perspective des monts étant verticale 20 frappe les yeux tout à la fois et bien plus puissamment que celle des plaines qui ne se voit qu'obliquement, en fuyant, et dont chaque objet vous en cache un autre.

J'attribuai, durant la première journée, aux agréments de cette variété le calme que je sentais renaître 25 en moi. J'admirais l'empire qu'ont sur nos passions les plus vives les êtres les plus insensibles, et je méprisais la philosophie de ne pouvoir pas même autant sur l'âme qu'une suite d'objets inanimés. Mais, cet état paisible ayant duré la nuit et augmenté le lendemain, je ne tar- 30 dai pas de juger qu'il y avait encore quelque autre cause qui ne m'était pas connue. J'arrivai ce jour-là sur des montagnes les moins élevées, et, parcourant ensuite leurs inégalités, sur celles des plus hautes qui étaient à ma portée. Après m'être promené dans les nuages, j'atteignais un séjour plus serein, d'où l'on voit dans la saison le tonnerre et l'orage se former au-dessous de soi; image trop vaine de l'âme du sage, dont l'exemple n'exista jamais, ou n'existe qu'aux mêmes lieux d'où l'on en a tiré l'emblème.

Ce fut là que je démêlai sensiblement dans la pureté de l'air où je me trouvais la véritable cause du changement de mon humeur, et du retour de cette paix intérieure que j'avais perdue depuis si longtemps. En effet, c'est une impression générale qu'éprouvent tous les hommes, quoiqu'ils ne l'observent pas tous, que sur les hautes montagnes, où l'air est pur et subtil, on se sent plus de facilité dans la respiration, plus de légèreté dans le corps, plus de sérénité dans l'esprit; les plaisirs y sont moins ardents, les passions plus modérées. Les méditations y prennent je ne sais quel caractère grand et sublime, proportionné aux objets qui nous frappent, je ne sais quelle volupté tranquille qui n'a rien d'âcre ni de sensuel. Il semble qu'en s'élevant au-dessus du séjour des hommes on y laisse tous les sentiments bas et terrestres, et qu'à mesure qu'on approche des régions éthérées, l'âme contracte quelque chose de leur inaltérable pureté. On y est grave sans mélancolie, paisible sans indolence, content d'être et de penser: tous les désirs trops vifs s'émoussent; ils perdent cette pointe aiguë qui les rend douloureux, ils ne laissent au fond du cœur qu'une émotion légère et douce; et c'est ainsi qu'un heureux climat fait servir à la félicité de l'homme les passions qui font ailleurs son tourment. Je doute qu'aucune agitation violente, aucune maladie de vapeurs, pût tenir contre un pareil séjour prolongé, et je suis surpris que des bains de l'air salutaire et bienfaisant des montagnes ne soient pas un des grands remèdes de la médecine et de la morale : 5

Quì non palazzi, non teatro o loggia;
Ma'n lor vece un' abete, un faggio, un pino,
Trà l' erba verde e 'l bel monte vicino 10
Levan di terra al ciel nostr' intelletto.[1]

Supposez les impressions réunies de ce que je viens de vous décrire, et vous aurez quelque idée de la situation délicieuse où je me trouvais. Imaginez la variété, la grandeur, la beauté de mille étonnants spectacles ; le 15 plaisir de ne voir autour de soi que des objets tout nouveaux, des oiseaux étranges, des plantes bizarres et inconnues ; d'observer en quelque sorte une autre nature, et de se trouver dans un nouveau monde. Tout cela fait aux yeux un mélange inexprimable, dont le charme 20 augmente encore par la subtilité de l'air, qui rend les couleurs plus vives, les traits plus marqués, rapproche tous les points de vue ; les distances paraissant moindres que dans les plaines, où l'épaisseur de l'air couvre la terre d'un voile, l'horizon présente aux yeux plus d'objets qu'il semble n'en pouvoir contenir ; enfin ce spectacle a je ne sais quoi de magique, de surnaturel, qui 25

[1] Au lieu des palais, des pavillons, des théâtres, les chênes, les noirs sapins, les hêtres, s'élancent de l'herbe verte au sommet des monts, et semblent élever au ciel, avec leurs têtes, les yeux et l'esprit des mortels. PÉTRARQUE.

ravit l'esprit et les sens; on oublie tout, on s'oublie soi-même, on ne sait plus où l'on est.

J'aurais passé tout le temps de mon voyage dans le seul enchantement du paysage si je n'en eusse éprouvé
5 un plus doux encore dans le commerce des habitants. Vous trouverez dans ma description un léger crayon de leur mœurs, de leur simplicité, de leur égalité d'âme, et de cette paisible tranquillité qui les rend heureux par l'exemption des peines plutôt que par le goût des plai-
10 sirs. Mais ce que je n'ai pu vous peindre et qu'on ne peut guère imaginer, c'est leur humanité désintéressée, et leur zèle hospitalier pour tous les étrangers que le hasard ou la curiosité conduisent parmi eux: j'en fis une épreuve surprenante, moi qui n'étais connu de per-
15 sonne, et qui ne marchais qu'à l'aide d'un conducteur. Quand j'arrivais le soir dans un hameau, chacun venait avec tant d'empressement m'offrir sa maison que j'étais embarrassé du choix; et celui qui obtenait la préférence en paraissait si content que la première fois je pris
20 cette ardeur pour de l'avidité. Mais je fus bien étonné quand, après en avoir usé chez mon hôte à peu près comme au cabaret, il refusa le lendemain mon argent, s'offensant même de ma proposition; et il en a partout été de même. Ainsi c'était le pur amour de l'hospi-
25 talité, communément assez tiède, qu'à sa vivacité j'avais pris pour l'âpreté du gain. Leur désintéressement fut si complet que dans tout le voyage je n'ai pu trouver à placer un patagon.[2] En effet, à quoi dépenser de l'argent dans un pays où les maîtres ne reçoivent point
30 le prix de leurs frais, ni les domestiques celui de leurs

[2] Écu du pays.

soins, et où l'on ne trouve aucun mendiant? Cependant l'argent est fort rare dans le Haut-Valais, mais c'est pour cela que les habitants sont à leur aise: car les denrées y sont abondantes sans aucun débouché au dehors, sans consommation de luxe au dedans, et sans que le cultivateur montagnard, dont les travaux sont les plaisirs, devienne moins laborieux. Si jamais ils ont plus d'argent, ils seront infailliblement plus pauvres; ils ont la sagesse de le sentir, et il y a dans le pays des mines d'or qu'il n'est pas permis d'exploiter.

J'étais d'abord fort surpris de l'opposition de ces usages avec ceux du Bas-Valais, où, sur la route d'Italie, on rançonne assez durement les passagers; et j'avais peine à concilier dans un même peuple des manières si différentes. Un Valaisan m'en expliqua la raison. "Dans la vallée," me dit-il, "les étrangers qui passent sont des marchands, et d'autres gens uniquement occupés de leur négoce et de leur gain; il est juste qu'ils nous laissent une partie de leur profit, et nous les traitons comme ils traitent les autres. Mais ici, où nulle affaire n'appelle les étrangers, nous sommes sûrs que leur voyage est désintéressé; l'accueil qu'on leur fait l'est aussi. Ce sont des hôtes qui nous viennent voir parce qu'ils nous aiment, et nous les recevons avec amitié.

"Au reste, ajouta-t-il en souriant, cette hospitalité n'est pas coûteuse, et peu de gens s'avisent d'en profiter."—"Ah! je le crois," lui répondis-je; "que ferait-on chez un peuple qui vit pour vivre, non pour gagner ni pour briller? Hommes heureux et dignes de l'être, j'aime à croire qu'il faut vous ressembler en quelque chose pour se plaire au milieu de vous."

Ce qui me paraissait le plus agréable dans leur accueil, c'était de n'y pas trouver le moindre vestige de gêne ni pour eux ni pour moi; ils vivaient dans leur maison comme si je n'y eusse pas été, et il ne tenait
5 qu'à moi d'y être comme si j'y eusse été seul. Ils ne connaissent point l'incommode vanité d'en faire les honneurs aux étrangers, comme pour les avertir de la présence d'un maître, dont on dépend au moins en cela. Si je ne disais rien, ils supposaient que je voulais vivre
10 à leur manière; je n'avais qu'à dire un mot pour vivre à la mienne, sans éprouver jamais de leur part la moindre marque de répugnance ou d'étonnement. Le seul compliment qu'ils me firent, après avoir su que j'étais Suisse, fut de me dire que nous étions frères, et que je
15 n'avais qu'à me regarder chez eux comme étant chez moi; puis ils ne s'embarrassèrent plus de ce que je faisais, n'imaginant pas même que je pusse avoir le moindre doute sur la sincérité de leurs offres, ni le moindre scrupule à m'en prévaloir. Ils en usent entre
20 eux avec la même simplicité: les enfants en âge de raison sont les égaux de leurs pères; les domestiques s'asseyent à table avec leurs maîtres; la même liberté règne dans les maisons et dans la république, et la famille est l'image de l'État.

25 La seule chose sur laquelle je ne jouissais pas de la liberté était la durée excessive des repas: j'étais bien le maître de ne pas me mettre à table; mais, quand j'y étais une fois, il y fallait rester une partie de la journée, et boire d'autant. Le moyen d'imaginer qu'un
30 homme, et un Suisse, n'aimât pas à boire? En effet, j'avoue que le bon vin me paraît une excellente chose,

et que je ne hais point à m'en égayer, pourvu qu'on ne m'y force pas. J'ai toujours remarqué que les gens faux sont sobres, et la grande réserve de la table annonce assez souvent des mœurs feintes et des âmes doubles. Un homme franc craint moins ce babil affectueux et ces tendres épanchements qui précèdent l'ivresse; mais il faut savoir s'arrêter et prévenir l'excès. Voilà ce qu'il ne m'était guère possible de faire avec d'aussi déterminés buveurs que les Valaisans, des vins aussi violents que ceux du pays, et sur des tables où l'on ne vit jamais d'eau. Comment se résoudre à jouer si sottement le sage et à fâcher d'aussi bonnes gens? Je m'enivrais donc par reconnaissance; et, ne pouvant payer mon écot de ma bourse, je le payais de ma raison.

Un autre usage qui ne me gênait guère moins, c'était de voir, même chez des magistrats, la femme et les filles de la maison, debout derrière ma chaise, servir à table comme des domestiques. La galanterie française se serait d'autant plus tourmentée à réparer cette incongruité qu'avec la figure des Valaisanes, des servantes mêmes rendraient leurs services embarrassants. Vous pouvez m'en croire, elles sont jolies puisqu'elles m'ont paru l'être. Des yeux accoutumés à vous voir sont difficiles en beauté. . . .

Je remarquai aussi un grand défaut dans l'habillement des Valaisanes: c'est d'avoir des corps de robe si élevés par derrière qu'elles en paraissent bossues; cela fait un effet singulier avec leurs petites coiffures noires plus ni de simplicité ni d'élégance. Je vous porte un et le reste de leur ajustement, qui ne manque au sur-

habit complet à la valaisane, et j'espère qu'il vous ira bien; il a été pris sur la plus jolie taille du pays.

Tandis que je parcourais avec extase ces lieux si peu connus et si dignes d'être admirés, que faisiez-vous cependant, ma Julie? Étiez-vous oubliée de votre ami? Julie oubliée! Ne m'oublierais-je pas plutôt moi-même? et que pourrais-je être un moment seul, moi qui ne suis plus rien que par vous? Je n'ai jamais mieux remarqué avec quel instinct je place en divers lieux notre existence commune selon l'état de mon âme. Quand je suis triste, elle se réfugie auprès de la vôtre, et cherche des consolations aux lieux où vous êtes; c'est ce que j'éprouvais en vous quittant. Quand j'ai du plaisir, je n'en saurais jouir seul, et pour le partager avec vous je vous appelle alors où je suis. Voilà ce qui m'est arrivé durant toute cette course, où la diversité des objets me rappelant sans cesse en moi-même, je vous conduisais partout avec moi. Je ne faisais pas un pas que nous ne le fissions ensemble. Je n'admirais pas une vue sans me hâter de vous la montrer. Tous les arbres que je rencontrais vous prêtaient leur ombre, tous les gazons vous servaient de siège. Tantôt, assis à vos côtés, je vous aidais à parcourir des yeux les objets; tantôt à vos genoux j'en contemplais un plus digne des regards d'un homme sensible. Rencontrais-je un pas difficile, je vous le voyais franchir avec la légèreté d'un faon qui bondit après sa mère. Fallait-il traverser un torrent, j'osais presser dans mes bras une si douce charge; je passais le torrent lentement, avec délices, et voyais à regret le chemin que j'allais atteindre. Tout me rappelait à vous dans ce séjour paisible, et les touchants attraits de la nature, et l'inaltérable pureté de l'air, et les mœurs simples des habitants, et leur sagesse égale et sûre, et l'aimable pudeur du sexe, et ses innocentes grâces; et tout ce qui frappait agréablement mes yeux et mon cœur leur peignait celle qu'ils cherchent. 5

"O ma Julie!" disais-je avec attendrissement, "que ne puis-je couler mes jours avec toi dans ces lieux ignorés, heureux de notre bonheur, et non du regard des hommes! Que ne puis-je ici rassembler toute mon âme en toi seule et devenir à mon tour l'univers pour 10 toi! Charmes adorés, vous jouiriez alors des hommages qui vous sont dus! Délices de l'amour, c'est alors que nos cœurs vous savoureraient sans cesse! Une longue et douce ivresse nous laisserait ignorer le cours des ans, et, quand enfin l'âge aurait calmé nos premiers feux, 15 l'habitude de penser et sentir ensemble ferait succéder à leurs transports une amitié non moins tendre. Tous les sentiments honnêtes, nourris dans la jeunesse avec ceux de l'amour, en rempliraient un jour le vide immense; nous pratiquerions au sein de cet heureux peuple, et à 20 son exemple, tous les devoirs de l'humanité; sans cesse nous nous unirions pour bien faire, et nous ne mourrions point sans avoir vécu."

La poste arrive; il faut finir ma lettre, et courir recevoir la vôtre. Que le cœur me bat jusqu'à ce mo- 25 ment! Hélas! j'étais heureux dans mes chimères: mon bonheur fuit avec elles; que vais-je être en réalité?

—Première Partie Lettre XXIII.

Criticism of the Eighteenth Century Theatre

(In the interest of Julie's happiness the lovers have been forced to separate and Saint-Preux, having visited Paris, gives his reflections on the conventionality and insincerity of its life and art.)

A Julie

....Comme il n'est pas possible que tous ces gens qui font exactement la même chose soient exactement affectés de même, il est clair qu'il faut les pénétrer par d'autres moyens pour les connaître; il est clair que tout
5 ce jargon n'est qu'un vain formulaire, et sert moins à juger des mœurs que du ton qui règne à Paris. On apprend ainsi les propos qu'on y tient, mais rien de ce qui peut servir à les apprécier. J'en dis autant de la plupart des écrits nouveaux; j'en dis autant de la scène
10 même, qui, depuis Molière, est bien plus un lieu où se débitent de jolies conversations que la représentation de la vie civile. Il y a ici trois théâtres, sur deux desquels, on représente des êtres chimériques, savoir: sur l'un,[1] des arlequins, des pantalons, des scaramouches;
15 sur l'autre,[2] des dieux, des diables, des sorciers. Sur le troisième,[3] on représente ces pièces immortelles dont la lecture nous faisait tant de plaisir, et d'autres plus nouvelles qui paraissent de temps en temps sur la scène. Plusieurs de ces pièces sont tragiques, mais peu tou-
20 chantes, et, si l'on y trouve quelques sentiments naturels

[1] The *Théâtre Italien,* which enjoyed great popularity.
[2] The *Opéra.*
[3] The *Comédie Française.*

et quelque vrai rapport au cœur humain, elles n'offrent aucune sorte d'instruction sur les mœurs particulières du peuple qu'elles amusent.

L'institution de la tragédie avait chez ses inventeurs, un fondement de religion qui suffisait pour l'autoriser: d'ailleurs, elle offrait aux Grecs un spectacle instructif et agréable dans les malheurs des Perses leurs ennemis,[4] dans les crimes et les folies des rois dont ce peuple s'était délivré. Qu'on représente à Berne, à Zurich, à la Haye, l'ancienne tyrannie de la maison d'Autriche, l'amour de la patrie et de la liberté nous rendra ces pièces intéressantes;[5] mais qu'on me dise de quel usage sont ici les tragédies de Corneille, et ce qu'importe au peuple de Paris Pompée ou Sertorius.[6] Les tragédies grecques roulaient sur des événements réels ou réputés tels par les spectateurs, et fondés sur des traditions historiques; mais que fait une flamme heroïque et pure dans l'âme des grands? Ne dirait-on pas que les combats de l'amour et de la vertu leur don-

[4] In the *Persae* of Æschylus.

[5] Rousseau is urging that the subjects treated should concern the lives of the spectators, in other words that they be given themes from their own history. Goethe whose *Werther* was much influenced by the *Nouvelle Héloïse* followed this line in his *Götz von Berlichingen* (1773). Manzoni in Italy who broke away from the unities of time and place also chose subjects from Italian history in *Il Conte di Carmagnola* (1820) and *Gli Adelchi* (1822). Mme de Staël in *De l'Allemagne* (1813), Stendhal in *Racine et Shakespeare* (1822) and Hugo in the *Préface de Cromwell* (1827) will in one form or another repeat this criticism of the classic dramatists.

[6] Pompey and Sertorius are the titles and heroes of two of Corneille's plays.

nent souvent de mauvaises nuits, et que le cœur a beaucoup à faire dans les mariages des rois? Juge de la vraisemblance et de l'utilité de tant de pièces, qui roulent toutes sur ce chimérique sujet!

5 Quant à la comédie, il est certain qu'elle doit représenter au naturel les mœurs du peuple pour lequel elle est faite, afin qu'il s'y corrige de ses vices et de ses défauts, comme on ôte devant un miroir les taches de son visage. Térence et Plaute se trompèrent dans leur 10 objet; mais avant eux Aristophane et Ménandre avaient exposé aux Athéniens les mœurs athéniennes; et, depuis, le seul Molière peignit plus naïvement[6a] encore celles des Français du siècle dernier à leurs propres yeux. Le tableau a changé, mais il n'est plus revenu 15 de peintre: maintenant on copie au théâtre[7] les conversations d'une centaine de maisons de Paris; hors de cela, on n'y apprend rien des mœurs des Français. Il y a dans cette grande ville cinq ou six cent mille âmes dont il n'est jamais question sur la scène. Molière osa 20 peindre des bourgeois et des artisans aussi bien que des marquis; Socrate faisait parler des cochers, menuisiers, cordonniers, maçons.[8] Mais les auteurs d'aujourd'hui, qui sont des gens d'un autre air, se croiraient déshonorés s'ils savaient ce qui se passe au comptoir

[6a] Naturally.

[7] Rousseau has in mind the plays of Marivaux and his school which reproduce the elegance and subtlety of the language of the *salons*.

[8] Rousseau here is reproducing a remark of Montaigne's (*Essais* Liv. III, Chap. XII) on whom he drew frequently. "Il (Socrate) n'a jamais dans la bouche que cochers, menuisiers, savetiers et massons."

d'un marchand ou dans la boutique d'un ouvrier; il ne leur faut que des interlocuteurs illustres, et ils cherchent dans le rang de leurs personnages l'élévation qu'ils ne peuvent tirer de leur génie.[9] Les spectateurs eux-mêmes sont devenus si délicats qu'ils craindraient de se 5 compromettre à la comédie comme en visite, et ne daigneraient pas aller voir en représentation des gens de moindre condition qu'eux. Il sont comme les seuls habitants de la terre; tout le reste n'est rien à leurs yeux. Avoir un carrosse, un suisse, un maître d'hôtel, 10 c'est être comme tout le monde. Pour être comme tout le monde, il faut être comme très peu de gens. Ceux qui vont à pied ne sont pas du monde; ce sont des bourgeois, des hommes du peuple, des gens de l'autre monde; et l'on dirait, qu'un carrosse n'est pas tant nécessaire 15 pour se conduire que pour exister. Il y a comme cela une poignée d'impertinents qui ne comptent qu'eux dans tout l'univers, et ne valent guère la peine qu'on les compte, si ce n'est pour le mal qu'ils font. C'est pour eux uniquement que sont faits les spectacles; ils s'y mon- 20 trent à la fois comme représentés au milieu du théâtre, et comme représentants aux deux côtés; ils sont per-

[9] The protest against the "exclusiveness" of the French theatre had begun before Rousseau. The partisans of Nivelle de la Chaussée's *comédie larmoyante* defended it on the ground that it presented characters like themselves and in situations like their own. They also found it more "moral." Diderot's criticism and practice as a playwright bears on the same point. See his *Fils Naturel* (1757) and *Père de Famille* (1758), also *Entretiens sur le Fils naturel* (1757), *De la poésie dramatique* (1758). Voltaire himself in *L'Enfant Prodigue, Nanine* and *Écossaise* seemed to be following this new trend. See Gaïffe, *Le Drame en France au XVIIIe siècle*, Paris, 1910.

sonnages sur la scène, et comédiens sur les bancs.[10] C'est ainsi que la sphére du monde et des auteurs se rétrécit, c'est ainsi que la scène moderne ne quitte plus son ennuyeuse dignité: on n'y sait plus montrer les 5 hommes qu'en habit doré. Vous diriez que la France n'est peuplée que de comtes et de chevaliers; et plus le peuple y est misérable et gueux, plus le tableau du peuple y est brillant et magnifique. Cela fait qu'en peignant le ridicule des états qui servent d'exemple aux 10 autres, on le répand plutôt que de l'éteindre, et que le peuple, toujours singe et imitateur des riches, va moins au théâtre pour rire de leur folies que pour les étudier, et devenir encore plus fou qu'eux en les imitant. Voilà de quoi fut cause Molière lui-même; il corrigea la 15 cour en infectant la ville; et ses ridicules marquis furent le premier modèle des petits-maîtres bourgeois qui leur succédèrent.[11]

En général, il y a beaucoup de discours et peu d'action sur la scène française: peut-être est-ce qu'en effet 20 le Français parle encore plus qu'il n'agit, ou du moins qu'il donne un bien plus grand prix à ce qu'on dit qu'à ce qu'on fait. Quelqu'un disait, en sortant d'une pièce de Denys le Tyran: "Je n'ai rien vu, mais j'ai entendu force paroles."[12] Voilà ce qu'on peut dire en sortant 25 des pièces françaises. Racine et Corneille, avec tout

10 Distinguished spectators sat on the French stage hemming in the actors. Voltaire protested vigorously against this custom and it was abolished in 1759.

11 This is one of the bases for Rousseau's condemnation of the theatre in his *Lettre à d'Alembert*.

12 This quotation probably came from Plutarch via Montaigne. cf. *Essais,* Liv. III, Chap. VIII.

leur génie, ne sont eux-mêmes que des parleurs; et leur successeur[13] est le premier qui, à l'imitation des Anglais, ait osé mettre quelquefois la scène en représentation. Communément tout se passe en beaux dialogues bien agencés, bien ronflants, où l'on voit d'abord que le 5 premier soin de chaque interlocuteur est toujours celui de briller. Presque tout s'énonce en maximes générales. Quelque agités qu'il puissent être, ils songent toujours plus au public qu'à eux-mêmes; une sentence leur coûte moins qu'un sentiment; les pièces de Racine 10 et de Molière exceptées, le *je* est presque aussi scrupuleusement banni de la scène française que des écrits de Port-Royal, et les passions humaines, aussi modestes que l'humilité chrétienne, n'y parlent jamais que par *on*. Il y a encore une certaine dignité maniérée dans 15 le geste et dans le propos, qui ne permet jamais à la passion de parler exactement son langage, ni à l'auteur de revêtir son personnage et de se transporter au lieu de la scène, mais le tient toujours enchaîné sur le théâtre et sous les yeux des spectateurs.[14] Aussi les 20

[13] Voltaire felt this defect in the French tradition, and in the presentation of his *Tancrède* (1760) tried to picture the action more graphically by having the stage setting represent a jousting field where there is to be a trial by combat. The limitation put upon the playwright by the unities of time and place made such action as appears in Shakespeare impossible. Yet it is to be noted that Rousseau does not take up the question of the unities.

[14] M. Mornet's painstaking researches have disclosed a few isolated protests against phases of the *style noble*, shortly before this date, in Gouges de Cessières (1758) and the *Mercure de France* (1758). Rousseau's objection *on principle* to the *whole theory* of that style at this early date was however an important element in the romantic revolt which was soon to find many supporters.

situations les plus vives ne lui font-elles jamais oublier un bel arrangement de phrases ni des attitudes élégantes; et si le désespoir lui plonge un poignard dans le cœur, non content d'observer la décence en tombant comme Polyxène,[15] il ne tombe point; la décence le maintient debout après sa mort, et tous ceux qui viennent d'expirer s'en retournent l'instant d'après sur leurs jambes.

Tout cela vient de ce que le Français ne cherche point sur la scène le naturel et l'illusion, et n'y veut que de l'esprit et des pensées; il fait cas de l'agrément et non de l'imitation, et ne se soucie pas d'être séduit, pourvu qu'on l'amuse. Personne ne va au spectacle pour le plaisir du spectacle, mais pour voir l'assemblée, pour en être vu, pour ramasser de quoi fournir au caquet après la pièce; et l'on ne songe à ce qu'on voit que pour savoir ce qu'on en dira. L'acteur pour eux est toujours l'acteur, jamais le personnage qu'il représente: cet homme qui parle en maître du monde n'est point Auguste, c'est Baron[16]; la veuve de Pompée est Adrienne[17]; Alzire[18] est Mlle. Gaussin, et ce fier sauvage[19] est Grandval. Les comédiens, de leur côté, négligent entièrement l'illusion, dont ils voient que per-

[15] The sacrifice of Polyxena was a classical example of dignity and poise in meeting death. It was a favorite subject in Greek plastic art and in tragedy, entering into the lost *Polyxena* of Sophocles, the *Hecuba* of Euripides and the *Troades* of Seneca. Rousseau probably had no particular play in mind.

[16] Baron, a well known actor appearing as Augustus in Corneille's *Cinna*.

[17] Adrienne Lecouvreur in Corneille's *Pompée*.

[18] Heroine in the play of the same name by Voltaire.

[19] The Indian Zamore in the same play.

sonne ne se soucie: ils placent les héros de l'antiquité entre six rangs de jeunes Parisiens; ils calquent les modes françaises sur l'habit romain; on voit Cornélie en pleurs avec deux doigts de rouge, Caton poudré à blanc, et Brutus[20] en panier. Tout cela ne choque personne, et ne fait rien au succès des pièces: comme on ne voit que l'acteur dans le personnage, on ne voit non plus que l'auteur dans le drame; et, si le costume est négligé, cela se pardonne aisément, car on sait bien que Corneille n'était pas tailleur, ni Crébillon perruquier.

Ainsi, de quelque sens qu'on envisage les choses, tout n'est ici que babil, jargon, propos sans conséquence. Sur la scène comme dans le monde, on a beau écouter ce qui se dit, on n'apprend rien de ce qui se fait: et qu'a-t-on besoin de l'apprendre? Sitôt qu'un homme a parlé, s'informe-t-on de sa conduite? n'a-t-il pas tout fait? n'est-il pas jugé? L'honnête homme d'ici n'est point celui qui fait de bonnes actions, mais celui qui dit de belles choses; et un seul propos inconsidéré, lâché sans réflexion, peut faire à celui qui le tient un tort irréparable que n'effaceraient pas quarante ans d'intégrité. En un mot, bien que les œuvres des hommes ne ressemblent guère à leurs discours, je vois qu'on ne les peint que par leurs discours, sans égard à leurs œuvres; je vois aussi que dans une grande ville la société paraît plus douce, plus facile, plus sûre même

[20] Actors were dressed in a conventional antique costume which approximated the fashions of the time, the *panier* was a flaring short skirt. Rousseau's irony is heightened by the fact that Cornelia (mother of the Gracchi), Cato and Brutus were regarded as Romans of the stern and simple type.

que parmi des gens moins étudiés; mais les hommes y sont-ils en effet plus humains, plus modérés, plus justes? Je n'en sais rien. Ce ne sont encore là que des apparences; et, sous ces dehors si ouverts et si agré-
5 ables, les cœurs sont peut-être plus cachés, plus enfoncés en dedans que les nôtres. Étranger, isolé, sans affaires, sans liaisons, sans plaisirs, et ne voulant m'en rapporter qu'à moi, le moyen de pouvoir prononcer?

—Deuxième Partie Lettre XVII.

Excursion on Lake Geneva

(After the separation of the lovers, Julie, on her father's insistence, had been released by Saint-Preux from her promise not to marry without his consent, in order from a sense of duty to marry M. de Wolmar, an undemonstrative man of honor and dignity to whom her father is under deep moral obligation. Saint-Preux, urged by his English friend, Lord Bomston, to whom the letter is addressed, had made a journey around the world on an English vessel. He has returned at the invitation of M. de Wolmar who knows of his earlier love for Julie. To show his confidence M. de Wolmar leaves for a few days and Saint-Preux and Julie set out from her home at Clarens for an excursion on the lake. They are caught in a storm and forced, after Saint-Preux and the boatmen are nearly exhausted, to land at Meillerie across the lake where Saint-Preux had sojourned on his return from his exile in the Valais (*cf. Première Partie, Lettre XXIII*). Notice in this selection Rousseau's description of romantic nature in its wilder aspects, his use of nature as a factor in the story and his lyric treatment of sentiment and virtue.)

De Saint-Preux à milord Édouard

. . . . Après le dîner, l'eau continuant d'être forte et le bateau ayant besoin de racommoder[1], je proposai un tour de promenade. Julie m'opposa le vent, le soleil, et songeait à ma lassitude. J'avais mes vues; ainsi je répondis à tout. "Je suis, lui dis-je, accoutumé dès l'enfance aux exercices pénibles; loin de nuire à ma santé, ils l'affermissent, et mon dernier voyage m'a rendu bien plus robuste encore. A l'égard du soleil et du vent, vous avez votre chapeau de paille; nous gagnerons des abris et des bois; il n'est question que de monter entre quelques rochers, et vous qui n'aimez pas la plaine en supporterez volontiers la fatigue." Elle fit ce que je voulais, et nous partîmes pendant le dîner de nos gens.

Vous savez qu'après mon exil du Valais, je revins, il y a dix ans, à Meillerie, attendre la permission de mon retour. C'est là que je passai des jours si tristes et si délicieux, uniquement occupé d'elle; et c'est de la que je lui écrivis une lettre dont elle fut si touchée. J'avais toujours désiré de revoir la retraite isolée qui me servit d'asile au milieu des glaces, et où mon cœur se plaisait à converser en lui-même avec ce qu'il eut de plus cher au monde. L'occasion de visiter ce lieu si chéri dans une saison plus agréable, et avec celle dont l'image l'habitait jadis avec moi, fut le motif secret de ma promenade. Je me faisais un plaisir de lui

[1] For *d'être raccommodé.*

montrer d'anciens monuments d'une passion si constante et si malheureuse.

Nous y parvînmes après une heure de marche par des sentiers tortueux et frais, qui, montant insensiblement
5 entre les arbres et les rochers, n'avaient rien de plus incommode que la longueur du chemin. En approchant et reconnaissant mes anciens renseignements,[2] je fus prêt à me trouver mal; mais je me surmontai, je cachai mon trouble, et nous arrivâmes. Ce lieu solitaire for-
10 mait un réduit sauvage et désert, mais plein de ces sortes de beautés qui ne plaisent qu'aux âmes sensibles, et paraissent horribles aux autres. Un torrent formé par la fonte des neiges roulait à vingt pas de nous une eau bourbeuse, et charriait avec bruit du limon, du
15 sable et des pierres. Derrière nous, une chaine de roches inaccessibles séparait l'esplanade où nous étions de cette partie des Alpes qu'on nomme les Glacières, parce que d'énormes sommets de glaces qui s'accroissent incessamment les couvrent depuis le commence-
20 ment du monde.[3] Des forêts de noirs sapins nous ombrageaient tristement à droite. Un grand bois de chênes était à gauche, au delà du torrent, et, au-dessous de nous, cette immense plaine d'eau que le lac forme au sein des Alpes nous séparait des riches côtes
25 du pays de Vaud, dont la cime du majestueux Jura couronnait le tableau.

[2] Markings, blazes to indicate his paths.

[3] Ces montagnes sont si hautes qu'une demi-heure après le soleil couché leurs sommets sont encore éclairés de ses rayons, dont le rouge forme sur ces cimes blanches une belle couleur de rose qu'on aperçoit de fort loin.

Au milieu de ces grands et superbes objets, le petit terrain où nous étions étalait les charmes d'un séjour riant et champêtre; quelques ruisseaux filtraient à travers les rochers et roulaient sur la verdure en filets de cristal; quelques arbres fruitiers sauvages penchaient 5 leurs têtes sur les nôtres; la terre, humide et fraîche, était couverte d'herbe et de fleurs. En comparant un si doux séjour aux objets qui l'environnaient il semblait que ce lieu désert dût être l'asile de deux amants échappés seuls au bouleversement de la nature. 10

Quand nous eûmes atteint ce réduit et que je l'eus quelque temps contemplé: "Quoi! dis-je à Julie en la regardant avec un œil humide, votre cœur ne vous dit-il rien ici, et ne sentez-vous point quelque émotion secrète à l'aspect d'un lieu si plein de vous?" Alors, sans 15 attendre sa réponse, je la conduisis vers le rocher, et lui montrai son chiffre gravé dans mille endroits, et plusieurs vers du[4] Pétrarque et du Tasse relatifs à la situation où j'étais en les traçant. En les revoyant moi-même après si longtemps, j'éprouvai combien la pré- 20 sence des objets peut ranimer puissamment les sentiments violents dont on fut agité près d'eux. Je lui dis avec un peu de véhémence: "O Julie! éternel charme de mon cœur, voici les lieux où soupira jadis pour toi le plus fidèle amant du monde; voici le séjour où ta chère 25 image faisait son bonheur, et préparait celui qu'il reçut enfin de toi-même. On n'y voyait alors ni ces fruits, ni ces ombrages, la verdure et les fleurs ne tapissaient

[4] Modernized texts read *de*. Rousseau, however wrote *du* as it was still customary at that time to write *le Pétrarque* as well as *le Tasse*.

point ces compartiments, le cours de ces ruisseaux n'en formait point les divisions, ces oiseaux n'y faisaient point entendre leurs ramages; le vorace épervier, le corbeau funèbre, et l'aigle terrible des Alpes, faisaient
5 seuls retentir de leurs cris ces cavernes; d'immenses glaces pendaient à tous ces rochers, des festons de neige étaient le seul ornement de ces arbres: tout respirait ici les rigueurs de l'hiver et l'horreur des frimas; les feux seuls de mon cœur me rendaient ce lieu sup-
10 portable, et les jours entiers s'y passaient à penser à toi. Voilà la pierre où je m'asseyais pour contempler au loin ton heureux séjour; sur celle-ci fut écrite la lettre qui toucha ton cœur; ces cailloux tranchants me servaient de burin pour graver ton chiffre; ici je passai
15 le torrent glacé pour reprendre une de tes lettres qu'emportait un tourbillon; là je vins relire et baiser mille fois la dernière que tu m'écrivis; voilà le bord où, d'un œil avide et sombre, je mesurais la profondeur de ces abîmes; enfin ce fut ici qu'avant mon triste départ je
20 vins te pleurer mourante, et jurer de ne te pas survivre. Fille trop constamment aimée, ô toi pour qui j'étais né, faut-il me retrouver avec toi dans les mêmes lieux, et regretter le temps que j'y passais à gémir de ton absence!..."[5] J'allais continuer; mais Julie, qui, me
25 voyant approcher du bord s'était effrayée et m'avait saisi la main, la serra sans mot dire en me regardant avec tendresse et retenant avec peine un soupir; puis

[5] To describe the revisiting of scenes in nature where the author had experienced love was to provide perhaps the greatest theme of the romantic lyrists. See Lamartine's *Le Lac,* Hugo's *Tristesse d'Olympio,* Musset's *Souvenir,* Ste. Beuve's *La Colline.*

tout à coup détournant la vue et me tirant par le bras: "Allons-nous-en, mon ami, me dit-elle d'une voix émue: l'air de ce lieu n'est pas bon pour moi."[6] Je partis avec elle en gémissant, mais sans lui répondre, et je quittai pour jamais ce triste réduit comme j'aurais quitté Julie 5 elle-même.

Revenus lentement au port après quelques détours, nous nous séparâmes. Elle voulut rester seule, et je continuai de me promener, sans trop savoir où j'allais. A mon retour, le bateau n'étant pas encore prêt, ni l'eau 10 tranquille, nous soupâmes tristement, les yeux baissés, l'air rêveur, mangeant peu et parlant encore moins. Après le souper, nous fûmes nous asseoir sur la grève, en attendant le moment du départ. Insensiblement la lune se leva, l'eau devint plus calme, et Julie me pro- 15 posa de partir. Je lui donnai la main[7] pour entrer dans le bateau, et, en m'asseyant à côté d'elle, je ne songeai plus à quitter sa main. Nous gardions un profond silence. Le bruit égal et mesuré des rames m'excitait à rêver. Le chant assez gai des bécassines[8], me retra- 20 çant les plaisirs d'un autre âge, au lieu de m'égayer m'attristait. Peu à peu je sentis augmenter la mélancolie dont j'étais accablé. Un ciel serein, la fraîcheur

[6] Notice the effective simplicity and naturalness of this reply with its absence of customary rhetoric.

[7] As Mornet points out this does not indicate familiarity. To give the hand to a lady at this time was quite as formal as to offer one's arm at present.

[8] La bécassine du lac de Genève n'est point l'oiseau qu'on appelle en France du même nom. Le chant plus vif et plus animé de la nôtre donne au lac, durant les nuits d'été, un air de vie et de fraîcheur qui rend ses rives encore plus charmantes.

de l'air, les doux rayons de la lune, le frémissement argenté dont l'eau brillait autour de nous, le concours des plus agréables sensations, la présence même de cet objet chéri, rien ne put détourner de mon cœur mille
5 réflexions douloureuses.[9]

Je commençai par me rappeler une promenade semblable faite autrefois avec elle durant le charme de nos premières amours. Tous les sentiments délicieux qui remplissaient alors mon âme s'y retracèrent pour l'af-
10 fliger; tous les événements de notre jeunesse, nos études, nos entretiens, nos lettres, nos rendez-vous, nos plaisirs,

E tanta fede, e sì dolci memorie,
E sì lungo costume![10]

15 ces foules de petits objets qui m'offraient l'image de mon bonheur passé, tout revenait, pour augmenter ma misère présente, prendre place en mon souvenir. "C'en est fait, disais-je en moi-même, ces temps, ces temps heureux ne sont plus; ils ont disparu pour jamais.
20 Hélas! ils ne reviendront plus; et nous vivons, et nous sommes ensemble, et nos cœurs sont toujours unis!" Il me semblait que j'aurais porté plus patiemment sa mort ou son absence, et que j'avais moins souffert tout le temps que j'avais passé loin d'elle. Quand je gémis-
25 sais dans l'éloignement, l'espoir de la revoir soulageait

[9] This celebrated passage with the paragraph following gives a striking example of Rousseau's use of nature to contribute to emotional effect. Notice the details employed, the rhythm of the prose, and compare the situation with *Le Lac*.

[10] "Et cette foi si pure, et ces doux souvenirs, et cette longue familiarité!" MÉTASTASIO.

mon cœur; je me flattais qu'un instant de sa présence effacerait toutes mes peines; j'envisageais au moins dans les possibles ut état moins cruel que le mien; mais se trouver auprès d'elle, mais la voir, la toucher, lui parler, l'aimer, l'adorer, et, presque en la possédant encore, la sentir perdue à jamais pour moi, voilà ce qui me jetait dans des accès de fureur et de rage qui m'agitèrent par degrés jusqu'au désespoir. Bientôt je commençai de rouler dans mon esprit des projets funestes, et, dans un transport dont je frémis en y pensant, je fus violemment tenté de la précipiter avec moi dans les flots et d'y finir dans ses bras ma vie et mes longs tourments. Cette horrible tentation devint à la fin si forte que je fus obligé de quitter brusquement sa main pour passer à la pointe du bateau.

Là mes vives agitations commencèrent à prendre un autre cours; un sentiment plus doux s'insinua peu à peu dans mon âme, l'attendrissement surmonta le désespoir, je me mis à verser des torrents de larmes; et cet état, comparé à celui dont je sortais, n'était pas sans quelque plaisir. Je pleurai fortement, longtemps, et fus soulagé. Quand je me trouvai bien remis, je revins auprès de Julie; je repris sa main. Elle tenait son mouchoir; je le sentis fort mouillé. "Ah! lui dis-je tout bas, je vois que nos cœurs n'ont jamais cessé de s'entendre! —— Il est vrai, dit-elle d'une voix altérée; mais que ce soit la dernière fois qu'ils auront parlé sur ce ton!" Nous recommençâmes alors à causer tranquillement, et, au bout d'une heure de navigation, nous arrivâmes sans autre accident. Quand nous fûmes rentrés, j'aperçus à la lumière qu'elle avait les yeux rouges et fort gonflés: elle ne dut pas trouver les miens en meilleur état. Après les fatigues de cette journée, elle avait grand besoin de repos; elle se retira, 5 et je fus me coucher.

Voilà, mon ami, le détail du jour de ma vie où, sans exception, j'ai senti les émotions les plus vives. J'espère qu'elles seront la crise qui me rendra tout à fait à moi. Au reste, je vous dirai que cette aventure m'a 10 plus convaincu que tous les arguments de la liberté de l'homme et du mérite de la vertu. Combien de gens sont faiblement tentés et succombent! Pour Julie, mes yeux le virent et mon cœur le sentit, elle soutint ce jour-là le plus grand combat qu'âme humaine ait pu soutenir: 15 elle vainquit pourtant. . . .

—Quatrième Partie, Lettre XVII.

The Ideal of Life

(Saint-Preux has come to live at the house of the Wolmars. M. de Wolmar has lost most of his fortune and with the help of Julie has developed a small estate at Clarens. Saint-Preux describes for his friend, Milord Édouard, the ideal life which the family leads, and discusses in detail questions of domestic economy which were received with keen interest at that time. This picture, as well as the description of life at the end of *Émile* gives Rousseau's matured ideal of happiness, and this should be remembered when reading his discourses of protest and his laudation of the state of nature. Though there existed and had been expressed protests against the hollowness and extravagance then in vogue, Rousseau's glorification of a modest and thrifty life in the home was new and important.)

De Saint-Preux à milord Édouard

Quelle retraite délicieuse! quelle charmante habitation! que la douce habitude d'y vivre en augmente le prix, et que, si l'aspect en paraît d'abord peu brillant, il est difficile de ne pas l'aimer aussitôt qu'on la connaît! Le goût que prend Mme de Wolmar à remplir ses nobles devoirs, à rendre heureux et bons ceux qui l'approchent, se communique à tout ce qui en est l'objet, à son mari, à ses enfants, à ses hôtes, à ses domestiques. Le tumulte, les jeux bruyants, les longs éclats de rire ne retentissent point dans ce paisible séjour, mais on y trouve partout des cœurs contents et des visages gais. Si quelquefois on y verse des larmes, elles sont d'attendrissement et de joie. Les noirs soucis, l'ennui, la tristesse, n'approchent pas plus d'ici que le vice et les remords dont ils sont le fruit. . . .

Les maîtres de cette maison jouissent d'un bien médiocre, selon les idées de fortune qu'on a dans le monde; mais, au fond, je ne connais personne de plus opulent qu'eux. Il n'y a point de richesse absolue. Ce mot ne signifie qu'un rapport de surabondance entre les désirs et les facultés de l'homme riche.[1] Tel est

[1] Schopenhauer in his *Aphorismen zur Lebensweisheit* has said that the measure of a man's unhappiness is the difference between what he desires and what he possesses. Later romantic

riche avec un arpent de terre; tel est gueux au milieu de ses monceaux d'or. Le désordre et les fantasies n'ont point de bornes et font plus de pauvres que les vrais besoins. Ici la proportion est établie sur un
5 fondement qui la rend inébranlable, savoir le parfait accord des deux époux. Le mari s'est chargé du recouvrement des rentes, la femme en dirige l'emploi, et c'est dans l'harmonie qui règne entre eux qu'est la source de leur richesse.

10 Ce qui m'a d'abord le plus frappé dans cette maison, c'est d'y trouver l'aisance, la liberté, la gaieté, au milieu de l'ordre et de l'exactitude. Le grand défaut des maisons bien réglées est d'avoir un air triste et contraint. L'extrême sollicitude des chefs sent toujours
15 un peu l'avarice; tout respire la gêne autour d'eux: la rigueur de l'ordre a quelque chose de servile qu'on ne supporte point sans peine. Les domestiques font leur devoir, mais ils le font d'un air mécontent et craintif. Les hôtes sont bien reçus, mais ils n'usent qu'avec dé-
20 fiance de la liberté qu'on leur donne; et, comme on s'y voit toujours hors de la règle, on n'y fait rien qu'en tremblant de se rendre indiscret. On sent que ces pères esclaves ne vivent point pour eux, mais pour leurs enfants, sans songer qu'ils ne sont pas seulement pères,
25 mais hommes, et qu'ils doivent à leurs enfants l'exemple de la vie de l'homme et du bonheur attaché à la sagesse. On suit ici des règles plus judicieuses: on y

pessimists like Senancour who retired to the simple life of nature felt that they could reduce their unhappiness by reducing their demands upon life. This, as well as the desire for independence, was an important factor in their decisions.

pense qu'un des principaux devoirs d'un bon père de famille n'est pas seulement de rendre son séjour riant afin que ses enfants s'y plaisent, mais d'y mener lui-même une vie agréable et douce, afin qu'ils sentent qu'on est heureux en vivant comme lui, et ne soient jamais tentés de prendre pour l'être une conduite opposée à la sienne. Une des maximes que M. de Wolmar répète le plus souvent au sujet des amusements des deux cousines est que la vie triste et mesquine des pères et mères est presque toujours la première source du désordre des enfants. . . .

Comme le premier pas vers le bien est de ne point faire de mal, le premier pas vers le bonheur est de ne point souffrir. Ces deux maximes, qui bien entendues épargneraient beaucoup de préceptes de morale, sont chères à Mme de Wolmar. Le mal-être lui est extrêmement sensible et pour elle et pour les autres; et il ne lui serait pas plus aisé d'être heureuse en voyant des misérables qu'à l'homme droit de conserver sa vertu toujours pure en vivant sans cesse au milieu des méchants Elle n'a point cette pitié barbare qui se contente de détourner les yeux des maux qu'elle pourrait soulager; elle les va chercher pour les guérir; c'est l'existence, et non la vue des malheureux, qui la tourmente; il ne lui suffit pas de ne point savoir qu'il y en a, il faut pour son repos qu'elle sache qu'il n'y en a pas, du moins autour d'elle, car ce serait sortir des termes de la raison que de faire dépendre son bonheur de celui de tous les hommes. Elle s'informe des besoins de son voisinage avec la chaleur qu'on met à son propre intérêt; elle en connaît tous les habitants; elle y étend pour ainsi dire l'enceinte de sa famille, et n'épargne aucun soin pour en écarter tous les sentiments de douleur et de peine auxquels la vie humaine est assujettie. . . .

Ce qui me plaît le plus dans les soins qu'on prend ici du bonheur d'autrui, c'est qu'ils sont tous dirigés par la sagesse, et qu'il n'en résulte jamais d'abus. N'est pas toujours bienfaisant qui veut; et souvent tel croit rendre de grands services, qui fait de grands maux qu'il ne voit pas, pour un petit bien qu'il aperçoit. Une qualité rare dans les femmes du meilleur caractère, et qui brille éminemment dans celui de Mme de Wolmar, c'est un discernement exquis dans la distribution de ses bienfaits, soit par le choix des moyens de les rendre utiles, soit par le choix des gens sur qui elle les répand. Elle s'est fait des règles dont elle ne se départ point. Elle sait accorder et refuser ce qu'on lui demande sans qu'il y ait ni faiblesse dans sa bonté, ni caprice dans son refus. Quiconque a commis en sa vie une méchante action n'a rien à espérer d'elle que justice, et pardon s'il l'a offensée; jamais faveur ni protection qu'elle puisse placer sur un meilleur sujet. Je l'ai vue refuser assez sèchement à un homme de cette espèce une grâce qui dépendait d'elle seule. "Je vous souhaite du bonheur, lui dit-elle, mais je n'y veux pas contribuer, de peur de faire du mal à d'autres en vous mettant en état d'en faire. Le monde n'est pas assez épuisé de gens de bien qui souffrent pour qu'on soit réduit à songer à vous." Il est vrai que cette dureté lui coûte extrêmement, et qu'il lui est rare de l'exercer. Sa maxime est de compter pour bons tous ceux dont la méchanceté ne lui est pas prouvée; et il y a bien peu de méchants qui n'aient l'adresse de se mettre à l'abri des preuves. Elle n'a point cette charité paresseuse des riches qui payent en argent aux malheureux le droit de rejeter leurs prières, et pour un bienfait imploré ne savent jamais donner que l'aumône. Sa bourse n'est pas inépuisable, 5 et, depuis qu'elle est mère de famille, elle en sait mieux régler l'usage. De tous les secours dont on peut soulager les malheureux, l'aumône est à la vérité celui qui coûte le moins de peine, mais il est aussi le plus passager et le moins solide; et Julie ne cherche pas à se 10 délivrer d'eux, mais à leur être utile.

Elle n'accorde pas non plus indistinctement des recommandations et des services sans bien savoir si l'usage qu'on en veut faire est raisonnable et juste. Sa protection n'est jamais refusée à quiconque en a un 15 véritable besoin et mérite de l'obtenir; mais pour ceux que l'inquiétude ou l'ambition porte à vouloir s'élever et quitter un état où ils sont bien, rarement peuvent-ils l'engager à se mêler de leurs affaires. La condition naturelle à l'homme est de cultiver la terre et de vivre 20 de ses fruits. Le paisible habitant des champs n'a besoin pour sentir son bonheur que de le connaître. Tous les vrais plaisirs de l'homme sont à sa portée; il n'a que les peines inséparables de l'humanité, des peines que celui qui croit s'en délivrer ne fait qu'échanger 25 contre d'autres plus cruelles.[2] Cet état est le seul nécessaire et le plus utile: il n'est malheureux que quand les autres le tyrannisent par leur violence, ou le séduisent

[2] L'homme sorti de sa première simplicité devient si stupide qu'il ne sait pas même désirer. Ses souhaits exaucés le mèneraient tous à la fortune, jamais à la félicité.

par l'exemple de leurs vices. C'est en lui que consiste la véritable prospérité d'un pays, la force et la grandeur qu'un peuple tire de lui-même, qui ne dépend en rien des autres nations, qui ne contraint jamais d'attaquer 5 pour se soutenir, et donne les plus sûrs moyens de se défendre. Quand il est question d'estimer la puissance publique, le bel esprit visite les palais du prince, ses ports, ses troupes, ses arsenaux, ses villes : le vrai politique parcourt les terres et va dans la chaumière du 10 laboureur. Le premier voit ce qu'on a fait, et le second ce qu'on peut faire.

Sur ce principe on s'attache ici, et plus encore à Étange, à contribuer autant qu'on peut à rendre aux paysans leur condition douce, sans jamais leur aider 15 à en sortir. Les plus aisés et les plus pauvres ont également la fureur d'envoyer leurs enfants dans les villes, les uns pour étudier et devenir un jour des messieurs, les autres pour entrer en condition et décharger leurs parents de leur entretien. Les jeunes gens, de leur côté, 20 aiment souvent à courir ; les filles aspirent à la parure bourgeoise ; les garçons s'engagent dans un service étranger : ils croient valoir mieux en rapportant dans leur village, au lieu de l'amour de la patrie et de la liberté, l'air à la fois rogue et rampant des soldats mer- 25 cenaires, et le ridicule mépris de leur ancien état. On leur montre à tous l'erreur de ces préjugés, la corruption des enfants, l'abandon des pères et les risques continuels de la vie, de la fortune et des mœurs, où cent périssent pour un qui réussit. S'ils s'obstinent, on ne 30 favorise point leur fantaisie insensée, on les laisse courir au vice et à la misère, et l'on s'applique à dédommager ceux qu'on a persuadés des sacrifices qu'ils font à la raison. On leur apprend à honorer leur condition naturelle en l'honorant soi-même; on n'a point avec les paysans les façons des villes, mais on use avec eux d'une honnête et grave familiarité, qui, maintenant 5 chacun dans son état, leur apprend pourtant à faire cas du leur. Il n'y a point de bon paysan qu'on ne porte à se considérer lui-même, en lui montrant la différence qu'on fait de lui à ces petits parvenus qui viennent briller un moment dans leur village et ternir leurs 10 parents de leur éclat. M. de Wolmar, et le baron[3], quand il est ici, manquent rarement d'assister aux exercices, aux prix, aux revues du village et des environs. Cette jeunesse, déjà naturellement ardente et guerrière, voyant de vieux officiers se plaire à ses assemblées, s'en 15 estime davantage, et prend plus de confiance en elle-même. On lui en donne encore plus en lui montrant des soldats retirés du service étranger en savoir moins qu'elle à tous égards: car, quoi qu'on fasse, jamais cinq sous de paye et la peur des coups de canne ne pro- 20 duiront une émulation pareille à celle que donne à un homme libre et sous les arbres la présence de ses parents, de ses voisins, de ses amis, de sa maîtresse, et la gloire de son pays.

La grande maxime de Mme de Wolmar est donc de 25 ne point favoriser les changements de condition, mais de contribuer à rendre heureux chacun dans la sienne, et surtout d'empêcher que la plus heureuse de toutes, qui est celle du villageois dans un état libre, ne se dépeuple en faveur des autres. 30

[3] Baron d'Etange, father of Julie.

Je lui faisais là-dessus l'objection des talents divers que la nature semble avoir partagés aux hommes pour leur donner à chacun leur emploi, sans égard à la condition dans laquelle ils sont nés. A cela elle me répon-
5 dit qu'il y avait deux choses à considérer avant le talent, savoir: les mœurs et la félicité. "L'homme, dit-elle, est un être trop noble pour devoir servir simplement d'instrument à d'autres, et l'on ne doit point l'employer à ce qui leur convient sans consulter aussi ce qui lui
10 convient à lui-même: car les hommes ne sont pas faits pour les places, mais les places sont faites pour eux; et, pour distribuer convenablement les choses, il ne faut pas tant chercher dans leur partage l'emploi auquel chaque homme est le plus propre que celui qui est le
15 plus propre à chaque homme pour le rendre bon et heureux autant qu'il est possible.[4] Il n'est jamais permis de détériorer une âme humaine pour l'avantage des autres, ni de faire un scélérat pour le service des honnêtes gens.

20 "Or, de mille sujets qui sortent du village, il n'y en a pas dix qui n'aillent se perdre à la ville ou qui n'en portent les vices plus loin que les gens dont ils les ont appris. Ceux qui réussissent et font fortune la font

[4] Kant was strongly influenced by this passage, and repeats its spirit and in part its phraseology in the development of his ethical system. It would be difficult to overestimate Rousseau's influence upon him and upon the later philosophical movement in Germany. Kant kept his portrait in his study and refers to his works frequently. Herder, Goethe, Lessing and Schiller strongly felt Rousseau's spell. Hegel makes Hume, Spinoza, and Rousseau the points of departure for modern German philosophy and sees in Rousseau's doctrine of free will as the essence of man's life the transition to and basis of Kant's doctrine.

presque tous par les voies déshonnêtes qui y mènent. Les malheureux qu'elle n'a point favorisés ne reprennent plus leur ancien état et se font mendiants ou voleurs plutôt que de redevenir paysans. De ces mille, s'il s'en trouve un seul qui résiste à l'exemple et se conserve 5 honnête homme, pensez-vous qu'à tout prendre celui-là passe une vie aussi heureuse qu'il l'eût passée à l'abri des passions violentes, dans la tranquille obscurité de sa première condition? . . .

"Je vous dirai plus, continua-t-elle: j'ai peine à croire 10 que tant de talents divers doivent être tous développés, car il faudrait pour cela que le nombre de ceux qui les possèdent fût exactement proportionné au besoin de la société; et, si l'on ne laissait au travail de la terre que ceux qui ont éminemment le talent de l'agriculture ou 15 qu'on enlevât à ce travail tous ceux qui sont plus propres à un autre, il ne resterait pas assez de laboureurs pour la cultiver et nous faire vivre. Je penserais que les talents des hommes sont comme les vertus des drogues, que la nature nous donne pour guérir nos 20 maux, quoique son intention soit que nous n'en ayons pas besoin. Il y a des plantes qui nous empoisonnent, des animaux qui nous dévorent, des talents qui nous sont pernicieux. S'il fallait toujours employer chaque chose selon ses principales propriétés, peut-être ferait- 25 on moins de bien que de mal aux hommes. Les peuples bons et simples n'ont pas besoin de tant de talents; ils se soutiennent mieux par leur seule simplicité que les autres par toute leur industrie; mais, à mesure qu'ils se corrompent, leurs talents se développent, comme pour 30 servir de supplément aux vertus qu'ils perdent, et pour forcer les méchants eux-mêmes d'être utiles en dépit d'eux." . . .

C'est ainsi, Milord, que cette âme angélique trouve toujours dans ses vertus de quoi combattre les vaines
5 subtilités dont les gens cruels pallient leurs vices. Tous ces soins et d'autres semblables sont mis par elle au rang de ses plaisirs, et remplissent une partie du temps que lui laissent ses devoirs les plus chéris. Quand, après s'être acquittée de tout ce qu'elle doit aux autres,
10 elle songe ensuite à elle-même, ce qu'elle fait pour se rendre la vie agréable peut encore être compté parmi ses vertus, tant son motif est toujours louable et honnête, et tant il y a de tempérance et de raison dans tout ce qu'elle accorde à ses désirs! Elle veut plaire à son
15 mari, qui aime à la voir contente et gaie; elle veut inspirer à ses enfants le goût des innocents plaisirs que la modération, l'ordre et la simplicité font valoir, et qui détournent le cœur des passions impétueuses. Elle s'amuse pour les amuser, comme la colombe amollit
20 dans son estomac le grain dont elle veut nourrir ses petits.

Julie a l'âme et le corps également sensibles.[5] La même délicatesse règne dans ses sentiments et dans ses organes. Elle était faite pour connaître et goûter tous
25 les plaisirs; et longtemps elle n'aima si chèrement la vertu même que comme la plus douce des voluptés. Aujourd'hui qu'elle sent en paix cette volupté suprême,

[5] *Sensible* meant merely the capacity for experiencing emotion. This was frequently looked upon as itself a virtue and on the moral side was often the ground of the most dangerous confusion of the romanticists.

elle ne se refuse aucune de celles qui peuvent s'associer avec celle-là; mais sa manière de les goûter ressemble à l'austérité de ceux qui s'y refusent, et l'art de jouir est pour elle celui des privations, non de ces privations pénibles et douloureuses qui blessent la nature et dont son auteur dédaigne l'hommage insensé, mais des privations passagères et modérées, qui conservent à la raison son empire, et, servant d'assaisonnement au plaisir, en préviennent le dégoût et l'abus. Elle prétend que tout ce qui tient aux sens et n'est pas nécessaire à la vie change de nature aussitôt qu'il tourne en habitude, qu'il cesse d'être un plaisir en devenant un besoin, que c'est à la fois une chaîne qu'on se donne et une jouissance dont on se prive, et que prévenir toujours les désirs n'est pas l'art de les contenter, mais de les éteindre. Tout celui qu'elle emploie à donner du prix aux moindres choses est de se les refuser vingt fois pour en jouir une. Cette âme simple se conserve ainsi son premier ressort: son goût ne s'use point; elle n'a jamais besoin de le ranimer par des excès, et je la vois souvent savourer avec délices un plaisir d'enfant qui serait insipide à tout autre.

Un objet plus noble qu'elle se propose encore en cela est de rester maîtresse d'elle-même, d'accoutumer ses passions à l'obéissance, et de plier tous ses désirs à la règle. C'est un nouveau moyen d'être heureuse, car on ne jouit sans inquiétude que de ce qu'on peut perdre sans peine; et si le vrai bonheur appartient au sage, c'est parce qu'il est de tous les hommes celui à qui la fortune peut le moins ôter.

Ce qui me paraît le plus singulier dans sa tempérance,

c'est qu'elle la suit sur les mêmes raisons qui jettent les voluptueux dans l'excès. "La vie est courte, il est vrai, dit-elle; c'est une raison d'en user jusqu'au bout, et de dispenser avec art sa durée afin d'en tirer le
5 meilleur parti qu'il est possible. Si un jour de satiété nous ôte un an de jouissance, c'est une mauvaise philosophie d'aller toujours jusqu'où le désir nous mène, sans considérer si nous ne serons point plus tôt au bout de nos facultés que de notre carrière, et si notre cœur
10 épuisé ne mourra point avant nous. Je vois que ces vulgaires épicuriens, pour ne vouloir jamais perdre une occasion, les perdent toutes, et, toujours ennuyés au sein des plaisirs, n'en savent jamais trouver aucun. Ils prodiguent le temps qu'ils pensent économiser, et se
15 ruinent comme les avares, pour ne savoir rien perdre à propos. Je me trouve bien de la maxime opposée, et je crois que j'aimerais encore mieux sur ce point trop de sévérité que de relâchement. Il m'arrive quelquefois de rompre une partie de plaisir, par la seule raison
20 qu'elle m'en fait trop; en la renouant j'en jouis deux fois. Cependant je m'exerce à conserver sur moi l'empire de ma volonté, et j'aime mieux être taxée de caprice que de me laisser dominer par mes fantaisies."

Voilà sur quel principe on fonde ici les douceurs
25 de la vie et les choses de pur agrément. Julie a du penchant à la gourmandise; et dans les soins qu'elle donne à toutes les parties du ménage, la cuisine surtout n'est pas négligée. La table se sent de l'abondance générale; mais cette abondance n'est point ruineuse:
30 il y règne une sensualité sans raffinement; tous les mets sont communs, mais excellents dans leurs espèces; l'ap

prêt en est simple et pourtant exquis. Tout ce qui n'est que d'appareil, tout ce qui tient à l'opinion, tous les plats fins et recherchés, dont la rareté fait tout le prix, et qu'il faut nommer pour les trouver bons, en sont bannis à jamais; et même, dans la délicatesse et le choix de ceux qu'on se permet, on s'abstient journellement de certaines choses qu'on réserve, pour donner à quelques repas un air de fête qui les rend plus agréables sans être plus dispendieux. Que croiriez-vous que sont ces mets si sobrement ménagés? du gibier rare? du poisson de mer? des productions étrangères? Mieux que tout cela: quelque excellent légume du pays, quelqu'un des savoureux herbages qui croissent dans nos jardins, certains poissons du lac apprêtés d'une certaine manière, certains laitages de nos montagnes, quelque pâtisserie à l'allemande, à quoi l'on joint quelque pièce de la chasse des gens de la maison; voilà tout l'extraordinaire qu'on y remarque; voilà ce qui couvre et orne la table, ce qui excite et contente notre appétit les jours de réjouissance. Le service est modeste et champêtre, mais propre et riant; la grâce et le plaisir y sont, la joie et l'appétit l'assaisonnent. Des surtouts dorés autour desquels on meurt de faim, des cristaux pompeux chargés de fleurs pour tout dessert, ne remplissent point la place des mets; on n'y sait point l'art de nourrir l'estomac par les yeux, mais on y sait celui d'ajouter du charme à la bonne chère, de manger beaucoup sans s'incommoder, de s'égayer à boire sans altérer sa raison, de tenir table longtemps sans ennui, et d'en sortir toujours sans dégoût.

Il y a au premier étage une petite salle à manger dif-

férente de celle où l'on mange ordinairement, laquelle est au rez-de-chaussée: cette salle particulière est à l'angle de la maison, et éclairée de deux côtés; elle donne par l'un sur le jardin, au delà duquel on voit le
5 lac à travers les arbres; par l'autre on aperçoit ce grand coteau de vignes qui commencent d'étaler aux yeux les richesses qu'on y recueillera dans deux mois. Cette pièce est petite, mais ornée de tout ce qui peut la rendre agréable et riante. C'est là que Julie donne ses petits
10 festins à son père, à son mari, à sa cousine, à moi, à elle-même, et quelquefois à ses enfants. Quand elle ordonne d'y mettre le couvert, on sait d'avance ce que cela veut dire, et M. de Wolmar l'appelle en riant le salon d'Apollon; mais ce salon ne diffère pas moins de
15 celui de Lucullus[6] par le choix des convives que par celui des mets. Les simples hôtes n'y sont point admis, jamais on n'y mange quand on a des étrangers; c'est l'asile inviolable de la confiance, de l'amitié, de la liberté; c'est la société des cœurs qui lie en ce lieu celle
20 de la table; elle est une sorte d'initiation à l'intimité, et jamais il ne s'y rassemble que des gens qui voudraient n'être plus séparés. Milord, la fête vous attend, et c'est dans cette salle que vous ferez ici votre premier repas.

25 Je n'eus pas d'abord le même honneur; ce ne fut qu'à mon retour de chez Madame d'Orbe que je fus traité dans le salon d'Apollon. Je n'imaginais pas qu'on pût rien ajouter d'obligeant à la réception qu'on m'avait faite, mais ce souper me donna d'autres idées;
30 j'y trouvai je ne sais quel délicieux mélange de famili-

[6] A Roman general noted for his sumptuous repasts.

arité, de plaisir, d'union, d'aisance, que je n'avais point encore éprouvé. Je me sentais plus libre sans qu'on m'eût averti de l'être; il me semblait que nous nous entendions mieux qu'auparavant. L'éloignement des domestiques m'invitait à n'avoir plus de réserve au 5 fond de mon cœur; et c'est là qu'à l'instance de Julie je repris l'usage, quitté depuis tant d'années, de boire avec mes hôtes du vin pur à la fin du repas.

Ce souper m'enchanta: j'aurais voulu que tous nos repas se fussent passés de même. "Je ne connaissais 10 point cette charmante salle, dis-je à Mme de Wolmar; pourquoi n'y mangez-vous pas toujours? — Voyez, dit-elle, elle est si jolie! ne serait-ce pas dommage de la gâter?" Cette réponse me parut trop loin de son caractère pour n'y pas soupçonner quelque sens caché. 15 "Pourquoi du moins, repris-je, ne rassemblez-vous pas toujours autour de vous les mêmes commodités qu'on trouve ici, afin de pouvoir éloigner vos domestiques et causer plus en liberté? — C'est, me répondit-elle encore, que cela serait trop agréable, et que l'ennui d'être tou- 20 jours à son aise est enfin le pire de tous." Il ne m'en fallut pas davantage pour concevoir son système; et je jugeai qu'en effet l'art d'assaisonner les plaisirs n'est que celui d'en être avare. . . .

Ce goût de parure s'étend de la maîtresse de la mai- 25 son à tout ce qui la compose. Le maître, les enfants, les domestiques, les chevaux, les bâtiments, les jardins, les meubles, tout est tenu avec un soin qui marque qu'on n'est pas au-dessous de la magnificence, mais qu'on la dédaigne; ou plutôt la magnificence y est en effet, s'il 30 est vrai qu'elle consiste moins dans la richesse de certaines choses que dans un bel ordre du tout, qui marque le concert des parties et l'unité d'intention de l'ordonnateur[7]. Pour moi, je trouve au moins que c'est une idée plus grande et plus noble de voir dans une maison simple et modeste un petit nombre de gens heureux d'un bonheur commun que de voir régner dans un palais la discorde et le trouble, et chacun de ceux qui l'habitent chercher sa fortune et son bonheur dans la ruine d'un autre et dans le désordre général. La maison bien réglée est une, et forme un tout agréable à voir: dans le palais on ne trouve qu'un assemblage confus de divers objets dont la liaison n'est qu'apparente. Au premier coup d'œil on croit voir une fin commune; en y regardant mieux, on est bientôt détrompé. . . .

Au contraire, un ordre de choses où rien n'est donné à l'opinion, où tout a son utilité réelle, et qui se borne aux vrais besoins de la nature, n'offre pas seulement un spectacle approuvé par la raison, mais qui contente les yeux et le cœur, en ce que l'homme ne s'y voit que sous des rapports agréables, comme se suffisant à lui-même, que l'image de sa faiblesse n'y paraît point, et que ce riant tableau n'excite jamais de réflexions attristantes. Je défie aucun homme sensé de contempler une heure durant le palais d'un prince et le faste qu'on y

[7] Cela me parait incontestable. Il y a de la magnificence dans la symétrie d'un grand palais, il n'y en a point dans une foule de maisons confusément entassées. Il y a de la magnificence dans l'uniforme d'un régiment en bataille, il n'y en a point dans le peuple qui le regarde, quoiqu'il ne s'y trouve peut-être pas un seul homme dont l'habit en particulier ne vaille mieux que celui d'un soldat. En un mot, la véritable magnificence n'est que l'ordre rendu sensible dans le grand; ce qui fait que, de tous les spectacles imaginables, le plus magnifique est celui de la nature.

voit briller sans tomber dans la mélancolie et déplorer le sort de l'humanité. Mais l'aspect de cette maison et de la vie uniforme et simple de ses habitants répand dans l'âme des spectateurs un charme secret qui ne fait qu'augmenter sans cesse. Un petit nombre de gens 5 doux et paisibles, unis par des besoins mutuels et par une réciproque bienveillance, y concourt par divers soins à une fin commune : chacun trouvant dans son état tout ce qu'il faut pour en être content et ne point désirer d'en sortir, on s'y attache comme y devant rester toute 10 la vie ; et la seule ambition qu'on garde est celle d'en bien remplir les devoirs. Il y a tant de modération dans ceux qui commandent et tant de zèle dans ceux qui obéissent que des égaux eussent pu distribuer entre eux les mêmes emplois sans qu'aucun se fût plaint de 15 son partage. Ainsi nul n'envie celui d'un autre ; nul ne croit pouvoir augmenter sa fortune que par l'augmentation du bien commun ; les maîtres mêmes ne jugent de leur bonheur que par celui des gens qui les environnent. On ne saurait qu'ajouter ni que retrancher ici, 20 parce qu'on n'y trouve que les choses utiles et qu'elles y sont toutes ; en sorte qu'on n'y souhaite rien de ce qu'on n'y voit pas, et qu'il n'y a rien de ce qu'on y voit dont on puisse dire : "Pourquoi n'y en a-t-il pas davantage ?" Ajoutez-y du galon, des tableaux, un lustre, de 25 la dorure, à l'instant vous appauvrirez tout. En voyant tant d'abondance dans le nécessaire et nulle trace de superflu, on est porté à croire que s'il n'y est pas, c'est qu'on n'a pas voulu qu'il y fût, et que si on le voulait, il y règnerait avec la même profusion ; en voyant con- 30 tinuellement les biens refluer au dehors par l'assistance du pauvre, on est porté à dire: "Cette maison ne peut contenir toutes ses richesses." Voilà, ce me semble, la véritable magnificence.

Cet air d'opulence m'effraya moi-même quand je 5 fus instruit de ce qui servait à l'entretenir. "Vous vous ruinez, dis-je à M. et Mme de Wolmar; il n'est pas possible qu'un si modique revenu suffise à tant de dépenses." Ils se mirent a rire, et me firent voir que, sans rien retrancher dans leur maison, il ne tiendrait 10 qu'à eux d'épargner beaucoup, et d'augmenter leur revenu plutôt que de se ruiner. "Notre grand secret pour être riches, me dirent-ils, est d'avoir peu d'argent, et d'éviter autant qu'il se peut, dans l'usage de nos biens, les échanges intermédiaires entre le produit et 15 l'emploi. Aucun de ces échanges ne se fait sans perte, et ces pertes multipliées réduisent presque à rien d'assez grands moyens, comme à force d'être brocantée une belle boîte d'or devient un mince colifichet. Le transport de nos revenus s'évite en les employant sur le lieu, 20 l'échange s'en évite encore en les consommant en nature[8]; et, dans l'indispensable conversion de ce que nous avons de trop en ce qui nous manque, au lieu des ventes et des achats pécuniaires qui doublent le préjudice, nous cherchons des échanges réels, où la commo- 25 dité de chaque contractant tienne lieu de profit à tous deux.

—Je conçois, leur dis-je, les avantages de cette méthode, mais elle ne me paraît pas sans inconvénient. Outre les soins importuns auxquels elle assujettit, le 30 profit doit être plus apparent que réel; et ce que vous

[8] "Goods" or produce.

perdez dans le détail de la régie de vos biens l'emporte probablement sur le gain que feraient avec vous vos fermiers, car le travail se fera toujours avec plus d'économie et la récolte avec plus de soin par un paysan que par vous. — C'est une erreur, me répondit Wolmar : le paysan se soucie moins d'augmenter le produit que d'épargner sur les frais, parce que les avances lui sont plus pénibles que les profits ne lui sont utiles ; comme son objet n'est pas tant de mettre un fonds en valeur que d'y faire peu de dépense, s'il s'assure un gain actuel, c'est bien moins en améliorant la terre qu'en l'épuisant ; et le mieux qui puisse arriver est qu'au lieu de l'épuiser, il la néglige.[9] Ainsi, pour un peu d'argent comptant recueilli sans embarras, un propriétaire oisif prépare à lui ou à ses enfants de grandes pertes, de grands travaux, et quelquefois la ruine de son patrimoine.

"D'ailleurs, poursuivit M. de Wolmar, je ne disconviens pas que je ne fasse la culture de mes terres à plus grands frais que ne ferait un fermier ; mais aussi le profit du fermier c'est moi qui le fais, et cette culture étant beaucoup meilleure, le produit est beaucoup plus grande ; de sorte qu'en dépensant davantage je ne laisse pas de gagner encore. Il y a plus : cet excès de dépense n'est qu'apparent, et produit réellement une très grande économie, car, si d'autres cultivaient nos terres, nous serions oisifs ; il faudrait demeurer à la ville ; la vie y

[9] French agriculture was in an unfortunate state in the eighteenth century as a result of this practice of farming out estates while the seigneur went to live in Paris. See Arthur Young's *Travels in France,* written on the eve of the French Revolution.

serait plus chère; il nous faudrait des amusements qui nous coûteraient beaucoup plus que ceux que nous trouvons ici, et nous seraient moins sensibles. Ces soins que vous appelez importuns font à la fois nos 5 devoirs et nos plaisirs: grâce à la prévoyance avec laquelle on les ordonne, ils ne sont jamais pénibles; ils nous tiennent lieu d'une foule de fantaisies ruineuses dont la vie champêtre prévient ou détruit le goût, et tout ce qui contribue à notre bien-être devient pour 10 nous un amusement.

"Jetez les yeux tout autour de vous, ajoutait ce judicieux père de famille, vous n'y verrez que des choses utiles, qui ne nous coûtent presque rien, et nous épargnent mille vaines dépenses. Les seules denrées du 15 cru couvrent notre table, les seules étoffes du pays composent presque nos meubles et nos habits: rien n'est méprisé parce qu'il est commun, rien n'est estimé parce qu'il est rare. Comme tout ce qui vient de loin est sujet à être déguisé ou falsifié, nous nous bornons, par 20 délicatesse autant que par modération, au choix de ce qu'il y a de meilleur auprès de nous, et dont la qualité n'est pas suspecte. Nos mets sont simples, mais choisis. Il ne manque à notre table, pour être somptueuse, que d'être servie loin d'ici: car tout y est bon, tout y serait 25 rare; et tel gourmand trouverait les truites du lac bien meilleures s'il les mangeait à Paris.[10]

"La même règle a lieu dans le choix de la parure,

[10] This is not an idle fancy. Rhine carp was a favorite delicacy on the table of Louis XVI, the king evidently being of one mind with that Roman emperor who would eat sea fish only when far from the sea.

qui, comme vous voyez, n'est pas négligée; mais l'élégance y préside seule, la richesse ne s'y montre jamais, encore moins la mode. Il y a une grande différence entre le prix que l'opinion donne aux choses et celui qu'elles ont réellement. C'est à ce dernier seul que Julie s'attache; et, quand il est question d'une étoffe, elle ne cherche pas tant si elle est ancienne ou nouvelle que si elle est bonne et si elle lui sied. Souvent même la nouveauté seule est pour elle un motif d'exclusion, quand cette nouveauté donne aux choses un prix qu'elles n'ont pas, ou qu'elles ne sauraient garder.

"Considérez encore qu'ici l'effet de chaque chose vient moins d'elle-même que de son usage et de son accord avec le reste; de sorte qu'avec des parties de peu de valeur Julie a fait un tout d'un grand prix. Le goût aime à créer, à donner seul la valeur aux choses. Autant la loi de la mode est inconstante et ruineuse, autant la sienne est économe et durable. Ce que le bon goût approuve une fois est toujours bien; s'il est rarement à la mode, en revanche il n'est jamais ridicule; et, dans sa modeste simplicité, il tire de la convenance des choses des règles inaltérables et sûres, qui restent quand les modes ne sont plus.

"Ajoutez, enfin, que l'abondance du seul nécessaire ne peut dégénérer en abus, parce que le nécessaire a sa mesure naturelle et que les vrais besoins n'ont jamais d'excès. On peut mettre la dépense de vingt habits en un seul, et manger en un repas le revenu d'une année; mais on ne saurait porter deux habits en même temps, ni dîner deux fois en un jour. Ainsi, l'opinion est illimitée, au lieu que la nature nous arrête de tous côtés;

et celui qui dans un état médiocre, se borne au bien-être, ne risque point de se ruiner.

"Voilà, mon cher, continuait le sage Wolmar, comment, avec de l'économie et des soins, on peut se mettre
5 au-dessus de sa fortune. Il ne tiendrait qu'à nous d'augmenter la nôtre sans changer notre manière de vivre, car il ne se fait ici presque aucune avance qui n'ait un produit pour objet, et tout ce que nous dépensons nous rend de quoi dépenser beaucoup plus." . . .

10 Bien plus, les privations qu'elle (Julie) s'impose par cette volupté tempérante dont j'ai parlé sont à la fois de nouveaux moyens de plaisir et de nouvelles ressources d'économie. Par exemple, elle aime beaucoup le café; chez sa mère elle en prenait tous les jours: elle en a
15 quitté l'habitude pour en augmenter le goût; elle s'est bornée à n'en prendre que quand elle a des hôtes, et dans le salon d'Apollon, afin d'ajouter cet air de fête à tous les autres. C'est une petite sensualité qui la flatte plus, qui lui coûte moins, et par laquelle elle aiguise et
20 règle à la fois sa gourmandise. . . .

Vous jugez bien q'au milieu de tant de soins divers le désœuvrement et l'oisiveté, qui rendent nécessaires la compagnie, les visites et les sociétés extérieures, ne trouvent guère ici de place. On fréquente les voisins
25 assez pour entretenir un commerce agréable, trop peu pour s'y assujettir. Les hôtes sont toujours bien venus et ne sont jamais désirés. On ne voit précisément qu'autant de monde qu'il faut pour se conserver le goût de la retraite; les occupations champêtres tiennent lieu
30 d'amusements; et, pour qui trouve au sein de sa famille une douce société, toutes les autres sont bien insipides.

La manière dont on passe ici le temps est trop simple et trop uniforme pour tenter beaucoup de gens,[11] mais c'est par la disposition du cœur de ceux qui l'ont adoptée qu'elle leur est intéressante. Avec une âme saine, peut-on s'ennuyer à remplir les plus chers et les plus 5 charmants devoirs de l'humanité et à se rendre mutuellement la vie heureuse? Tous les soirs, Julie, contente de sa journée, n'en désire point une différente pour le lendemain, et tous les matins elle demande au Ciel un jour semblable à celui de la veille: elle fait 10 toujours les mêmes choses parce qu'elles sont bien et qu'elle ne connaît rien de mieux à faire. Sans doute elle jouit ainsi de toute la félicité permise à l'homme. Se plaire dans la durée de son état, n'est-ce pas un signe assuré qu'on y vit heureux? 15

Si l'on voit rarement ici de ces tas de désœuvrés qu'on appelle bonne compagnie, tout ce qui s'y rassemble intéresse le cœur par quelque endroit avantageux et rachète quelques ridicules par mille vertus. De paisibles campagnards sans monde et sans politesse, mais bons, 20 simples, honnêtes et contents de leur sort; d'anciens officiers retirés du service, des commerçants ennuyés de s'enrichir, de sages mères de famille qui amènent leurs filles à l'école de la modestie et des bonnes mœurs,

[11] Je crois qu'un de nos beaux esprits voyageant dans ce pays-là, reçu et caressé dans cette maison à son passage, ferait ensuite à ses amis une relation bien plaisante de la vie de manants qu'on y mène. Au reste, je vois par les lettres de milady Catesby* que ce goût n'est pas particulier à la France, et que c'est apparemment aussi l'usage en Angleterre de tourner ses hôtes en ridicule pour prix de leur hospitalité.

* Rousseau is in error in believing these letters translated from the English. They were fiction written in 1759 by Mme Riccoboni.

voilà le cortège que Julie aime à rassembler autour d'elle. Son mari n'est pas fâché d'y joindre quelquefois de ces aventuriers corrigés par l'âge et l'expérience, qui, devenus sages à leurs dépens, reviennent
5 sans chagrin cultiver le champ de leur père, qu'ils voudraient n'avoir point quitté. Si quelqu'un récite à table les événements de sa vie, ce ne sont point les aventures merveilleuses du riche Sindbad, racontant au sein de la mollesse orientale comment il a gagné ses
10 trésors: ce sont les relations plus simples de gens sensés que les caprices du sort et les injustices des hommes ont rebutés des faux biens vainement poursuivis, pour leur rendre le goût des véritables.

Croiriez-vous que l'entretien même des paysans a des
15 charmes pour ces âmes élevées, avec qui le sage aimerait à s'instruire? Le judicieux Wolmar trouve dans la naïveté villageoise des caractères plus marqués, plus d'hommes pensant par eux-mêmes, que sous le masque uniforme des habitants des villes, où chacun se montre
20 comme sont les autres plutôt que comme il est lui-même. La tendre Julie trouve en eux des cœurs sensibles aux moindres caresses, et qui s'estiment heureux de l'intérêt qu'elle prend à leur bonheur. Leur cœur ni leur esprit ne sont point façonnés par l'art; ils n'ont point
25 appris à se former sur nos modèles, et l'on n'a pas peur de trouver en eux l'homme de l'homme, au lieu de celui de la nature.

Souvent, dans ses tournées, M. de Wolmar rencontre quelque bon vieillard dont le sens et la raison le frap-
30 pent, et qu'il se plaît à faire causer. Il l'amène à sa femme; elle lui fait un accueil charmant, qui marque

non la politesse et les airs de son état, mais la bienveillance et l'humanité de son caractère. On retient le bonhomme à diner: Julie le place à côté d'elle, le sert, le caresse, lui parle avec intérêt, s'informe de sa famille, de ses affaires, ne sourit point de son embarras, ne 5 donne point une attention gênante à ses manières rustiques, mais le met à son aise par la facilité des siennes, et ne sort point avec lui de ce tendre et touchant respect dû à la viellesse infirme qu'honore une longue vie passée sans reproche. Le vieillard, enchanté, se livre 10 à l'épanchement de son cœur, il semble reprendre un moment la vivacité de sa jeunesse. Le vin bu à la santé d'une jeune dame en réchauffe mieux son sang à demi glacé. Il se ranime à parler de son ancien temps, de ses amours, de ses campagnes, des combats où il 15 s'est trouvé, du courage de ses compatriotes, de son retour au pays, de sa femme, de ses enfants, des travaux champêtres, des abus qu'il a remarqués, des remèdes qu'il imagine. Souvent des long discours de son âge sortent d'excellents préceptes moraux ou des 20 leçons d'agriculture; et, quand il n'y aurait dans les choses qu'il dit que le plaisir qu'il prend à les dire, Julie en prendrait à les écouter.

Elle passe après le dîner dans sa chambre, et en rapporte un petit présent de quelque nippe convenable à la 25 femme ou aux filles du vieux bonhomme. Elle le lui fait offrir par les enfants, et, réciproquement, il rend aux enfants quelque don simple et de leur goût, dont elle l'a secrètement chargé pour eux. Ainsi se forme de bonne heure l'étroite et douce bienveillance qui fait 30 la liaison des états divers. Les enfants s'accoutument

à honorer la vieillesse, à estimer la simplicité et à distinguer le mérite dans tous les rangs. Les paysans, voyant leurs vieux pères fêtés dans une maison respectable et admis à la table des maîtres, ne se tiennent point
5 offensés d'en être exclus; ils ne s'en prennent point à leur rang, mais à leur âge: ils ne disent point: "Nous sommes trop pauvres," mais: "Nous sommes trop jeunes pour être ainsi traités." L'honneur qu'on rend à leurs vieillards, et l'espoir de le partager un jour, les
10 consolent d'en être privés et les excitent à s'en rendre dignes.

Cependant le vieux bonhomme, encore attendri des caresses qu'il a reçues, revient dans sa chaumière, empressé de montrer à sa femme et à ses enfants les dons
15 qu'il leur apporte. Ces bagatelles répandent la joie dans toute une famille, qui voit qu'on a daigné s'occuper d'elle. Il leur raconte avec emphase la réception qu'on lui a faite, les mets dont on l'a servi, les vins dont il a goûté, les discours obligeants qu'on lui a tenus,
20 combien on s'est informé d'eux, l'affabilité des maîtres, l'attention des serviteurs, et généralement ce qui peut donner du prix aux marques d'estime et de bonté qu'il a reçues; en le racontant il en jouit une seconde fois, et toute la maison croit jouir aussi des honneurs rendus
25 à son chef. Tous bénissent de concert cette famille illustre et généreuse qui donne exemple aux grands et refuge aux petits, qui ne dédaigne point le pauvre et rend honneur aux cheveux blancs. Voilà l'encens qui plaît aux âmes bienfaisantes. S'il est des bénédictions
30 humaines que le Ciel daigne exaucer, ce ne sont point celles qu'arrachent la flatterie et la bassesse en pré-

sence des gens qu'on loue, mais celles que dicte en secret un cœur simple et reconnaissant au coin d'un foyer rustique.

C'est ainsi qu'un sentiment agréable et doux peut couvrir de son charme une vie insipide à des cœurs in- 5 différents; c'est ainsi que les soins, les travaux, la retraite, peuvent devenir des amusements par l'art de les diriger. Une âme saine peut donner du goût à des occupations communes, comme la santé du corps fait trouver bons les aliments les plus simples. Tous ces 10 gens ennuyés qu'on amuse avec tant de peine doivent leur dégoût à leurs vices, et ne perdent le sentiment du plaisir qu'avec celui du devoir. Pour Julie, il lui est arrivé précisément le contraire, et des soins qu'une certaine langueur d'âme lui eût laissé négliger autrefois 15 lui deviennent intéressants par le motif qui les inspire. Il faudrait être insensible pour être toujours sans vivacité. La sienne s'est développée par les mêmes causes qui la réprimaient autrefois. Son cœur cherchait la retraite et la solitude pour se livrer en paix aux affec- 20 tions dont il était pénétré; maintenant elle a pris une activité nouvelle en formant de nouveaux liens. Elle n'est point de ces indolentes mères de famille, contentes d'étudier quand il faut agir, qui perdent à s'instruire des devoirs d'autrui le temps qu'elles devraient mettre 25 à remplir les leurs. Elle pratique aujourd'hui ce qu'elle apprenait autrefois. Elle n'étudie plus, elle ne lit plus: elle agit. Comme elle se lève une heure plus tard que son mari, elle se couche aussi plus tard d'une heure. Cette heure est le seul temps qu'elle donne encore à 30 l'étude, et la journée ne lui paraît jamais assez longue pour tous les soins dont elle aime à la remplir.

Voilà, Milord, ce que j'avais à vous dire sur l'économie de cette maison et sur la vie privée des maîtres qui la gouvernent. Contents de leur sort, ils en jouissent paisiblement; contents de leur fortune, ils ne travaillent pas à l'augmenter pour leurs enfants, mais à leur laisser, avec l'héritage qu'ils ont reçu, des terres en bon état, des domestiques affectionnés, le goût du travail, de l'ordre, de la modération, et tout ce qui peut rendre douce et charmante à des gens sensés la jouissance d'un bien médiocre, aussi sagement conservé qu'il fut honnêtement acquis.

—*Cinquième Partie, Lettre II.*

Joys of the Vintage

(This letter, also from Saint-Preux to Milord Édouard, gives in more concrete form a picture of the simple joys of country life.)

De Saint-Preux à Milord Édouard

. . . Vous ne sauriez concevoir avec quel zèle, avec quelle gaieté tout cela se fait. On chante, on rit toute la journée, et le travail n'en va que mieux. Tout vit dans la plus grande familiarité; tout le monde est égal, et personne ne s'oublie. Les dames sont sans airs, les paysannes sont décentes, les hommes badins et non grossiers. C'est à qui trouvera les meilleures chansons, à qui fera les meilleurs contes, à qui dira les meilleurs traits. L'union même engendre les folâtres querelles, et l'on ne s'agace mutuellement que pour montrer combien on est sûr les uns des autres. On ne revient point ensuite faire chez soi les messieurs; on passe aux vignes toute la journée: Julie y a fait faire une loge où l'on va se chauffer quand on a froid et dans laquelle on se réfugie en cas de pluie. On dîne avec les paysans et à leur heure, aussi bien qu'on travaille avec eux. On mange avec appétit leur soupe un peu grossière, mais bonne, saine et chargée d'excellents légumes. On ne ricane point orgueilleusement de leur air gauche et de leurs compliments rustauds: pour les mettre à leur aise, on s'y prête sans affectation. Ces complaisances ne leur échappent pas, ils y sont sensibles; et, voyant qu'on veut bien sortir pour eux de sa place, ils s'en tiennent d'autant plus volontiers dans la leur. A dîner on amène les enfants, et ils passent le reste de la journée à la vigne. Avec quelle joie ces bons villageois les voient arriver! "O bienheureux enfants! disent-ils en les pressant dans leurs bras robustes, que le bon Dieu prolonge vos jours aux dépens des nôtres! ressemblez à vos pères et mères, et soyez comme eux la bénédiction du pays!" Souvent, en songeant que la plupart de ces hommes ont porté les armes et savent manier l'épée et le mousquet aussi bien que la serpette et la houe, en voyant Julie au milieu d'eux, si charmante et si respectée, recevoir, elle et ses enfants, leurs touchantes acclamations, je me rappelle l'illustre et vertueuse Agrippine montrant son fils[12] aux troupes de Germanicus. Julie! femme incomparable! vous exercez dans la simplicité de la vie privée le despotique empire de la sagesse et des bienfaits; vous êtes pour tout le pays un dépôt cher et sacré que chacun voudrait défendre et conserver au prix de son sang, et vous vivez

[12] Caligula.

plus sûrement, plus honorablement, au milieu d'un peuple entier qui vous aime, que les rois entourés de tous leurs soldats.

Le soir, on revient gaiement tous ensemble. On nourrit et loge les ouvriers tout le temps de la vendange; et même le dimanche, après le prêche du soir, on se rassemble avec eux et l'on danse jusqu'au souper. Les autres jours on ne se sépare point non plus en rentrant au logis, hors le baron, qui ne soupe jamais et se couche de fort bonne heure, et Julie, qui monte avec ses enfants chez lui jusqu'à ce qu'il s'aille coucher. A cela près, depuis le moment qu'on prend le métier de vendangeur jusqu'à celui qu'on le quitte, on ne mêle plus la vie citadine à la vie rustique. Ces saturnales sont bien plus agréables et plus sages que celles des Romains. Le renversement qu'ils affectaient était trop vain pour instruire le maître ni l'esclave; mais la douce égalité qui règne ici rétablit l'ordre de la nature, forme une instruction pour les uns, une consolation pour les autres, et un lien d'amitié pour tous.[13]

[13] Si de là naït un commun état de fête, non moins doux à ceux qui descendent qu'à ceux qui montent, ne s'ensuit-il pas que tous les états sont presque indifférents par eux-mêmes, pourvu qu'on puisse et qu'on veuille en sortir quelquefois? Les gueux sont malheureux parce qu'ils sont toujours gueux; les rois sont malheureux parce qu'ils sont toujours rois. Les états moyens, dont on sort plus aisément, offrent des plaisirs au-dessus et au-dessous de soi; ils étendent aussi les lumières de ceux qui les remplissent, en leur donnant plus de préjugés à connaître, et plus de degrés à comparer. Voilà, ce me semble, la principale raison pourquoi c'est généralement dans les conditions médiocres qu'on trouve les hommes les plus heureux et du meilleur sens.

Le lieu d'assemblée est une salle à l'antique avec une grande cheminée où l'on fait bon feu. La pièce est éclairée de trois lampes, auxquelles M. de Wolmar a seulement fait ajouter des capuchons de fer-blanc pour intercepter la fumée et réfléchir la lumière. Pour prévenir l'envie et les regrets, on tâche de ne rien étaler aux yeux de ces bonnes gens qu'ils ne puissent retrouver chez eux, de ne leur montrer d'autre opulence que le choix du bon dans les choses communes et un peu plus de largesse dans la distribution. Le souper est servi sur deux longues tables. Le luxe et l'appareil des festins n'y sont pas, mais l'abondance et la joie y sont. Tout le monde se met à table: maîtres, journaliers, domestiques; chacun se lève indifféremment pour servir sans exclusion, sans préférence, et le service se fait toujours avec grâce et avec plaisir. On boit à discrétion; la liberté n'a point d'autres bornes que l'honnêteté. La présence de maîtres si respectés contient tout le monde et n'empêche pas qu'on ne soit à son aise et gai. Que s'il arrive à quelqu'un de s'oublier, on ne trouble point la fête par des réprimandes, mais il est congédié sans rémission dès le lendemain.

Je me prévaux aussi des plaisirs du pays et de la saison. Je reprends la liberté de vivre à la valaisane et de boire assez souvent du vin pur; mais je n'en bois point qui n'ait été versé de la main d'une des deux cousines. Elles se chargent de mesurer ma soif à mes forces et de ménager ma raison. Qui sait mieux qu'elles comment il la faut gouverner et l'art de me l'ôter et de me la rendre? Si le travail de la journée, la durée et la gaieté du repas, donnent plus de force au vin versé de ces mains chéries, je laisse exhaler mes transports sans contrainte; ils n'ont plus rien que je doive taire, rien que gêne la présence du sage Wolmar. Je ne crains point que son œil éclairé lise au fond de 5 mon cœur, et, quand un tendre souvenir y veut renaître, un regard de Claire lui donne le change, un regard de Julie m'en fait rougir.

Après le souper, on veille encore une heure ou deux en teillant du chanvre; chacun dit sa chanson tour à 10 tour. Quelquefois les vendangeuses chantent en chœur toutes ensemble, ou bien alternativement à voix seule et en refrain. La plupart de ces chansons sont de vieilles romances dont les airs ne sont pas piquants, mais ils ont je ne sais quoi d'antique et de doux qui 15 touche à la longue. Les paroles sont simples, naïves, souvent tristes; elles plaisent pourtant. Nous ne pouvons nous empêcher, Claire de sourire, Julie de rougir, moi de soupirer, quand nous retrouvons dans ces chansons des tours et des expressions dont nous nous 20 sommes servis autrefois. Alors, en jetant les yeux sur elles et me rappelant les temps éloignés, un tressaillement me prend, un poids insupportable me tombe tout à coup sur le cœur et me laisse une impression funeste qui ne s'efface qu'avec peine. Cependant je trouve à 25 ces veillés une sorte de charme que je ne puis vous expliquer, et qui m'est pourtant fort sensible. Cette réunion des différents états, la simplicité de cette occupation, l'idée de délassement, d'accord, de tranquillité, le sentiment de paix qu'elle porte à l'âme, a quelque 30 chose d'attendrissant qui dispose à trouver ces chansons plus intéressantes. Ce concert des voix de femmes n'est pas non plus sans douceur. Pour moi, je suis convaincu que de toutes les harmonies il n'y en a point d'aussi agréable que le chant à l'unisson, et que, s'il nous faut des accords, c'est parce que nous avons le goût dépravé. En effet, toute l'harmonie ne se trouve- 5 t-elle pas dans un son quelconque? et qu'y pouvons-nous ajouter sans altérer les proportions que la nature a établies dans la force relative des sons harmonieux? En doublant les uns et non pas les autres, en ne les renforçant pas en même rapport, n'ôtons-nous pas à 10 l'instant ces proportions? La nature a tout fait le mieux qu'il était possible; mais nous voulons mieux faire encore, et nous gâtons tout.

Il y a une grande émulation pour ce travail du soir aussi bien que pour celui de la journée, et la filouterie 15 que j'y voulais employer m'attira hier un petit affront. Comme je ne suis pas des plus adroits à teiller et que j'ai souvent des distractions, ennuyé d'être toujours noté pour avoir fait le moins d'ouvrage je tirais doucement avec le pied des chènevottes de mes voisins pour 20 grossir mon tas; mais cette impitoyable Mme d'Orbe s'en étant aperçue, fit signe à Julie, qui, m'ayant pris sur le fait, me tança sévèrement. "Monsieur le fripon, me dit-elle tout haut, point d'injustice, même en plaisantant; c'est ainsi qu'on s'accoutume à devenir mé- 25 chant tout de bon, et, qui pis est, à plaisanter encore."

Voilà comment se passe la soirée. Quand l'heure de la retraite approche, Mme de Wolmar dit: "Allons tirer le feu d'artifice." A l'instant chacun prend son paquet de chènevottes, signe honorable de son travail; 30 on les porte en triomphe au milieu de la cour; on les

rassemble en un tas; on en fait un trophée; on y met le feu; mais n'a pas cet honneur qui veut; Julie l'adjuge en présentant le flambeau à celui ou celle qui a fait ce soir-là le plus d'ouvrage; fût-ce elle-même, elle se l'at-
5 tribue sans façon. L'auguste cérémonie est accompagnée d'acclamations et de battements de mains. Les chènevottes font un feu clair et brillant qui s'élève jusqu'aux nues, un vrai feu de joie, autour duquel on saute, on rit. Ensuite on offre à boire à toute l'assem-
10 blée: chacun boit à la santé du vainqueur, et va se coucher content d'une journée passée dans le travail, la gaieté, l'innocence, et qu'on ne serait pas fâché de recommencer le lendemain, le surlendemain, et toute sa vie.

15 —*Cinquième Partie, Lettre VII.*

Reasons for the Popularity of Julie

(At the close of *Julie* Rousseau added this note which gives his views on his own work and the novel in general.)

20 En achevant de relire ce recueil, je crois voir pourquoi l'intérêt, tout faible qu'il est, m'en est si agréable, et le sera, je pense, à tout lecteur d'un bon naturel: c'est qu'au moins ce faible intérêt est pur et sans mélange de peine; qu'il n'est point excité par des noir-
25 ceurs, par des crimes, ni mêlé du tourment de haïr. Je ne saurais concevoir quel plaisir on peut prendre à imaginer et composer le personnage d'un scélérat, à se mettre à sa place tandis qu'on le représente, à lui prêter l'éclat le plus imposant. Je plains beaucoup les auteurs

de tant de tragédies pleines d'horreurs, lesquels passent
leur vie à faire agir et parler des gens qu'on ne peut
écouter ni voir sans souffrir. Il me semble qu'on
devrait gémir d'être condamné à un travail si cruel:
ceux qui s'en font un amusement doivent être bien 5
dévorés du zèle de l'utilité publique. Pour moi, j'admire de bon cœur leurs talents et leurs beaux génies.
mais je remercie Dieu de ne me les avoir pas donnés.

EMILE

It is difficult for us to understand the keen interest and wide discussion aroused by the publication of *Émile ou de l'Éducation* in 1762. The popularity of the treatise was due in part to the vogue of works on education in the decade preceding its appearance.[1] In even larger part it was due to the fact that it was presented as the romance of a child's development, his progress from infancy to maturity and marriage, from helplessness and dependence to complete mastery of self and assurance in independent activity. The love interest, though to later tastes somewhat forced, was supplied by the introduction of Sophie, Emile's feminine counterpart, and the volume concluded with a picture of the ideal life in the little house with the green shutters, not unlike the account of Julie's days at Clarens.

Of the influence of the volume upon even the greatest thinkers, especially in Germany, there can be no question. It was Kant's favorite. Goethe called it the "Bible of teachers," and Herder, Lessing and Schiller were among its admirers. Owing to its somewhat abstract presentation of Rousseau's general views on life its influence was greater on the pedagogical and philosophical than on the purely literary side.

[1] For a list of such works see Mornet's *Jean-Jacques Rousseau, Morceaux Choisis*, 3e édition, pp. 42-43.

True to his belief in nature's goodness, Rousseau held that the first part of education until his pupil's tenth or twelfth year, should be "negative." It should close the door to vice and protect his charge from vicious contacts while developing his body and his senses which are to be the instruments of his later knowledge.

After this period instruction proper is to be given in those subjects on which the pupil's curiosity has been stimulated. This instruction is inculcated through example rather than theory. It is drawn from experiment and experience and its end is frankly utilitarian.

After the age of fifteen begins the time of Emile's moral education. This section of the work contained the famous confession of faith of the Savoyard Vicar who showed that the principles of Christianity could be derived from the contemplation of the harmonies of nature, thus doing away with the necessity for revelation. For this reason the work was condemned by the Parliament of Paris, and Rousseau was forced to leave France. Rousseau's reply, *Lettre à Christophe de Beaumont,* is one of the best expositions of his theory of education. It was, however, ineffective. Geneva was likewise hostile, and Rousseau was forced or believed himself forced to a long period of wandering.

Of the criticisms of that time, or of later times, those which attack the work on the ground that it is impossible to apply the system in detail are beside the point. Rousseau did not intend that his treatise should provide a practical manual but merely the broad lines of a system. He realized, and indeed admits, that it would be impossible to find an ideal tutor who could spend twenty years with every, or indeed any, child. He would likewise admit that it would be impossible entirely to ignore "moral" education until the pupil reached the age of fifteen. What he tried to do was to apply his general principles to education. He insists everywhere on the natural, the normal, and the favor which these words have since enjoyed in connection with education is sufficient testimony to his influence.[2]

The Need of Education

Tout est bien, sortant des mains de l'Auteur des choses; tout dégénère entre les mains de l'homme. Il force une terre à nourrir les productions d'une autre, un arbre à porter les fruits d'un autre; il mêle et con-
5 fond les climats, les éléments, les saisons; il mutile son chien, son cheval, son esclave; il bouleverse tout, il défigure tout; il aime la difformité, les monstres; il ne veut rien tel que la fait la nature, pas même l'homme; il le faut dresser pour lui, comme un cheval de manège;
10 il le faut contourner à sa mode, comme un arbre de son jardin.

Sans cela, tout irait plus mal encore, et notre espèce ne veut pas être façonnée à demi. Dans l'état où sont désormais les choses, un homme abandonné dès sa
15 naissance à lui-même parmi les autres serait le plus

[2]The most important studies on Rousseau's educational theories are those of Compayré. See especially *J.-J. Rousseau et l'éducation de la nature,* Paris, 3e edition; also his *Histoire critique des doctrines de l'éducation en France.* On Rousseau's relation to his predecessors see P. Villey, *L'Influence de Montaigne sur les idées pédagogiques de Locke et de Rousseau,* Paris, 1911.

défiguré de tous. Les préjugés. l'autorité, la nécessité, l'exemple, toutes les institutions sociales dans lesquelles nous nous trouvons submergés étoufferaient en lui la nature, et ne mettraient rien à la place. Elle y serait comme un arbrisseau que le hasard fait naître au milieu 5 d'un chemin, et que les passants font bientôt périr, en le heurtant de toutes parts et le pliant dans tous les sens.

—*Livre I.*

THE LIMITS OF INDIVIDUAL RIGHTS 10

(This passage provides a good example of what Rousseau means by negative education.)

Nos premiers devoirs sont envers nous; nos sentiments primitifs se concentrent en nous-mêmes; tous nos mouvements naturels se rapportent d'abord à notre 15 conservation et à notre bien-être. Ainsi le premier sentiment de la justice ne nous vient pas de celle que nous devons, mais de celle qui nous est due; et c'est encore un des contresens des éducations communes, que, parlant d'abord aux enfants de leurs devoirs, 20 jamais de leurs droits, on commence par leur dire le contraire de ce qu'il faut, ce qu'ils ne sauraient entendre, et ce qui ne peut les intéresser. . . .

Il s'agit donc de remonter à l'origine de la propriété; car c'est de là que la première idée en doit naître. L'en- 25 fant, vivant à la campagne, aura pris quelque notion des travaux champêtres; il ne faut pour cela que des yeux, du loisir; il aura l'un et l'autre. Il est de tout âge, surtout du sien, de vouloir créer, imiter, produire, donner des signes de puissance et d'activité. Il n'aura 30 pas vu deux fois labourer un jardin, semer, lever, croître des légumes, qu'il voudra jardiner à son tour.

Je ne m'oppose point à son envie: au contraire, je la favorise, je partage son goût, je travaille avec lui, non pour son plaisir, mais pour le mien; du moins il le
5 croit ainsi: je deviens son garçon jardinier; en attendant qu'il ait des bras, je laboure pour lui la terre: il en prend possession en y plantant une fêve; et sûrement cette possession est plus sacrée et plus respectable que celle que prenait Nunès Balboa de l'Amérique
10 méridionale au nom du roi d'Espagne, en plantant son étendard sur les côtes de la mer du Sud.

On vient tous les jours arroser les fèves, on les voit lever dans des transports de joie. J'augmente cette joie en lui disant, Cela vous appartient; et lui expliquant
15 alors ce terme d'appartenir, je lui fais sentir qu'il a mis là son temps, son travail, sa peine, sa personne enfin; qu'il y a dans cette terre quelque chose de lui-même qu'il peut réclamer contre qui que ce soit, comme il pourrait retirer son bras de la main d'un autre homme
20 qui voudrait le retenir malgré lui.

Un beau jour il arrive empressé et l'arrosoir à la main. O spectacle! ô douleur! toutes les fèves sont arrachées, tout le terrain est bouleversé, la place même ne se reconnaît plus. Ah! qu'est devenu mon travail,
25 mon ouvrage, le doux fruit de mes soins et de mes sueurs? Qui m'a ravi mon bien? qui m'a pris mes fèves? Ce jeune cœur se soulève; le premier sentiment de l'injustice y vient verser sa triste amertume; les larmes coulent en ruisseaux; l'enfant désolé remplit
30 l'air de gémissements et de cris. On prend part à sa peine, à son indignation; on cherche, on s'informe, on

fait des perquisitions. Enfin l'on découvre que le jardinier a fait le coup: on le fait venir.

Mais nous voici bien loin de compte. Le jardinier, apprenant de quoi l'on se plaint, commence à se plaindre plus haut que nous. Quoi, messieurs, c'est vous 5
qui m'avez ainsi gâté mon ouvrage! J'avais semé là des melons de Malte, dont la graine m'avait été donnée comme un trésor, et desquels j'espérais vous régaler quand il seraient mûrs; mais voilà que, pour y planter vos misérables fèves, vous m'avez détruit mes melons 10
déjà tout levés, et que je ne remplacerai jamais. Vous m'avez fait un tort irréparable, et vous vous êtes privés vous-mêmes du plaisir de manger des melons exquis.

JEAN-JACQUES

Excusez-nous, mon pauvre Robert. Vous aviez mis 15
là votre travail, votre peine. Je vois bien que nous avons eu tort de gâter votre ouvrage; mais nous vous ferons venir d'autre graine de Malte, et nous ne travaillerons plus la terre avant de savoir si quelqu'un n'y a point mis la main avant nous. 20

ROBERT

Oh bien! messieurs, vous pouvez donc vous reposer; car il n'y a plus guère de terre en friche. Moi, je travaille celle que mon père a bonifiée, chacun en fait autant de son côté, et toutes les terres que vous voyez 25
sont occupées depuis longtemps.

ÉMILE

Monsieur Robert, il y a donc souvent de la graine de melons perdue?

ROBERT

Pardonnez-moi, mon jeune cadet; car il ne vous vient pas souvent de petits messieurs aussi étourdis que vous. Personne ne touche au jardin de son voisin; chacun 5 respecte le travail des autres, afin que le sien soit en sûreté.

ÉMILE

Mais moi je n'ai point de jardin.

ROBERT

10 Que m'importe? si vous gâtez le mien, je ne vous y laisserai plus promener; car, voyez-vous, je ne veux pas perdre ma peine.

JEAN-JACQUES

Ne pourrait-on pas proposer un arrangement au bon 15 Robert? Qu'il nous accorde, à mon petit ami et à moi, un coin de son jardin pour le cultiver, à condition qu'il aura la moitié du produit.

ROBERT

Je vous l'accorde sans condition. Mais souvenez-20 vous que j'irai labourer vos fèves, si vous touchez à mes melons.

Dans cet essai de la manière d'inculquer aux enfants les notions primitives, on voit comment l'idée de la propriété remonte naturellement au droit du premier oc-25 cupant par le travail. Cela est clair, net, simple, et toujours à la portée de l'enfant. De là jusqu'au droit de propriété et aux échanges il n'y a plus qu'un pas, après lequel il faut s'arrêter tout court.

On voit encore qu'une explication que je renferme 30 ici dans deux pages d'écriture sera peut-être l'affaire d'un an pour la pratique; car, dans la carrière des idées morales, on ne peut avancer trop lentement, ni trop bien s'affermir à chaque pas. Jeunes maîtres, pensez, je vous prie, à cet exemple, et souvenez-vous qu'en toute chose vos leçons doivent être plus en actions qu'en discours; car les enfants oublient aisément ce qu'ils ont dit et ce qu'on leur a dit, mais non pas ce qu'ils ont fait et ce qu'on leur a fait.

De pareilles instructions se doivent donner, comme je l'ai dit, plus tôt ou plus tard, selon que le naturel paisible ou turbulent de l'élève en accélère ou retarde le besoin; leur usage est d'une évidence qui saute aux yeux: mais, pour ne rien omettre d'important dans les choses difficiles, donnons encore un exemple.

Votre enfant dyscole gâte tout ce qu'il touche: ne vous fâchez point; mettez hors de sa portée ce qu'il peut gâter. Il brise les meubles dont il se sert; ne vous hâtez point de lui en donner d'autres: laissez-lui sentir le préjudice de la privation. Il casse les fenêtres de sa chambre; laissez le vent souffler sur lui nuit et jour, sans vous soucier des rhumes; car il vaut mieux qu'il soit enrhumé que fou. Ne vous plaignez jamais des incommodités qu'il vous cause, mais faites qu'il les sente le premier. A la fin vous faites raccommoder les vitres, toujours sans rien dire. Il les casse encore? changez alors de méthode; dites-lui sèchement, mais sans colère: Les fenêtres sont à moi; elles ont été mises là par mes soins; je veux les garantir. Puis vous l'enfermerez à l'obscurité dans un lieu sans fenêtre. A ce procédé si nouveau il commence par crier, tempêter: personne ne l'écoute. Bientôt il se lasse et change de ton; il se

plaint, il gémit: un domestique se présente, le mutin le prie de le délivrer. Sans chercher de prétexte pour n'en rien faire, le domestique répond: *J'ai aussi des vitres à conserver*, et s'en va. Enfin, après que l'enfant
5 aura demeuré là plusieurs heures, assez longtemps pour s'y ennuyer et s'en souvenir, quelqu'un lui suggérera de vous proposer un accord au moyen duquel vous lui rendriez la liberté, et il ne casserait plus de vitre. Il ne demandera pas mieux. Il vous fera prier de le venir
10 voir: vous viendrez; il vous fera sa proposition, et vous l'accepterez à l'instant, en lui disant: C'est très bien pensé; nous y gagnerons tous deux: que n'avez-vous eu plus tôt cette bonne idée! Et puis, sans lui demander ni protestation ni confirmation de sa promesse, vous
15 l'embrasserez avec joie et l'emmènerez sur-le-champ dans sa chambre, regardant cet accord comme sacré et inviolable autant que si le serment y avait passé. Quelle idée pensez-vous qu'il prendra, sur ce procédé, de la foi des engagements et de leur utilité? Je suis trompé
20 s'il y a sur la terre un seul enfant, non déjà gâté, à l'épreuve de cette conduite, et qui s'avise après cela de casser une fenêtre à dessein. Suivez la chaîne de tout cela. Le petit méchant ne songeait guère, en faisant un trou pour planter sa fêve, qu'il se creusait
25 un cachot où sa science ne tarderait pas à le faire enfermer.

—*Livre II.*

A Lesson in Courtesy and the Ways of Magnetized Ducks

Depuis longtemps nous nous étions aperçus, mon élève et moi, que l'ambre, le verre, la cire, divers corps frottés, attiraient les pailles, et que d'autres ne les attiraient pas. Par hasard nous en trouvons un qui a une vertu plus singulière encore : c'est d'attirer à quelque distance, et sans être frotté, la limaille et d'autres brins de fer. Combien de temps cette qualité nous amuse, sans que nous puissions y rien voir de plus ! Enfin nous trouvons qu'elle se communique au fer même, aimanté dans un certain sens. Un jour nous allons à la foire ; un joueur de gobelets attire avec un morceau de pain un canard de cire flottant sur un bassin d'eau. Fort surpris, nous ne disons pourtant pas, C'est un sorcier, car nous ne savons ce que c'est qu'un sorcier. Sans cesse frappés d'effets dont nous ignorons les causes, nous ne nous pressons de juger de rien, et nous restons en repos dans notre ignorance jusqu'à ce que nous trouvions l'occasion d'en sortir.

De retour au logis, à force de parler du canard de la foire, nous allons nous mettre en tête de l'imiter : nous prenons une bonne aiguille bien aimantée, nous l'entourons de cire blanche, que nous façonnons de notre mieux en forme de canard, de sorte que l'aiguille traverse le corps et que la tête fasse le bec. Nous posons sur l'eau le canard, nous approchons du bec un anneau de clef, et nous voyons, avec une joie facile à comprendre, que notre canard suit la clef précisément comme celui de la foire suivait le morceau de pain.

Observer dans quelle direction le canard s'arrête sur l'eau quand on l'y laisse en repos, c'est ce que nous pourrons faire une autre fois. Quant à présent, tout occupés de notre objet, nous n'en voulons pas davan-5 tage.

Dès le même soir nous retournons à la foire avec du pain préparé dans nos poches; et, sitôt que le joueur de gobelets a fait son tour, mon petit docteur, qui se contenait à peine, lui dit que ce tour n'est pas difficile, et 10 que lui-même en fera bien autant. Il est pris au mot: à l'instant il tire de sa poche le pain où est caché le morceau de fer; en approchant de la table, le cœur lui bat; il présente le pain presque en tremblant; le canard vient et le suit: l'enfant s'écrie et tressaillit d'aise. Aux 15 battements de mains, aux acclamations de l'assemblée, la tête lui tourne, il est hors de lui. Le bateleur interdit vient pourtant l'embrasser, le féliciter, et le prie de l'honorer encore le lendemain de sa présence, ajoutant qu'il aura soin d'assembler plus de monde encore pour 20 applaudir à son habileté. Mon petit naturaliste enorgueilli veut babiller; mais sur-le-champ je lui ferme la bouche, et l'emmène comblé d'éloges.

L'enfant, jusqu'au lendemain, compte les minutes avec une risible inquiétude. Il invite tout ce qu'il ren-25 contre; il voudrait que tout le genre humain fût témoin de sa gloire; il attend l'heure avec peine, il la devance: on vole au rendez-vous; la salle est déjà pleine. En entrant son jeune cœur s'épanouit. D'autres jeux doivent précéder; le joueur de gobelets se surpasse et 30 fait des choses surprenantes. L'enfant ne voit rien de tout cela; il s'agite, il sue, il respire à peine; il passe son temps à manier dans sa poche son morceau de pain, d'une main tremblante d'impatience. Enfin son tour vient; le maître l'annonce au public avec pompe. Il s'approche un peu honteux, il tire son pain... Nouvelle vicissitude des choses humaines! le canard, si privé la veille, est devenu sauvage aujourd'hui; au lieu de présenter le bec, il tourne la queue et s'enfuit; il évite le pain et la main qui le présente avec autant de soin qu'il les suivait auparavant. Après mille essais inutiles et toujours hués, l'enfant se plaint, dit qu'on le trompe, que c'est un autre canard qu'on a substitué au premier, et défie le joueur de gobelets d'attirer celui-ci.

Le joueur de gobelets, sans répondre, prend un morceau de pain, le présente au canard; à l'instant le canard suit le pain, et vient à la main qui le retire. L'enfant prend le même morceau de pain; mais, loin de réussir mieux qu'auparavant, il voit le canard se moquer de lui, et faire des pirouettes tout autour du bassin; il s'éloigne enfin tout confus, et n'ose plus s'exposer aux huées.

Alors le joueur de gobelets prend le morceau de pain que l'enfant avait apporté, et s'en sert avec autant de succès que du sien: il en tire le fer devant tout le monde, autre risée à nos dépens; puis de ce pain ainsi vidé il attire le canard comme auparavant. Il fait la même chose avec un autre morceau coupé devant tout le monde par une main tierce; il en fait autant avec son gant; avec le bout de son doigt; enfin il s'éloigne au milieu de la chambre, et, du ton d'emphase propre à ces gens-là, déclarant que son canard n'obéira pas moins à sa voix qu'à son geste, il lui parle, et le canard

obéit; il lui dit d'aller à droite et il va à droite, de revenir, et il revient, de tourner et il tourne; le mouvement est aussi prompt que l'ordre. Les applaudissements redoublés sont autant d'affronts pour nous.
5 Nous nous évadons sans être aperçus, et nous nous renfermons dans notre chambre sans aller raconter nos succès à tout le monde, comme nous l'avions projété.

Le lendemain l'on frappe à notre porte: j'ouvre; c'est l'homme aux gobelets. Il se plaint modestement
10 de notre conduite. Que nous avait-il fait pour nous engager à vouloir décréditer ses jeux et lui ôter son gagne-pain? Qu'y a-t-il donc de si merveilleux dans l'art d'attirer un canard de cire, pour acheter cet honneur aux dépens de la subsistance d'un honnête homme?
15 Ma foi, messieurs, si j'avais quelque autre talent pour vivre, je ne me glorifierais guère de celui-ci. Vous deviez croire qu'un homme qui a passé sa vie à s'exercer dans cette chétive industrie en sait là-dessus plus que vous, qui ne vous en occupez que quelques moments. Si je
20 ne vous ai pas d'abord montré mes coups de maître, c'est qu'il ne faut pas se presser d'étaler étourdiment ce qu'on sait: j'ai toujours soin de conserver mes meilleurs tours pour l'occasion, et après celui-ci j'en ai d'autres encore pour arrêter de jeunes indiscrets. Au reste,
25 messieurs, je viens de bon cœur vous apprendre ce secret qui vous a tant embarrassés, vous priant de n'en pas abuser pour me nuire, et d'être plus retenus une autre fois.

Alors il nous montre sa machine, et nous voyons
30 avec la dernière surprise qu'elle ne consiste qu'en un aimant fort et bien armé, qu'un enfant caché sous la table faisait mouvoir sans qu'on s'en aperçût.

L'homme replie sa machine; et, après lui avoir fait nos remerciments et nos excuses, nous voulons lui faire un présent; il le refuse. "Non, messieurs, je n'ai pas assez à me louer de vous pour accepter vos dons; je vous laisse obligés à moi malgré vous; c'est ma seule 5 vengeance. Apprenez qu'il y a de la générosité dans tous les états; je fais payer mes tours et non mes leçons."

En sortant, il m'adresse à moi nommément et tout haut une réprimande: J'excuse volontiers, me dit-il, 10 cet enfant; il n'a péché que par ignorance. Mais vous, monsieur, qui deviez connaître sa faute, pourquoi la lui avoir laissé faire? Puisque vous vivez ensemble, comme le plus âgé vous lui devez vos soins, vos conseils; votre experience est l'autorité qui doit le conduire. 15 En se reprochant, étant grand, les torts de sa jeunesse, il vous reprochera sans doute ceux dont vous ne l'aurez pas averti.

Il part, et nous laisse tous deux très confus. Je me blâme de ma molle facilité; je promets à l'enfant de la 20 sacrifier une autre fois à son intérêt, et de l'avertir de ses fautes avant qu'il en fasse; car le temps approche où nos rapports vont changer, et où la sévérité du maître doit succéder à la complaisance du camarade; ce changement doit s'amener par degrés; il faut tout 25 prévoir, et tout prévoir de fort loin.

Le lendemain nous retournons à la foire pour revoir le tour dont nous avons appris le secret. Nous abordons avec un profond respect notre bateleur Socrate; à peine osons-nous lever les yeux sur lui: il nous comble 30 d'honnêtetés, et nous place avec une distinction qui nous humilie encore. Il fait ses tours comme à l'ordinaire; mais il s'amuse et se complaît longtemps à celui du canard, en nous regardant souvent d'un air assez fier. Nous savons tout, et nous ne soufflons pas. Si mon 5 élève osait seulement ouvrir la bouche, ce serait un enfant à écraser.

Tout le détail de cet exemple importe plus qu'il ne semble. Que de leçons dans une seule! que de suites mortifiantes attire le premier mouvement de vanité! 10 Jeune maître, épiez ce premier mouvement avec soin. Si vous savez en faire sortir ainsi l'humiliation, les disgrâces, soyez sûr qu'il n'en reviendra de longtemps un second. Que d'apprêts! direz-vous. J'en conviens, et le tout pour nous faire une boussole qui nous tienne 15 lieu de méridienne.

Ayant appris que l'aimant agit à travers les autres corps, nous n'avons rien de plus pressé que de faire une machine semblable à celle que nous avons vue: une table évidée, un bassin très-plat ajusté sur cette table, 20 et rempli de quelques lignes d'eau, un canard fait avec un peu plus de soin, etc. Souvent attentifs autour du bassin, nous remarquons enfin que le canard en repos affecte toujours à peu près la même direction. Nous suivons cette expérience, nous examinons cette direc- 25 tion: nous trouvons qu'elle est du midi au nord. Il n'en faut pas davantage; notre boussole est trouvée, ou autant vaut; nous voilà dans la physique.

—*Livre III.*

A Lesson in Cosmography

30 Je n'aime point les explications en discours; les jeunes gens y font peu d'attention et ne les retiennent

guère. Les choses! les choses! Je ne répéterai jamais assez que nous donnons trop de pouvoir aux mots: avec notre éducation babillarde nous ne faisons que des babillards.

Supposons que, tandis que j'étudie avec mon élève 5 le cours du soleil et la manière de s'orienter, tout à coup il m'interrompe pour me demander à quoi sert tout cela. Quel beau discours je vais lui faire! de combien de choses je saisis l'occasion de l'instruire en répondant à sa question, surtout si nous avons des té- 10 moins de notre entretien![3] Je lui parlerai de l'utilité des voyages, des avantages du commerce, des productions particulières à chaque climat, des mœurs des différents peuples, de l'usage du calendrier, de la supputation du retour des saisons pour l'agriculture, de l'art 15 de la navigation, de la manière de se conduire sur mer et de suivre exactement sa route, sans savoir où l'on est. La politique, l'histoire naturelle, l'astronomie, la morale même et le droit des gens entreront dans mon explication, de manière à donner à mon élève une 20 grande idée de toutes ces sciences et un grand désir de les apprendre. Quand j'aurai tout dit, j'aurai fait l'étalage d'un vrai pédant, auquel il n'aura pas compris une seule idée. Il aurait grande envie de me demander comme auparavant à quoi sert de s'orienter; mais il 25 n'ose, de peur que je ne me fâche. Il trouve mieux

[3] J'ai souvent remarqué que, dans les doctes instructions qu'on donne aux enfants, on songe moins à se faire écouter d'eux que des grandes personnes qui sont présentes. Je suis très sûr de ce que je dis là, car j'en ai fait l'observation sur moi-même.

son compte à feindre d'entendre ce qu'on l'a forcé d'écouter. Ainsi se pratiquent les belles éducations.

Mais notre Émile, plus rustiquement élevé, et à qui nous donnons avec tant de peine une conception dure, 5 n'écoutera rien de tout cela. Du premier mot qu'il n'entendra pas il va s'enfuir, il va folâtrer par la chambre, et me laisser pérorer tout seul. Cherchons une solution plus grossière; mon appareil scientifique ne vaut rien pour lui.

10 Nous observions la position de la forêt au nord de Montmorency, quand il m'a interrompu par son importune question, *A quoi sert cela?* Vous avez raison, lui dis-je; il y faut penser à loisir; et si nous trouvons que ce travail n'est bon à rien, nous ne le reprendrons plus, 15 car nous ne manquons pas d'amusements utiles. On s'occupe d'autre chose, et il n'est plus question de géographie du reste de la journée.

Le lendemain matin je lui propose un tour de promenade avant le déjeuner: il ne demande pas mieux; pour 20 courir, les enfants sont toujours prêts, et celui-ci a de bonnes jambes. Nous montons dans la forêt, nous parcourons les champeaux, nous nous égarons, nous ne savons plus où nous sommes; et, quand il s'agit de revenir, nous ne pouvons plus retrouver notre chemin. 25 Le temps se passe, la chaleur vient, nous avons faim; nous nous pressons, nous errons vainement de côté et d'autre, nous ne trouvons partout que des bois, des carrières, des plaines, nul renseignement pour nous reconnaître. Bien échauffés, bien recrus, bien affamés, 30 nous ne faisons avec nos courses que nous égarer davantage. Nous nous asseyons enfin pour nous reposer, pour délibérer. Émile, que je suppose élevé comme un autre enfant, ne délibère point, il pleure; il ne sait pas que nous sommes à la porte de Montmorency, et qu'un simple taillis nous le cache; mais ce taillis est une forêt pour lui, un homme de sa stature est enterré dans des 5 buissons.

Après quelques moments de silence, je lui dis d'un air inquiet: Mon cher Émile, comment ferons-nous pour sortir d'ici?

ÉMILE, *en nage, et pleurant à chaudes larmes,* 10

Je n'en sais rien. Je suis las; j'ai faim, j'ai soif; je n'en puis plus.

JEAN-JACQUES

Me croyez-vous en meilleur état que vous? et pensez-vous que je me fisse faute de pleurer, si je pouvais 15 déjeuner de mes larmes? Il ne s'agit pas de pleurer, il s'agit de se reconnaître. Voyons votre montre; quelle heure est-il?

ÉMILE

Il est midi, et je suis à jeun. 20

JEAN-JACQUES

Cela est vrai, il est midi, et je suis à jeun.

ÉMILE

Oh! que vous devez avoir faim!

JEAN-JACQUES 25

Le malheur est que mon dîner ne viendra pas me chercher ici. Il est midi: c'est justement l'heure où nous observions hier de Montmorency la position de la forêt. Si nous pouvions de même observer de la forêt la position de Montmorency?... 30

ÉMILE

Oui ; mais hier nous voyions la forêt, et d'ici nous ne voyons pas la ville.

JEAN-JACQUES

5 Voilà le mal... Si nous pouvions nous passer de la voir, pour trouver sa position !...

ÉMILE

O mon bon ami !

JEAN-JACQUES

10 Ne disions-nous pas que la forêt était...

ÉMILE

Au nord de Montmorency.

JEAN-JACQUES

Par conséquent Montmorency doit être...

15 ÉMILE

Au sud de la forêt.

JEAN-JACQUES

Nous avons un moyen de trouver le nord à midi.

ÉMILE

20 Oui, par la direction de l'ombre.

JEAN-JACQUES

Mais le sud ?

ÉMILE

Comment faire ?

25 JEAN-JACQUES

Le sud est l'opposé du nord.

ÉMILE

Cela est vrai ; il n'y a qu'à chercher l'opposé de l'ombre. Oh ! voilà le sud ! voilà le sud ! sûrement
30 Montmorency est de ce côté : cherchons de ce côté.

JEAN-JACQUES

Vous pouvez avoir raison; prenons ce sentier à travers le bois.

ÉMILE, *frappant des mains et poussant un cri de joie,*

Ah! je vois Montmorency! le voilà tout devant nous, 5 tout à découvert. Allons déjeuner, allons dîner, courons vite: l'astronomie est bonne à quelque chose.

Prenez garde que s'il ne dit pas cette dernière phrase, il la pensera; peu importe, pourvu que ce ne soit pas moi qui la dise. Or soyez sûr qu'il n'oubliera de sa vie 10 la leçon de cette journée; au lieu que, si je n'avais fait que lui supposer tout cela dans sa chambre, mon discours eût été oublié dès le lendemain. Il faut parler tant qu'on peut par les actions, et ne dire que ce qu'on ne saurait faire. 15

—*Livre III.*

Robinson Crusoe as a Text Book

N'y aurait-il point moyen de rapprocher tant de leçons éparses dans tant de livres, de les réunir sous un objet commun qui pût être facile à voir, intéressant à 20 suivre, et qui pût servir de stimulant, même à cet âge? Si l'on peut inventer une situation où tous les besoins naturels de l'homme se montrent d'une manière sensible à l'esprit d'un enfant, et où les moyens de pourvoir à ces mêmes besoins se développent successivement 25 avec la même facilité, c'est par la peinture vive et naïve de cet état qu'il faut donner le premier exercice à son imagination.

Philosophe ardent, je vois déjà s'allumer la vôtre. Ne vous mettez pas en frais; cette situation est trouvée, 30

elle est décrite, et, sans vous faire tort, beaucoup mieux que vous ne la décririez vous-même, du moins avec plus de vérité et de simplicité. Puis-qu'il nous faut absolument des livres, il en existe un qui fournit, à mon gré,
5 le plus heureux traité d'éducation naturelle. Ce livre sera le premier que lira mon Émile; seul il composera durant longtemps toute sa bibliothèque, et il y tiendra toujours une place distinguée. Il sera le texte auquel tous nos entretiens sur les sciences naturelles ne ser-
10 viront que de commentaire. Il servira d'épreuve durant nos progrès à l'état de notre jugement; et, tant que notre goût ne sera pas gâté, sa lecture nous plaira toujours. Quel est donc ce merveilleux livre? Est-ce Aristote? est-ce Pline? est-ce Buffon? Non; c'est
15 Robinson Crusoé.

Robinson Crusoé dans son île, seul, dépourvu de l'assistance de ses semblables et des instruments de tous les arts, pourvoyant cependant à sa subsistance, à sa conservation, et se procurant même une sorte de
20 bien-être: voilà un objet intéressant pour tout âge, et qu'on a mille moyens de rendre agréable aux enfants. Voilà comment nous réalisons l'île déserte qui me servait d'abord de comparaison. Cet état n'est pas, j'en conviens, celui de l'homme social; vraisemblablement
25 il ne doit pas être celui d'Émile: mais c'est sur ce même état qu'il doit apprécier tous les autres. Le plus sûr moyen de s'élever au-dessus des préjugés et d'ordonner ses jugements sur les vrais rapports des choses, est de se mettre à la place d'un homme isolé, et de juger de
30 tout comme cet homme en doit juger lui-même, eu égard à sa propre utilité.

Ce roman, débarrassé de tout son fatras, commençant au naufrage de Robinson près de son île, et finissant à l'arrivée du vaisseau qui vient l'en tirer, sera tout à la fois l'amusement et l'instruction d'Émile durant l'époque dont il est ici question. Je veux que la tête lui en tourne, qu'il s'occupe sans cesse de son château, de ses chèvres, de ses plantations; qu'il apprenne en détail, non dans des livres, mais sur les choses, tout ce qu'il faut savoir en pareil cas; qu'il pense être Robinson lui-même; qu'il se voie habillé de peaux, portant un grand bonnet, un grand sabre, tout le grotesque équipage de la figure, au parasol près, dont il n'aura pas besoin. Je veux qu'il s'inquiète des mesures à prendre, si ceci ou cela venait à lui manquer; qu'il examine la conduite de son héros, qu'il cherche s'il n'a rien omis, s'il n'y avait rien de mieux à faire; qu'il marque attentivement ses fautes, et qu'il en profite pour n'y pas tomber lui-même en pareil cas: car ne doutez point qu'il ne projette d'aller faire un établissement semblable; c'est le vrai château en Espagne de cet heureux âge, où l'on ne connaît d'autre bonheur que le nécessaire et la liberté.

Quelle ressource que cette folie pour un homme habile, qui n'a su la faire naître qu'afin de la mettre à profit! L'enfant, pressé de se faire un magasin pour son île, sera plus ardent pour apprendre, que le maître pour enseigner. Il voudra savoir tout ce qui est utile, et ne voudra savoir que cela: vous n'aurez plus besoin de le guider, vous n'aurez qu'à le retenir. Au reste, dépêchons-nous de l'établir dans cette île, tandis qu'il y borne sa félicité; car le jour approche où, s'il y veut vivre encore, il n'y voudra plus vivre seul; et où *Vendredi,* qui maintenant ne le touche guère, ne lui suffira pas longtemps.[4]

—*Livre III.*

5 THE IMMORALITY OF IDLENESS

(Rousseau in several passages prophesied the coming revolution.[5] In this selection he is demanding that his pupil shall learn a trade, both for his own sake and the sake of society. He makes it plain that he con-
10 siders the existing order unstable and likely soon to be overthrown. The trade he prefers for his charge is that of carpenter. The moral attitude and the tone here assumed is very similar to that more recently taken by Tolstoi who may in this as in many other re-
15 spects be regarded as Rousseau's disciple. (See Benrubi, *Tolstoi continuateur de J.-J. Rousseau.* Annales J.-J. R., Vol. III, pp. 83-118.)

Vous vous fiez à l'ordre actuel de la société, sans songer que cet ordre est sujet à des révolutions inévitables,
20 et qu'il vous est impossible de prévoir ni de prévenir celle qui peut regarder vos enfants Le grand devient petit, le riche devient pauvre, le monarque devient sujet; les coups du sort sont-ils si rares que vous puissiez compter d'en être exempt? Nous approchons de l'état
25 de crise et du siècle des révolutions.[6] Qui peut vous

[4] An artistic touch by which Rousseau is preparing for the later introduction of Sophie.

[5] Cf. F. Rocquain, *L'Esprit révolutionnaire avant la Révolution,* Paris, 1875.

[6] Je tiens pour impossible que les grandes monarchies de l'Europe aient encore longtemps à durer: toutes ont brillé, et tout État qui brille est sur son déclin. J'ai de mon opinion des

répondre de ce que vous deviendrez alors? Tout ce qu'ont fait les hommes, les hommes peuvent le détruire: il n'y a de caractères ineffaçables que ceux qu'imprime la nature, et la nature ne fait ni princes, ni riches, ni grands seigneurs. Que fera donc, dans la bassesse, ce satrape que vous n'avez élevé que pour la grandeur? Que fera, dans la pauvreté, ce publicain qui ne sait vivre que d'or? Que fera, dépourvu de tout, ce fastueux imbécile qui ne sait point user de lui-même, et ne met son être que dans ce qui est étranger à lui? Heureux celui qui sait quitter alors l'état qui le quitte, et rester homme en dépit du sort! Qu'on loue tant qu'on voudra ce roi vaincu qui veut s'enterrer en furieux sous les débris de son trône; moi je le méprise; je vois qu'il n'existe que par sa couronne, et qu'il n'est rien du tout s'il n'est roi: mais celui qui la perd et s'en passe est alors au-dessus d'elle....

L'homme et le citoyen, quel qu'il soit, n'a d'autre bien à mettre dans la société que lui-même, tous ses autres biens y sont malgré lui; et quand un homme est riche, ou il ne jouit pas de sa richesse, ou le public en jouit aussi. Dans le premier cas il vole aux autres ce dont il se prive; et dans le second il ne leur donne rien. Ainsi la dette sociale lui reste tout entière tant qu'il ne paye que de son bien. Mais mon père, en le gagnant, a servi la société... Soit; il a payé sa dette, mais non pas la vôtre. Vous devez plus aux autres que si vous fussiez né sans bien, puisque vous êtes né favorisé. Il

raisons plus particulières que cette maxime; mais il n'est pas à propos de les dire, et chacun ne les voit que trop.

n'est point juste que ce qu'un homme a fait pour la société en décharge un autre de ce qu'il lui doit ; car chacun, se devant tout entier, ne peut payer que pour lui, et nul père ne peut transmettre à son fils le droit
5 d'être inutile à ses semblables : or c'est pourtant ce qu'il fait, selon vous, en lui transmettant ses richesses, qui sont la preuve et le prix du travail. Celui qui mange dans l'oisiveté ce qu'il n'a pas gagné lui-même le vole ; et un rentier que l'État paye pour ne rien faire ne diffère
10 guère, à mes yeux, d'un brigand qui vit aux dépens des passants. Hors de la société, l'homme isolé, ne devant rien à personne, a droit de vivre comme il lui plaît ; mais dans la société, où il vit nécessairement aux dépens des autres, il leur doit en travail le prix de son
15 entretien ; cela est sans exception. Travailler est donc un devoir indispensable à l'homme social. Riche ou pauvre, puissant ou faible, tout citoyen oisif est un fripon.

—*Livre III.*

DU CONTRAT SOCIAL

The most important, at least the most systematic, of Rousseau's works on political science is the *Contrat Social.* Rousseau had as early as 1743, during his stay at the French embassy in Venice, become interested in political questions. In the following decade, exactly when it is impossible to say, he had planned and begun to write his *Institutions politiques* which he never completed. It seems from the statement in the *Confessions* (Partie II, Livre IX) that he had done considerable work upon it by 1756. Later, in 1759, he decided to extract from the unfinished larger work the section which he revised and published as the *Contrat Social.* It appeared in April, 1762, in an edition published by Rey, at Amsterdam. Although the last chapter on *La Réligion Civile* was written in 1757, the main body of the work was composed, at least in a first draft, considerably earlier, most probably about 1754, and dates, therefore, from about the time of his writing the *Discours sur l'Inégalité.* Much has been written on the contradictions between these two works, especially the difference in attitude toward the state of nature which in the *Contrat* is dismissed briefly.[1]

[1] Students interested in this question and that of the date of composition should consult the discussion between A. Schinz and G. Beaulavon in the *Revue d'histoire littéraire de la France* (1912-1913), also Dreyfus-Brisac, *Du Contrat Social,* Paris, 1896; Beaulavon *Du Contrat Social,* Paris, 2e édition, 1914; Vaughan, *Political Writings of Rousseau,* London, 1915. The two latter contain excellent bibliographies.

Some of this confusion will be obviated if it is remembered that Rousseau's purpose and intention in the two works were quite different; the *Discours* was critical and destructive, the *Contrat* idealistic and constructive.

The idea that the state was based upon a contract was not original with Rousseau. Indeed it was a commonplace of political discussion and could be found in one form or another in Hobbes, Locke, and Jurieu, to mention but a few with whom Rousseau was familiar. What distinguishes Rousseau's contract is the fact that it is made not between the people and a "prince" or ruler, but between the people and themselves, each individual agreeing to surrender his rights to the state, in the government of which he is in return to possess an equal right with his fellows.

When later political historians assert that *historically* there never was any such contract, they are merely saying what Rousseau would himself have admitted. His point is that in order that a state should have the *moral* right to govern its citizens it must be based upon "the consent of the governed." When these same critics, as occasionally happens, employ the above phrase, they are themselves asserting that democratic government exists only where there is at least an implied agreement between the governing body and the governed. How far Rousseau is right as to the terms of this implied contract is however quite a different question and one where he is certainly open to serious criticism.

The heart of Rousseau's political theory may be said

to be found, however, in his conception of the *"volonté générale,"* and it is his most important single contribution to political theory. Locke had made the distinction between "public will" and "private will" (*On Civil Government,* Chapter XIII). The conception of Rousseau is, however, far more clearly developed and becomes central to his system. The doctrine of the *volonté générale* is first stated by Rousseau in his article on *Économie Politique* published in Vol. V of Diderot's *Encyclopédie* (1755). He there refers to an article by Diderot himself in the same volume on *Droit Naturel.* Whether the conception originated with Diderot or with Rousseau and what each owed to the other is uncertain. There can be no question, however, that the development of the idea and its later prominence are due to Jean-Jacques. According to him it is with the creation of this general will that the state comes to have a corporate existence of its own. This will expresses itself in the spirit and patriotism of the citizens and in the laws of the state. In a state properly constituted citizens actuated by the general will are capable, according to Rousseau, of acting against their selfish interest as private citizens, and the general will is, therefore, not the same as the will of all, considered as private individuals. This idea has been attacked severely by many political historians as chimerical and mystical. Mystical it may be, chimerical it certainly is not. Rousseau had been profoundly impressed by Plutarch's heroes who sacrificed themselves to their city or state, and it was the city states of antiquity as much as the Republic of Geneva that he had before himself as his ideal. When today we speak of a good citizen as one actuated by "public spirit," we are very near Rousseau's conception of the *volonté générale*. It is true that Rousseau seems to contradict himself when he demands of citizens that they surrender to the state virtually every one of those individual rights which, on other occasions, he so eloquently extolls.[2] It is also true that through his consequent failure to safeguard adequately the rights of individuals, a minority would be completely at the mercy of the majority, and his system could be made, as it was in the French Revolution, an excuse or pretext for the worst forms of mob tyranny.[3]

Sujet de ce Premier Livre

L'homme est né libre, et partout il est dans les fers. Tel se croit le maître des autres qui ne laisse pas d'être plus esclave qu'eux. Comment ce changement s'est-il
5 fait? Je l'ignore. Qu'est-ce qui peut le rendre légitime? Je crois pouvoir résoudre cette question.

Si je ne considérais que la force et l'effet qui en dérive, je dirais: Tant qu'un peuple est contraint d'obéir et qu'il obéit, il fait bien; sitôt qu'il peut secouer le joug
10 et qu'il le secoue, il fait encore mieux; car, en recouvrant sa liberté par le même droit qui la lui a ravie,

[2] It should be remembered that Rousseau had in mind, in writing the *Contrat*, a small compact city state, and that he never expected the *Contrat*, as it stood, to be used as a constitution. When he was planning constitutions for Corsica and Poland, he himself proceeded quite differently.

[3] On this whole question see Vaughan, *Political Writings of Rousseau*, Vol. I, pp. 422-428.

ou il est fondé à la reprendre, ou l'on ne l'était pas à la lui ôter. Mais l'ordre social est un droit sacré qui sert de base à tous les autres. Cependant ce droit ne vient point de la nature; il est donc fondé sur des conventions. Il s'agit de savoir quelles sont ces conventions. Avant d'en venir là, je dois établir ce que je viens d'avancer.

—*Livre I, Chap. I.*

Du Droit du Plus Fort

Le plus fort n'est jamais assez fort pour être toujours le maître, s'il ne transforme sa force en droit et l'obéissance en devoir. De là le droit du plus fort, droit pris ironiquement en apparence et réellement établi en principe.[4] Mais ne nous expliquera-t-on jamais ce mot? La force est une puissance physique; je ne vois point quelle moralité peut résulter de ses effets. Céder à la force est un acte de nécessité, non de volonté; c'est tout au plus un acte de prudence. En quel sens pourra-ce être un devoir?

Supposons un moment ce prétendu droit. Je dis qu'il n'en résulte qu'un galimatias inexplicable; car sitôt que c'est la force qui fait le droit, l'effet change avec la cause; toute force qui surmonte la première succède à son droit. Sitôt qu'on peut désobéir impunément, on le peut légitimement; et puisque le plus fort a toujours raison, il ne s'agit que de faire en sorte qu'on soit le plus fort. Or, qu'est-ce qu'un droit qui périt quand la force cesse? S'il faut obéir par force, on n'a pas besoin d'obéir par devoir; et si l'on n'est

[4] Rousseau is here criticising Hobbes's theory.

plus forcé d'obéir, on n'y est plus obligé. On voit donc que le mot *droit* n'ajoute rien à la force; il ne signifie ici rien du tout.

Obéissez aux puissances. Si cela veut dire: cédez à 5 la force, le précepte est bon, mais superflu; je réponds qu'il ne sera jamais violé. Toute puissance vient de Dieu, je l'avoue; mais toute maladie en vient aussi: est-ce à dire qu'il soit défendu d'appeler le médecin?[5] Qu'un brigand me surprenne au coin d'un bois, non-10 seulement il faut par force donner la bourse, mais quand je pourrai la soustraire, suis-je en conscience obligé de la donner? Car enfin le pistolet qu'il tient est aussi une puissance.

Convenons donc que force ne fait pas droit, et qu'on 15 n'est obligé d'obéir qu'aux puissances légitimes. Ainsi, ma question primitive revient toujours.

—*Livre I, Chap. III.*

Du Pacte Social

Je suppose les hommes parvenus à ce point où les ob-20 stacles qui nuisent à leur conservation dans l'état de nature l'emportent par leur résistance sur les forces que chaque individu peut employer pour se maintenir dans cet état. Alors cet état primitif ne peut plus subsister, et le genre humain périrait s'il ne changeait de 25 manière d'être.

Or, comme les hommes ne peuvent engendrer de nouvelles forces, mais seulement unir et diriger celles qui existent, ils n'ont plus d'autre moyen pour se con-

[5] The theory of "divine right" was still widely held in the eighteenth century. Rousseau here adroitly brushes it aside.

server, que de former, par agrégation, une somme de forces qui puisse l'emporter sur la résistance, de les mettre en jeu par un seul mobile, et de les faire agir de concert.

Cette somme de forces ne peut naître que du concours de plusieurs; mais la force et la liberté de chaque homme étant les premiers instruments de sa conservation, comment les engagera-t-il sans se nuire, sans négliger les soins qu'il se doit? Cette difficulté, ramenée à mon sujet, peut s'énoncer en ces termes:

"Trouver une forme d'association qui défende et protège de toute la force commune la personne et les biens de chaque associé, et par laquelle chacun, s'unissant à tous, n'obéisse pourtant qu'à lui-même, et reste aussi libre qu'auparavant." Tel est le problème fondamental dont le Contrat social donne la solution.

Les clauses de ce Contrat sont tellement déterminées par la nature de l'acte, que la moindre modification les rendrait vaines et de nul effet; en sorte que, bien qu'elles n'aient peut-être jamais été formellement énoncées, elles sont partout les mêmes, partout tacitement admises et reconnues, jusqu'à ce que, le pacte social étant violé, chacun rentre alors dans ses premiers droits et reprenne sa liberté naturelle en perdant la liberté conventionnelle pour laquelle il y renonça.

Ces clauses, bien entendues, se réduisent toutes à une seule, savoir: l'aliénation totale de chaque associé avec tous ses droits à toute la communauté; car, premièrement, chacun se donnant tout entier, la condition est égale pour tous, et, la condition étant égale pour tous, nul n'a intérêt de la rendre onéreuse aux autres.

De plus l'aliénation se faisant sans réserve, l'union est aussi parfaite qu'elle peut l'être, et nul associé n'a plus rien à réclamer: car, s'il restait quelques droits aux paarticuliers, comme il n'y aurait aucun supérieur
5 commun qui pût prononcer entre eux et le public, chacun, étant en quelque point son propre juge, prétendrait bientôt l'être en tout; l'état de nature subsisterait, et l'association deviendrait nécessairement tyrannique ou vaine.

10 Enfin, chacun se donnant à tous, ne se donne à personne; et, comme il n'y a pas un associé sur lequel on n'acquière le même droit qu'on lui cède sur soi, on gagne l'équivalent de tout ce qu'on perd, et plus de force pour conserver ce qu'on a.

15 Si donc on écarte du pacte social ce qui n'est pas de son essence, on trouvera qu'il se réduit aux termes suivants: "Chacun de nous met en commun sa personne et toute sa puissance sous la suprème direction de la volonté générale, et nous recevons en corps chaque
20 membre comme partie indivisible du tout."

A l'instant, au lieu de la personne particulière de chaque contractant, cet acte d'association produit un corps moral et collectif, composé d'autant de membres que l'assemblée a de voix, lequel reçoit de ce même
25 acte son unité, son *moi* commun, sa vie et sa volonté. Cette personne publique, qui se forme ainsi par l'union de toutes les autres, prenait autrefois le nom de *Cité,* et prend maintenant celui de *République,* ou de *Corps politique,* lequel est appelé par ses membres *État,* quand
30 il est passif; *Souverain,* quand il est actif; *Puissance,* en le comparant à ses semblables. A l'égard des asso-

ciés, ils prennent collectivement le nom de *peuple,* et s'appellent en particulier *citoyens,* comme participants à l'autorité souveraine, et *sujets,* comme soumis aux lois de l'État. Mais ces termes se confondent souvent et se prennent l'un pour l'autre; il suffit de les savoir distinguer quands ils sont employés dans toute leur précision. 5

—*Livre I, Chap. VI.*

De l'État Civil

Ce passage de l'état de nature à l'état civil produit dans l'homme un changement très remarquable, en substituant dans sa conduite la justice à l'instinct, et donnant à ses actions la moralité qui leur manquait auparavant.[6] C'est alors seulement que la voix du devoir, succédant à l'impulsion physique, et le droit à l'appetit, l'homme, qui, jusque-là, n'avait regardé que lui-même, se voit forcé d'agir sur d'autres principes, et de consulter sa raison avant d'écouter ses penchants. Quoiqu'il se prive dans cet état de plusieurs avantages qu'il tient de la nature, il en regagne de si grands, ses facultés s'exercent et se développent, ses idées s'étendent, ses sentiments s'ennoblissent, son âme tout entière s'élève à tel point, que, si les abus de cette nouvelle condition ne le dégradaient souvent au-dessous de celle dont il est sorti, il devrait bénir sans cesse l'instant heureux qui l'en arracha pour jamais, et qui, d'un animal stupide et borné, fit un être intelligent et un homme. 10 15 20 25

[6] It has frequently been objected that morality is not the result of social or political organization but its indispensable antecedent condition.

Réduisons toute cette balance à des termes faciles à comparer. Ce que l'homme perd par le contrat social, c'est sa liberté naturelle et un droit illimité à tout ce qui le tente et qu'il peut atteindre; ce qu'il gagne, c'est
5 la liberté civile et la propriété de tout ce qu'il possède. Pour ne pas se tromper dans ces compensations, il faut bien distinguer la liberté naturelle, qui n'a pour borne que les forces de l'individu, de la liberté civile, qui est limitée par la volonté générale, et la possession, qui
10 n'est que l'effet de la force ou le droit du premier occupant, de la propriété, qui ne peut être fondée que sur un titre positif.

On pourrait sur ce qui précède ajouter à l'acquit de l'état civil la liberté morale, qui seule rend l'homme
15 vraiment maître de lui, car l'impulsion du seul appétit est l'esclavage, et l'obéissance à la loi qu'on s'est prescrite est la liberté. Mais je n'en ai déjà que trop dit sur cet article, et le sens philosophique du mot *liberté* n'est pas ici de mon sujet.
20
—Livre I, Chap. VIII.

Si la Volonté Générale Peut Errer

Il s'ensuit de ce qui précède que la volonté générale est toujours droite et tend toujours à l'utilité publique; mais il ne s'ensuit pas que les délibérations du peuple
25 aient toujours la même rectitude. On veut toujours son bien, mais on ne le voit pas toujours; jamais on ne corrompt le peuple mais souvent on le trompe, et c'est alors seulement qu'il paraît vouloir ce qui est mal.

Il y a souvent bien de la différence entre la volonté
30 de tous et la volonté générale: celle-ci ne regarde qu'à

l'intérêt commun, l'autre regarde à l'intérêt privé, et n'est qu'une somme de volontés particulières; mais ôtez de ces mêmes volontés les plus et les moins qui s'entre-détruisent,[7] reste pour somme des différences la volonté générale. 5

Si, quand le peuple, suffisamment informé, délibère, les citoyens n'avaient aucune communication entre eux, du grand nombre de petites différences resulterait toujours la volonté générale, et la délibération serait toujours bonne. Mais quand il se fait des brigues, des 10 associations partielles aux dépens de la grande, la volonté de chacune de ces associations devient générale par rapport à ses membres, et particulière par rapport à l'État; on peut dire alors qu'il n'y a plus autant de votants que d'hommes, mais seulement autant que d'as- 15 sociations: les différences deviennent moins nombreuses et donnent un résultat moins général. Enfin, quand une de ces associations est si grande qu'elle l'emporte sur toutes les autres, vous n'avez plus pour résultat une somme de petites différences, mais une différence 20 unique; alors il n'y a plus de volonté générale, et l'avis qui l'emporte n'est qu'un avis particulier.

Il importe donc, pour avoir bien l'énoncé de la volonté générale, qu'il n'y ait pas de société partielle dans

[7] "Chaque intérêt, dit le Marquis d'Argenson, a des principes différents. L'accord de deux intérêts particuliers se forme par opposition à celui d'un tiers."* Il eut pu ajouter que l'accord de tous les intérêts se forme par opposition à celui de chacun. S'il n'y avait point d'intérêts différents, à peine sentirait-on l'intérêt commun qui ne trouverait jamais d'obstacle: tout irait de lui-même, et la politique cesserait d'être un art.

* *Considerations sur le Gouvernement de la France,* Chap. II.

l'État, et que chaque citoyen n'opine que d'après lui. Telle fut l'unique et sublime institution du grand Lycurgue. Que s'il y a des sociétés partielles, il en faut multiplier le nombre et en prévenir l'inégalité, comme
5 firent Solon, Numa, Servius. Ces précautions sont les seules bonnes pour que la volonté générale soit toujours éclairée et que le peuple ne se trompe point.

—Livre II, Chap. III.

De la Loi

Par le pacte social, nous avons donné l'existence et
10 la vie au corps politique; il s'agit maintenant de lui donner le mouvement et la volonté par la legislation. Car l'acte primitif par lequel ce corps se forme et s'unit ne détermine rien encore de ce qu'il doit faire pour se conserver.

15 Ce qui est bien et conforme à l'ordre est tel par la nature des choses et indépendamment des conventions humaines. Toute justice vient de Dieu, lui seul en est la source; mais si nous savions la recevoir de si haut, nous n'aurions besoin ni de gouvernement ni de lois.
20 Sans doute il est une justice universelle, émanée de la raison seule; mais cette justice, pour être admise entre nous, doit être réciproque. A considérer humainement les choses, faute de sanction naturelle, les lois de la justice sont vaines parmi les hommes; elles ne font
25 que le bien du méchant et le mal du juste, quand celui-ci les observe avec tout le monde, sans que personne les observe avec lui. Il faut donc des conventions et des lois pour unir les droits aux devoirs, et ramener la justice à son objet. Dans l'état de nature, où tout est

commun, je ne dois rien à ceux à qui je n'ai rien promis; je ne reconnais pour être à autrui que ce qui m'est inutile. Il n'en est pas ainsi dans l'état civil, où tous les droits sont fixés par la loi.

Mais qu'est-ce donc enfin qu'une loi?[8] Tant qu'on se contentera de n'attacher à ce mot que des idées métaphysiques, on continuera de raisonner sans s'entendre; et quand on aura dit ce que c'est qu'une loi de la nature, on n'en saura pas mieux ce que c'est qu'une loi de l'État.

J'ai déjà dit qu'il n'y avait point de volonté générale sur un objet particulier. En effet, cet objet particulier est dans l'État ou hors de l'État: une volonté qui lui est étrangère n'est point générale par rapport à lui, et si cet objet est dans l'État, il en fait partie; alors il se forme entre le tout et sa partie une relation qui en fait deux êtres séparés, dont la partie est l'un, et le tout moins cette même partie est l'autre. Mais le tout moins une partie n'est point le tout, et tant que ce rapport subsiste, il n'y a plus de tout, mais deux parties inégales; d'où il suit que la volonté de l'une n'est point non plus générale par rapport à l'autre.

Mais quand tout le peuple statue sur tout le peuple, il ne considère que lui-même; et s'il se forme alors un rapport, c'est de l'objet entier sous un point de vue à l'objet entier sous un autre point de vue, sans aucune division du tout. Alors, la matière sur laquelle on sta-

[8] Rousseau is criticising the metaphysical definition of law given by Montesquieu in the first book of *L'Esprit des Lois,* where he defines a law as a statement of the relations that exist between things.

tue est générale comme la volonté qui statue. C'est cet acte que j'appelle une loi.

Quand je dis que l'objet des lois est toujours général, j'entends que la Loi considère les sujets en corps et les 5 actions comme abstraites, jamais un homme comme individu, ni une action particulière. Ainsi, la Loi peut bien statuer qu'il y aura des privilèges, mais elle n'en peut donner nommément à personne; la Loi peut faire plusieurs classes de citoyens, assigner même les qualités 10 qui donneront droit à ces classes, mais elle ne peut nommer tels et tels pour y être admis; elle peut établir un Gouvernement royal et une succession héréditaire, mais elle ne peut élire un roi ni nommer une famille royale: en un mot, toute fonction qui se rapporte à un objet 15 individuel n'appartient point à la puissance législative.

Sur cette idée, on voit à l'instant qu'il ne faut plus demander à qui il appartient de faire des lois, puisqu'elles sont des actes de la volonté générale; ni si le prince est au-dessus des lois, puisqu'il est membre de 20 l'État ni si la Loi peut être injuste, puisque nul n'est injuste envers lui-même; ni comment on est libre et soumis aux lois, puisqu'elles ne sont que des registres de nos volontés.

On voit encore que la Loi réunissant l'universalité 25 de la volonté et celle de l'objet, ce qu'un homme, quel qu'il puisse être, ordonne de son chef n'est point une loi. Ce qu'ordonne même le souverain sur un objet particulier n'est pas non plus une loi, mais un décret; ni un acte de souveraineté, mais de magistrature.

30 J'appelle donc République tout État régi par des lois, sous quelque forme d'administration que ce puisse

être; car alors seulement l'intérêt public gouverne, et la chose publique est quelque chose. Tout Gouvernement légitime est républicain.[9] J'expliquerai ci-après ce que c'est que Gouvernement.

Les lois ne sont proprement que les conditions de l'association civile. Le peuple soumis aux lois en doit être l'auteur: il n'appartient qu'à ceux qui s'associent de régler les conditions de la société; mais comment les régleront-ils? Sera-ce d'un commun accord, par une inspiration subite? Le corps politique a-t-il un organe pour énoncer ses volontés? Qui lui donnera la prévoyance nécessaire pour en former les actes et les publier d'avance ou comment les prononcera-t-il au moment du besoin? Comment une multitude aveugle, qui souvent ne sait ce qu'elle veut, parce qu'elle sait rarement ce qui lui est bon, exécuterait-elle d'elle-même une entreprise aussi grande, aussi difficile, qu'un système de législation? De lui-même, le peuple veut toujours le bien; mais, de lui-même, il ne le voit pas toujours. La volonté générale est toujours droite; mais le jugement qui la guide n'est pas toujours éclairé. Il faut lui faire voir les objets tels qu'ils sont, quelquefois tels qu'ils doivent lui paraître; lui montrer le bon chemin qu'elle cherche, la garantir des séductions des volontés particulières, rapprocher à ses yeux les lieux et les temps, balancer l'attrait des avantages présents

[9] Je n'entends pas seulement, par ce mot, une aristocratie ou une démocratie, mais en général tout gouvernement guidé par la volonté générale, qui est la loi. Pour être légitime, il ne faut pas que le gouvernement se confonde avec le souverain, mais qu'il en soit le ministre; alors la monarchie elle-même est république. Ceci s'éclaircira dans le livre suivant.

et sensibles, par le danger des maux éloignés et cachés. Les particuliers voient le bien qu'ils rejettent, le public veut le bien qu'il ne voit pas. Tous ont également besoin de guides; il faut obliger les uns à conformer
5 leurs volontés à leur raison; il faut apprendre à l'autre à connaître ce qu'il veut. Alors, des lumières publiques résulte l'union de l'entendement et de la volonté dans le corps social; de là l'exact concours des parties, et enfin la plus grande force du tout. Voilà d'où naît la
10 nécessité d'un Législateur.

—Livre II, Chap. VI.

LES CONFESSIONS

The question of the *Confessions* is bound up with that of Rousseau's quarrel with Diderot, into the details of which it is impossible here to enter. The first suggestion that he write the story of his life undoubtedly came to him from his publisher, Rey, who requested him to prepare a sketch as an introduction to an edition of his works. The plan changed and grew under Rousseau's hand in the years from 1763-1770. Though known to a circle of admirers before his death, Books I-VI were not published until 1781. The remaining sections appeared in 1788.

Their purpose and spirit, as Rousseau saw it, is explained in the introduction printed below. As the autobiographical side of his work is well represented in only the account of his writing of *La Nouvelle Héloïse* the *Lettres à M. de Malesherbes* and the *Cinquième Rêverie* printed in complete form, we give in addition during his retirement at the Ermitage.

Introduction

Je forme une entreprise qui n'eut jamais d'exemple, et dont l'exécution n'aura point d'imitateur. Je veux montrer à mes semblables un homme dans toute la vérité de la nature; et cet homme, ce sera moi.

Moi seul. Je sens mon cœur, et je connais les 5 hommes. Je ne suis fait comme aucun de ceux que j'ai vus; j'ose croire n'être fait comme aucun de ceux qui existent. Si je ne vaux pas mieux, au moins je suis autre. Si la nature a bien ou mal fait de briser le moule dans lequel elle m'a jeté, c'est ce dont on ne peut juger qu'après m'avoir lu.

5 Que la trompette du jugement dernier sonne quand elle voudra, je viendrai, ce livre à la main, me présenter devant le souverain juge. Je dirai hautement: "Voilà ce que j'ai fait, ce que j'ai pensé, ce que je fus. J'ai dit le bien et le mal avec la même franchise. Je 10 n'ai rien tu de mauvais, rien ajouté de bon; et s'il m'est arrivé d'employer quelque ornement indifferent, ce n'a jamais été que pour remplir un vide occasionné par mon défaut de mémoire. J'ai pu supposer vrai ce que je savais avoir pu l'être, jamais ce que je savais être faux. 15 Je me suis montré tel que je fus: méprisable et vil quand je l'ai été; bon, généreux, sublime, quand je l'ai été: j'ai dévoilé mon intérieur tel que tu l'as vu toi-même Être éternel. Rassemble autour de moi l'innombrable foule de mes semblables; qu'ils écoutent 20 mes confessions, qu'ils gémissent de mes indignités, qu'ils rougissent de mes misères. Que chacun d'eux découvre à son tour son cœur au pied de ton trône avec la même sincérité; et puis qu'un seul te dise, s'il l'ose: *Je fus meilleur que cet homme-là.*

25 —*Partie I., Livre I.*

The Genesis of la Nouvelle Héloise

Ce fut le 9 avril 1756 que je quittai la ville pour n'y plus habiter;[1] car je ne compte pas pour habitation

[1] Rousseau had already written the *Confessions* before his unexpected return to Paris in 1770.

quelques courts séjours que j'ai faits depuis, tant à Paris qu'à Londres et dans d'autres villes, mais toujours de passage, ou toujours malgré moi. Mme d'Épinay vint nous prendre tous trois[2] dans son carrosse; son fermier vint charger mon petit bagage, et je fus installé dès le même jour. Je trouvai ma petite retraite arrangée et meublée simplement, mais proprement et même avec goût. La main qui avait donné ses soins à cet ameublement le rendait à mes yeux d'un prix inestimable, et je trouvais délicieux d'être l'hôte de mon amie, dans une maison de mon choix, qu'elle avait bâtie exprès pour moi.[2]

Quoiqu'il fît froid et qu'il y eût même encore de la neige, la terre commençait à végéter; on voyait des violettes et des primevères; les bourgeons des arbres commençaient à poindre, et la nuit même de mon arrivée fut marquée par le premier chant du rossignol, qui se fit entendre presque à ma fenêtre, dans un bois qui touchait la maison. Après un léger sommeil, oubliant à mon réveil ma transplantation, je me croyais encore dans la rue de Grenelle,[3] quand tout à coup ce ramage me fit tressaillir, et je m'écriai dans mon transport: "Enfin tous mes vœux sont accomplis!" Mon premier soin fut de me livrer à l'impression des objets champêtres dont j'étais entouré. Au lieu de commen-

[2] Some time before, on a visit to Mme d'Épinay's estate, La Chevrette, near the forest of Montmorency, Rousseau had admired the site of a dilapidated cottage and exclaimed, *"Voilà un asile tout fait pour moi!"* Unknown to him she had it rebuilt, offered it to him as a residence, and he came to occupy it with Thérèse Le Vasseur and her mother.

[3] Where he had lived in Paris at the Hôtel de Languedoc.

cer à m'arranger dans mon logement, je commençai par m'arranger pour mes promenades, et il n'y eut pas un sentier, pas un taillis, pas un bosquet, pas un réduit autour de ma demeure, que je n'eusse parcouru dès le lendemain. Plus j'examinais cette charmante retraite, plus je la sentais faite pour moi. Ce lieu solitaire plutôt que sauvage me transportait en idée au bout du monde. Il avait de ces beautés touchantes qu'on ne trouve guère auprès des villes; et jamais, en s'y trouvant transporté tout d'un coup, on n'eût pu se croire à quatre lieues de Paris....

Les souvenirs des divers temps de ma vie m'amenèrent à réfléchir sur le point où j'étais parvenu, et je me vis déjà sur le déclin de l'âge, en proie à des maux douloureux,[4] et croyant approcher du terme de ma carrière sans avoir goûté dans sa plénitude presque aucun des plaisirs dont mon cœur était avide, sans avoir donné l'essor aux vifs sentiments que j'y sentais en réserve, sans avoir savouré, sans avoir effleuré du moins cette enivrante volupté que je sentais dans mon âme en puissance, et qui, faute d'objet, s'y trouvait toujours comprimée, sans pouvoir s'exhaler autrement que par mes soupirs.

Comment se pouvait-il qu'avec une âme naturellement expansive, pour qui vivre c'était aimer, je n'eusse pas trouvé jusqu'alors un ami tout à moi, un véritable ami, moi qui me sentais si bien fait pour l'être. Comment se pouvait-il qu'avec des sens si combustibles, avec un cœur tout pétri d'amour, je n'eusse pas du moins une fois brûlé de sa flamme pour un objet dé-

[4] Rousseau believed himself seriously ill.

terminé? Dévoré du besoin d'aimer, sans jamais l'avoir pu bien satisfaire, je me voyais atteindre aux portes de la vieillesse, et mourir sans avoir vécu.

Ces rèflexions tristes, mais attendrissantes, me faisaient replier sur moi-même avec un regret qui n'était 5 pas sans douceur. Il me semblait que la destinée me devait quelque chose qu'elle ne m'avait pas donné. A quoi bon m'avoir fait naître avec des facultés exquises, pour les laisser jusqu'à la fin sans emploi? Le sentiment de mon prix interne, en me donnant celui de cette 10 injustice, m'en dédommageait en quelque sorte, et me faisait verser des larmes que j'aimais à laisser couler.

Je faisais ces méditations dans la plus belle saison de l'année, au mois de juin, sous des bocages frais, au chant du rossignol, au gazouillement des ruisseaux. 15 Tout concourut à me replonger dans cette mollesse trop séduisante, pour laquelle j'étais né, mais dont le ton dur et sévère où venait de me monter une longue effervescence m'aurait dû délivrer pour toujours. J'allai malheureusement me rappeler le dîner du château de 20 Toune,[5] et ma rencontre avec ces deux charmantes filles, dans la même saison et dans des lieux à peu près semblables à ceux où j'étais dans ce moment. Ce souvenir, que l'innocence qui s'y joignait me rendait plus doux encore, m'en rappela d'autres de la même 25 espèce. Bientôt je vis rassemblés autour de moi tous les objets qui m'avaient donné de l'émotion dans ma jeunesse, Mlle Galley, Mlle de Graffenried, Mlle de

[5] Rousseau, as a lad, met one day in early summer two young ladies, Mlles de Graffenried and Galley, and accompanied them to Toune (see *Confessions,* Partie I, Livre IV).

Breil, Mme Bazile, Mme de Larnage, mes jolies écolières, et jusqu'à la piquante Zulietta,[6] que mon cœur ne peut oublier. Je me vis entouré d'un sérail de houris, de mes anciennes connaissances, pour qui le goût le plus
5 vif ne m'était pas un sentiment nouveau. Mon sang s'allume et pétille, la tête me tourne, malgré mes cheveux déjà grisonnants, et voilà le grave citoyen de Genève,[6a] voilà l'austère Jean-Jacques, à près de quarante-cinq ans, redevenu tout à coup le berger extrava-
10 gant. L'ivresse dont je fus saisi, quoique si prompte et si folle, fut si durable et si forte, qu'il n'a pas moins fallu, pour m'en guérir, que la crise imprévue et terrible des malheurs où elle m'a précipité....

Que fis-je en cette occasion? Déjà mon lecteur l'a
15 deviné, pour peu qu'il m'ait suivi jusqu'ici. L'impossibilité d'atteindre aux êtres réels me jeta dans le pays des chimères: et ne voyant rien d'existant qui fût digne de mon délire, je le nourris dans un monde idéal, que mon imagination créatrice eut bientôt peuplé d'êtres
20 selon mon cœur. Jamais cette ressource ne vint plus à propos, et ne se trouva si féconde. Dans mes continuelles extases, je m'enivrais à torrents des plus délicieux sentiments qui jamais soient entrés dans un cœur d'homme. Oubliant tout à fait la race humaine, je me
25 fis des sociétés de créatures parfaites, aussi célestes par leurs vertus que par leurs beautés, d'amis sûrs, tendres,

[6] Women of various types whom Rousseau had met in his wanderings and to whose memory he had a sentimental attachment. The *écolières* are the pupils to whom he taught music.

[6a] During Rousseau's visit to Geneva in 1754, citizenship in the republic had been conferred upon him, an honor of which he was proud.

fidèles, tels que je n'en trouvai jamais ici-bas. Je pris un tel goût à planer ainsi dans l'empyrée, au milieu des objets charmants dont je m'étais entouré, que j'y passais les heures, les jours sans compter; et perdant le souvenir de toute autre chose, à peine avais-je mangé un morceau à la hâte, que je brûlais de m'échapper pour courir retrouver mes bosquets....

Je me figurai l'amour, l'amitié, les deux idoles de mon cœur, sous les plus ravissantes images. Je me plus à les orner de tous les charmes du sexe que j'avais toujours adoré. J'imaginai deux amies plutôt que deux amis, parce que si l'exemple est plus rare, il est aussi plus aimable. Je les douai de deux caractères analogues, mais différents; de deux figures non pas parfaites, mais de mon goût, qu'animaient la bienveillance et la sensibilité. Je fis l'une[7] brune et l'autre[8] blonde, l'une vive et l'autre douce, l'une sage et l'autre faible; mais d'une si touchante faiblesse, que la vertu semblait y gagner. Je donnai à l'une des deux un amant[9] dont l'autre fut la tendre amie, et même quelque chose de plus; mais je n'admis ni rivalité, ni querelles, ni jalousie, parce que tout sentiment pénible me coûte à imaginer, et que je ne voulais ternir ce riant tableau par rien qui dégradât la nature. Epris de mes deux charmants modèles, je m'identifiais avec l'amant et l'ami le plus qu'il m'était possible; mais je le fis aimable et jeune, lui donnant au surplus les vertus et les défauts que je me sentais.

[7] Claire d'Orbe.
[8] Julie d'Étange.
[9] Saint-Preux.

Pour placer mes personnages dans un séjour qui leur convînt, je passai successivement en revue les plus beaux lieux que j'eusse vus dans mes voyages. Mais je ne trouvai point de bocage assez frais, point de 5 paysage assez touchant à mon gré. Les vallées de la Thessalie m'auraient pu contenter, si je les avais vues; mais mon imagination, fatiguée à inventer, voulait quelque lieu réel qui pût lui servir de point d'appui, et me faire illusion sur la réalité des habitants que j'y 10 voulais mettre. Je songeai longtemps aux îles Borromées,[9a] dont l'aspect délicieux m'avait transporté; mais j'y trouvai trop d'ornement et d'art pour mes personnages. Il me fallait cependant un lac, et je finis par choisir celui autour duquel mon cœur n'a jamais cessé 15 d'errer. Je me fixai sur la partie des bords de ce lac à laquelle depuis longtemps mes vœux ont placé ma résidence dans le bonheur imaginaire auquel le sort m'a borné. Le lieu natal de ma pauvre maman[10] avait encore pour moi un attrait de prédilection. Le con-20 traste des positions, la richesse et la variété des sites, la magnificence, la majesté de l'ensemble qui ravit les sens, émeut le cœur, élève l'âme, achevèrent de me déterminer, et j'établis à Vevey mes jeunes pupilles. Voilà tout ce que j'imaginai du premier bond; le reste n'y fut 25 ajouté que dans la suite.

Je me bornai longtemps à un plan si vague, parce qu'il suffisait pour remplir mon imagination d'objets agréables, et mon cœur de sentiments dont il aime à se nourrir. Ces fictions, à force de revenir, prirent enfin

[9a] In the Lago Maggiore.

[10] Mme de Warens.

plus de consistance, et se fixèrent dans mon cerveau sous une forme déterminée. Ce fut alors que la fantaisie me prit d'exprimer sur le papier quelques-unes des situations qu'elles m'offraient; et rappelant tout ce que j'avais senti dans ma jeunesse, de donner ainsi l'essor en quelque sorte au désir d'aimer, que je n'avais pu satisfaire, et dont je me sentais dévoré. 5

—*Partie II, Livre IX.*

LETTRES À M. DE MALESHERBES

(After Rousseau had retired from the life of Paris and of society, and had broken with Diderot and his circle, he seems to have felt the need of justifying or at least explaining himself. To this end, in 1762, he wrote four letters to M. de Malesherbes, president of the Cour des Aides. As the second of these is of particular interest to students of the First Discourse, and the third throws much light on his "reformation," they have been included here. April 9, 1756, was the date when, as we have seen, he left Paris, as he thought, for good, and decided to live the rest of his life close to nature. On this day he accepted the offer of Mme d'Épinay and established himself at l'Ermitage, a little cottage in the forest of Montmorency. In this region, he passed the most fruitful years of his life, and wrote his *La Nouvelle Héloïse, Émile ou le Traité de l'éducation,* and rewrote his *Contrat Social.* Cf. Rousseau, *Œuvres,* Vol. VIII, pp. 277-351; Ducros, *De Genève à l'Hermitage,* 1908, pp. 323 et seq; Rey, *J.-J. Rousseau dans la vallée de Montmorency,* 1909.)

À M. de Malesherbes

À Montmorency, le 12 janvier, 1762.

Je continue, monsieur, à vous rendre compte de moi, puisque j'ai commencé; car ce qui peut m'être le plus défavorable est d'être connu à demi; et, puisque mes fautes ne m'ont point ôté votre estime, je ne présume pas que ma franchise me la doive ôter.

Une âme paresseuse qui s'effraye de tout soin, un tempérament ardent, bilieux, facile à s'affecter, et sen-
10 sible à l'excès à tout ce qui l'affecte, semblent ne pouvoir s'allier dans le même caractère; et ces deux contraires composent pourtant le fond du mien. Quoique je ne puisse résoudre cette opposition par des principes, elle existe pourtant; je le sens, rien n'est plus certain, et
15 j'en puis du moins donner par les faits une espèce d'historique qui peut servir à la concevoir. J'ai eu plus d'activité dans l'enfance, mais jamais comme un autre enfant. Cet ennui de tout m'a de bonne heure jeté dans la lecture. A six ans, Plutarque me tomba sous
20 la main; à huit, je le savais par cœur; j'avais lu tous les romans; ils m'avaient fait verser des seaux de larmes avant l'âge où le cœur prend intérêt aux romans. De là se forma dans le mien ce goût héroïque et romanesque qui n'a fait qu'augmenter jusqu'à présent, et
25 qui acheva de me dégoûter de tout, hors de ce qui ressemblait à mes folies. Dans ma jeunesse, que je croyais trouver dans le monde les mêmes gens que j'avais connus dans mes livres, je me livrais sans réserve à quiconque savait m'en imposer par un certain jargon dont
30 j'ai toujours été la dupe. J'étais actif, parce que j'étais fou; à mesure que j'étais détrompé, je changeais de

goûts, d'attachements, de projets; et dans tous ces changements, je perdais toujours ma peine et mon temps, parce que je cherchais toujours ce qui n'était point. En devenant plus expérimenté, j'ai perdu peu à peu l'espoir de le trouver, et par conséquent le zèle de le chercher. Aigri par les injustices que j'avais éprouvées, par celles dont j'avais été le témoin, souvent affligé du désordre où l'exemple et la force des choses m'avaient entraîné moi-même, j'ai pris en mépris mon siècle et mes contemporains; et, sentant que je ne trouverais point au milieu d'eux une situation qui pût contenter mon cœur, je l'ai peu à peu détaché de la société des hommes, et je m'en suis fait une autre dans mon imagination, laquelle m'a d'autant plus charmé, que je la pouvais cultiver sans peine, sans risque, et la trouver toujours sûre et telle qu'il me la fallait.

Après avoir passé quarante ans de ma vie ainsi mécontent de moi-même et des autres, je cherchais inutilement à rompre les liens qui me tenaient attaché à cette société que j'estimais si peu, et qui m'enchaînaient aux occupations le moins de mon goût, par des besoins que j'estimais ceux de la nature, et qui n'étaient que ceux de l'opinion: tout à coup un heureux hasard vint m'éclairer sur ce que j'avais à faire pour moi-même, et à penser de mes semblables, sur lesquels mon cœur était sans cesse en contradiction avec mon esprit, et que je me sentais encore porté à aimer, avec tant de raisons de les haïr. Je voudrais, monsieur, vous pouvoir peindre ce moment qui a fait dans ma vie une si singulière époque, et qui me sera toujours présent quand je vivrais éternellement.

J'allais voir Diderot, alors prisonnier à Vincennes, j'avais dans ma poche un *Mercure de France*, que je me mis à feuilleter le long du chemin. Je tombe sur la question de l'Académie de Dijon, qui a donné lieu à
5 mon premier écrit. Si jamais quelque chose a ressemblé à une inspiration subite, c'est le mouvement qui se fit en moi à cette lecture: tout à coup je me sens l'esprit ébloui de mille lumières; des foules d'idées vives s'y présentent à la fois avec une force et une
10 confusion qui me jeta dans un trouble inexprimable; je sens ma tête prise par un étourdissement semblable à l'ivresse. Une violente palpitation m'oppresse, soulève ma poitrine; ne pouvant plus respirer en marchant, je me laisse tomber sous un des arbres de l'avenue, et
15 j'y passe une demi-heure dans une telle agitation, qu'en me relevant j'aperçus tout le devant de ma veste mouillé de mes larmes, sans avoir senti que j'en répandais. O monsieur! si j'avais jamais pu écrire le quart de ce que j'ai vu et senti sous cet arbre, avec
20 quelle clarté j'aurais fait voir toutes les contradictions du système social! avec quelle force j'aurais exposé tous les abus de nos institutions! avec quelle simplicité j'aurais démontré que l'homme est bon naturellement, et que c'est par ces institutions seules que les hommes
25 deviennent méchants! Tout ce que j'ai pu retenir de ces foules de grandes vérités, qui, dans un quart d'heure, m'illuminèrent sous cet arbre, a été bien faiblement épars dans les trois principaux de mes écrits; savoir, ce premier *Discours*, celui sur *l'Inégalité*, et le *Traité de*
30 *l'éducation*, lesquels trois ouvrages sont inséparables, et forment ensemble un même tout. Tout le reste a

été perdu ; et il n'y eut d'écrit là-dessus que la Prosopopée de Fabricius. Voilà comment, lorsque j'y pensais le moins, je devins auteur presque malgré moi. Il est aisé de concevoir comment l'attrait d'un premier succès et les critiques des barbouilleurs me jetèrent tout de bon dans la carrière. Avais-je quelque vrai talent pour écrire ? je ne sais. Une vive persuasion m'a toujours tenu lieu d'éloquence, et j'ai toujours écrit lâchement et mal quand je n'ai pas été fortement persuadé : ainsi c'est peut-être un retour caché d'amour-propre qui m'a fait choisir et mériter ma devise,[1] et m'a si passionnément attaché à la vérité ou à tout ce que j'ai pris pour elle. Si je n'avais écrit que pour écrire, je suis convaincu que l'on ne m'aurait jamais lu.

Après avoir découvert, ou cru découvrir, dans les fausses opinions des hommes, la source de leurs misères et de leur méchanceté, je sentis qu'il n'y avait que ces mêmes opinions qui m'eussent rendu malheureux moi-même, que mes maux et mes vices me venaient bien plus de ma situation que de moi-même. Dans le même temps, une maladie,[2] dont j'avais dès l'enfance senti les premières atteintes, s'étant déclarée absolument incurable, malgré toutes les promesses des faux guérisseurs dont je n'ai pas été longtemps la dupe, je jugeai que si je voulais être conséquent, et secouer une fois de

[1] Rousseau's motto was *vitam impendere vero.*

[2] Rousseau had believed himself ill at various times during his youth and had made ineffectual journeys in search of relief. At about the time when his first discourse was published, and again in 1762, his affliction, or at least his discomfort, became more distressing. Though he was undoubtedly ill, he believed his malady more dangerous than was really the case.

dessus mes épaules le pesant joug de l'opinion, je n'-avais pas un moment à perdre. Je pris brusquement mon parti avec assez de courage, et je l'ai assez bien soutenu jusqu'ici avec une fermeté dont moi seul peux
5 sentir le prix, parce qu'il n'y a que moi seul qui sache quels obstacles j'ai eus et j'ai encore tous les jours à combattre pour me maintenir sans cesse contre le courant. Je sens pourtant bien que depuis dix ans j'ai un peu dérivé; mais si j'estimais seulement en avoir encore
10 quatre à vivre, on me verrait donner une deuxième secousse, et remonter tout au mons à mon premier niveau, pour n'en plus guère redescendre; car toutes les grandes épreuves sont faites, et il est désormais démontré pour moi, par l'expérience, que l'état où je me suis mis est
15 le seul où l'homme puisse vivre bon et heureux, puisqu'il est le plus indépendant de tous, et le seul où on ne se trouve jamais pour son propre avantage dans la nécessité de nuire à autrui.

J'avoue que le nom que m'ont fait mes écrits a beau-
20 coup facilité l'exécution du parti que j'ai pris. Il faut être cru bon auteur, pour se faire impunément mauvais copiste,[3] et ne pas manquer de travail pour cela. Sans ce premier titre, on m'eût pu trop prendre au mot sur l'autre, et peut-être cela m'aurait-il mortifié; car je
25 brave aisément le ridicule, mais je ne supporterais pas si bien le mépris. Mais si quelque réputation me donne à cet égard un peu d'avantage, il est bien compensé par tous les inconvénients attachés à cette même réputation. quand on ne veut point être esclave, et qu'on veut

[3] Rousseau earned his living, or at least attempted to, at this and later times by copying music at ten sous a page.

vivre isolé et indépendant. Ce sont ces inconvénients en partie qui m'ont chassé de Paris, et qui, me poursuivant encore dans mon asile, me chasseraient très certainement plus loin, pour peu que ma santé vînt à se raffermir. Un autre de mes fléaux dans cette grande ville était ces foules de prétendus amis qui s'étaient emparés de moi, et qui, jugeant de mon cœur par les leurs, voulaient absolument me rendre heureux à leur mode, et non pas à la mienne. Au désespoir de ma retraite, ils m'y ont poursuivi pour m'en tirer. Je n'ai pu m'y maintenir sans tout rompre. Je ne suis vraiment libre que depuis ce temps-là.

Libre! non, je ne le suis point encore; mes derniers écrits ne sont point encore imprimés; et, vu le déplorable état de ma pauvre machine, je n'espère plus survivre à l'impression du recueil de tous: mais si, contre mon attente, je puis aller jusque-là et prendre une fois congé du public, croyez, monsieur, qu'alors je serai libre, ou que jamais homme ne l'aura été. *O utinam!* O jour trois fois heureux! Non, il ne me sera pas donné de le voir.

Je n'ai pas tout dit, monsieur, et vous aurez peut-être encore au moins une lettre à essuyer. Heureusement rien ne vous oblige de les lire, et peut-être y seriez-vous bien embarrassé. Mais pardonnez, de grâce; pour recopier ces longs fatras, il faudrait les refaire, et en vérité, je n'en ai pas le courage. J'ai sûrement bien du plaisir à vous écrire, mais je n'en ai pas moins à me reposer, et mon état ne me permet pas d'écrire longtemps de suite.

À M. de Malesherbes

À Montmorency, le 26 janvier 1762.

Après vous avoir exposé, monsieur, les vrais motifs de ma conduite, je voudrais vous parler de mon état moral dans ma retraite. Mais je sens qu'il est bien tard; mon âme aliénée d'elle-même est tout à mon corps: le délabrement de ma pauvre machine l'y tient de jour en jour plus attachée, et jusqu'à ce quelle s'en sépare enfin tout à coup. C'est de mon bonheur que je voudrais vous parler, et l'on parle mal du bonheur quand on souffre.

Mes maux sont l'ouvrage de la nature, mais mon bonheur est le mien. Quoi qu'on en puisse dire, j'ai été sage, puisque j'ai été heureux autant que ma nature m'a permis de l'être: je n'ai point été chercher ma félicité au loin, je l'ai cherchée auprès de moi, et l'y ai trouvée. Spartien[4] dit que Similis, courtisan de Trajan, ayant sans mécontentement personnel quitté la cour et tous ses emplois pour aller vivre paisiblement à la campagne, fit mettre ces mots sur sa tombe: *J'ai demeuré soixante-seize ans sur la terre, et j'en ai vécu sept.* Voilà ce que je puis dire à quelque égard, quoique mon sacrifice ait été moindre: je n'ai commencé de vivre que le 9 avril 1756.

Je ne saurais vous dire, monsieur, combien j'ai été touché de voir que vous m'estimiez le plus malheureux des hommes. Le public sans doute en jugera comme vous,

[4] Ælius Spartianus, a minor Roman historian, who wrote in the reign of Diocletian. The reference is probably taken from Dio Cassius, *Historia Romana,* LXIX. Similis is merely referred to in Aelius, *De Vita Hadriani,* IX, 5-6.

et c'est encore ce qui m'afflige. Oh! que le sort dont j'ai joui n'est-il connu de tout l'univers! chacun voudrait s'en faire un semblable; la paix règnerait sur la terre; les hommes ne songeraient plus à se nuire, et il n'y aurait plus de méchants quand nul n'aurait intérêt à l'être. Mais de quoi jouissais-je enfin quand j'étais seul? De moi, de l'univers entier, de tout ce qui est, de tout ce qui peut être, de tout ce qu'a de beau le monde sensible, et d'imaginable le monde intellectuel: je rassemblais autour de moi tout ce qui pouvait flatter mon cœur; mes désirs étaient la mesure de mes plaisirs. Non, jamais les plus voluptueux n'ont connu de pareilles délices, et j'ai cent fois plus joui de mes chimères qu'ils ne font des réalités.

Quand mes douleurs me font tristement mesurer la longueur des nuits, et que l'agitation de la fièvre m'empêche de goûter un seul instant de sommeil, souvent je me distrais de mon état présent, en songeant aux divers événements de ma vie; et les repentirs, les doux souvenirs, les regrets, l'attendrissement, se partagent le soin de me faire oublier quelques moments mes souffrances. Quels temps croiriez-vous, monsieur, que je me rapelle le plus souvent et le plus volontiers dans mes rêves? Ce ne sont point les plaisirs de ma jeunesse; ils furent trop rares, trop mêlés d'amertume, et sont déjà trop loin de moi. Ce sont ceux de ma retraite; ce sont mes promenades solitaires, ce sont ces jours rapides, mais délicieux, que j'ai passés tout entiers avec moi seul, avec ma bonne et simple gouvernante,[5]

[5] Thérèse Le Vasseur, an unattractive and almost illiterate servant to whom Rousseau became attached, by whom he had sev-

avec mon chien bien-aimé, ma vieille chatte, avec les oiseaux de la campagne et les biches de la forêt, avec la nature entière et son inconcevable auteur. En me levant avant le soleil pour aller voir, contempler son
5 lever dans mon jardin; quand je voyais commencer une belle journée, mon premier souhait était que ni lettres, ni visites, n'en vinssent troubler le charme. Après avoir donné la matinée à divers soins que je remplissais tous avec plaisir, parce que je pouvais les
10 remettre à un autre temps, je me hâtais de dîner pour échapper aux importuns, et me ménager un plus long après-midi. Avant une heure, même les jours les plus ardents, je partais par le grand soleil avec le fidèle Achate,[6] pressant le pas dans la crainte que quelqu'un
15 ne vînt s'emparer de moi avant que j'eusse pu m'esquiver; mais quand une fois j'avais pu doubler un certain coin, avec quel battement de cœur, avec quel pétillement de joie je commençais à respirer en me sentant sauvé, en me disant: "Me voilà maître de moi pour
20 le reste de ce jour!" J'allais alors d'un pas plus tranquille chercher quelque lieu sauvage dans la forêt, quelque lieu désert où rien ne montrant la main des hommes n'annonçât la servitude et la domination.

eral children and whom he later married. She followed him in all his wanderings and survived him. Opinions on her character and influence on Rousseau's life differ widely. M. Ritter defends her. M. Faguet (*J.-J. Rousseau* 1911) on the contrary is inclined to see in her the cause of many of Rousseau's misfortunes. Rousseau speaks of her here and later as his *"gouvernante."*

[6] His dog, *Turc*. The dog's name had been changed from *Duc* to *Turc* through fear of offending M. le Duc de Luxembourg, his patron, on whose estate he was living.

quelque asile où je pusse croire avoir pénétré le premier, et où nul tiers importun ne vînt s'interposer entre la nature et moi. C'etait là qu'elle semblait déployer à mes yeux une magnificence toujours nouvelle. L'or des genêts et la pourpre des bruyères frappaient mes 5 yeux d'un luxe qui touchait mon cœur; la majesté des arbres qui me couvraient de leur ombre, la délicatesse des arbustes qui m'environnaient, l'étonnante variété des herbes et des fleurs que je foulais sous mes pieds, tenaient mon esprit dans une alternative continuelle 10 d'observation et d'admiration: le concours de tant d'objets intéressants qui se disputaient mon attention, m'attirant sans cesse de l'un à l'autre, favorisait mon humeur rêveuse et paresseuse, et me faisait souvent redire en moi-même: "Non, Salomon dans toute sa 15 gloire ne fut jamais vêtu comme l'un d'eux."

Mon imagination ne laissait pas longtemps déserte la terre ainsi parée. Je la peuplais bientôt d'êtres selon mon cœur, et, chassant bien loin l'opinion, les préjugés, toutes les passions factices, je transportais dans les 20 asiles de la nature des hommes dignes de les habiter. Je m'en formais une société charmante dont je ne me sentais pas indigne, je me faisais un siècle d'or à ma fantaisie, et remplissant ces beaux jours de toutes les scènes de ma vie qui m'avaient laissé de doux sou- 25 venirs, et de toutes celles que mon cœur pouvait désirer encore, je m'attendrissais jusqu'aux larmes sur les vrais plaisirs de l'humanité, plaisirs si délicieux, si purs, et qui sont désormais si loin des hommes. Oh! si dans ces moments, quelque idée de Paris, de mon 30 siècle, et de ma petite gloriole d'auteur, venait troubler mes rêveries, avec quel dédain je la chassais à l'instant pour me livrer, sans distractions, aux sentiments exquis dont mon âme était pleine! Cependant au milieu de tout cela, je l'avoue, le néant de mes chimères venait 5 quelquefois la contrister tout à coup. Quand tous mes rêves se seraient tournés en réalités, ils ne m'auraient pas suffi; j'aurais imaginé, rêvé, désiré encore. Je trouvais en moi un vide inexplicable que rien n'aurait pu remplir, un certain élancement de cœur vers une 10 autre sorte de jouissance dont je n'avais pas d'idée, et dont pourtant je sentais le besoin. Hé bien, monsieur, cela même était jouissance, puisque j'en étais pénétré d'un sentiment très vif, et d'une tristesse attirante, que je n'aurais pas voulu ne pas avoir.

15 Bientôt de la surface de la terre j'élevais mes idées à tous les êtres de la nature, au système universel des choses, à l'être incompréhensible qui embrasse tout. Alors, l'esprit perdu dans cette immensité je ne pensais pas, je ne raisonnais pas, je ne philosophais pas, 20 je me sentais, avec une sorte de volupté, accablé du poids de cet univers, je me livrais avec ravissement à la confusion de ces grandes idées, j'aimais à me perdre en imagination dans l'espace, mon cœur resserré dans les bornes des êtres s'y trouvait trop à l'étroit; j'étouf- 25 fais dans l'univers; j'aurais voulu m'élancer dans l'infini. Je crois que, si j'eusse dévoilé tous les mystères de la nature, je me serais senti dans une situation moins délicieuse que cette étourdissante extase à laquelle mon esprit se livrait sans retenue, et qui, dans l'agitation 30 de mes transports, me faisait écrier quelquefois: "O grand Être! ô grand Être!" sans pouvoir dire ni penser rien de plus.

Ainsi s'écoulaient dans un délire continuel les journées les plus charmantes que jamais créature humaine ait passées: et quand le coucher du soleil me faisait songer à la retraite, étonné de la rapidité du temps, je croyais n'avoir pas assez mis à profit ma journée, 5
je pensais en pouvoir jouir davantage encore; et, pour réparer le temps perdu, je me disais: "Je reviendrai demain."

Je revenais à petits pas, la tête un peu fatiguée, mais le cœur content; je me reposais agréablement au retour, 10
en me livrant à l'impression des objets, mais sans penser, sans imaginer, sans rien faire autre chose que sentir le calme et le bonheur de ma situation. Je trouvais mon couvert mis sur ma terrasse. Je soupais de grand appétit dans mon petit domestique; nulle 15
image de servitude et de dépendance ne troublait la bienveillance qui nous unissait tous. Mon chien luimême était mon ami, non mon esclave; nous avions toujours la même volonté, mais jamais il ne m'a obéi. Ma gaieté durant toute la soirée témoignait que j'avais 20
vécu seul tout le jour; j'étais bien différent quand j'avais vu de la compagnie: j'étais rarement content des autres, et jamais de moi. Le soir, j'étais grondeur et taciturne: cette remarque est de ma gouvernante, et, depuis qu'elle me l'a dite, je l'ai toujours trouvée juste 25
en m'observant. Enfin, après avoir fait encore quelques tours dans mon jardin, ou chanté quelque air sur mon épinette, je trouvais dans mon lit un repos de corps et d'âme cent fois plus doux que le sommeil même.

Ce sont là les jours qui ont fait le vrai bonheur de 30
ma vie, bonheur sans amertune, sans ennuis, sans re-

grets, et auquel j'aurais borné volontiers tout celui de mon existence. Oui, monsieur, que de pareils jours remplissent pour moi l'éternité, je n'en demande point d'autres, et n'imagine pas que je sois beaucoup moins
5 heureux dans ces ravissantes contemplations que les intelligences célestes. Mais un corps qui souffre ôte à l'esprit sa liberté; désormais je ne suis plus seul, j'ai un hôte qui m'importune, il faut m'en délivrer pour être à moi; et l'essai que j'ai fait de ces douces jouis-
10 sances ne sert plus qu'à me faire attendre avec moins d'effroi le moment de les goûter sans distraction.

Mais me voici déjà à la fin de ma seconde feuille. Il m'en faudrait pourtant encore une. Encore une lettre donc, et puis plus. Pardon, monsieur; quoique j'aime
15 trop à parler de moi, je n'aime pas à en parler avec tout le monde: c'est ce qui me fait abuser de l'occasion quand je l'ai et qu'elle me plaît. Voilà mon tort et mon excuse. Je vous prie de la prendre en gré.

LES REVERIES DU PROMENEUR SOLITAIRE

(The *Cinquième Promenade* of the *Rêveries* recounts the story of Rousseau's brief sojourn at the Ile de Saint-Pierre where he found asylum for six weeks (September-October, 1765) from his real or imagined persecutors. He had already received the visit of David Hume who in all good faith had invited him to come to England, an invitation which Rousseau was to accept with disastrous results. His house at Motiers had been stoned. How serious this "lapidation" was and what had caused it, is a question on which biographers disagree. This account was written, not fifteen, but at latest thirteen years after the events recorded, in 1777. His sense of being unjustly persecuted by all mankind had now become deeply rooted in his spirit and amounted to an obsession. The situation will be clearer to anyone who reads the *Confessions, Œuvres,* Vol. IX, pp. 66-82; cf. also Metzger, *J.-J. Rousseau à l'île de Saint-Pierre* 1875, also *Mémoires de la Société Archéologique Savoisienne* 1905.)

Cinquième Promenade

Description de l'île de Saint-Pierre. Rousseau regrette de n'avoir pu y fixer son séjour. Il y travaille à la botanique. Détail de ses amusements dans cette île. Il y fonde une colonie.

De toutes les habitations où j'ai demeuré (et j'en ai eu de charmantes), aucune ne m'a rendu si véritablement heureux et ne m'a laissé de si tendres regrets que l'île de Saint-Pierre au milieu du lac de Bienne. Cette
5 petite île, qu'on appelle à Neuchâtel l'île de La Motte, est bien peu connue, même en Suisse. Aucun voyageur, que je sache, n'en fait mention. Cependant elle est très agréable, et singulièrement située pour le bonheur d'un homme qui aime à se circonscrire; car, quoique je
10 sois peut-être le seul au monde à qui sa destinée en ait fait une loi, je ne puis croire être le seul qui ait un goût si naturel, quoique je ne l'ais trouvé jusqu'ici chez nul autre.

Les rives du lac de Bienne sont plus sauvages et ro-
15 mantiques[1] que celles du lac de Genève, parce que les rochers et les bois y bordent l'eau de plus près; mais elles ne sont pas moins riantes. S'il y a moins de culture de champs et de vignes, moins de villes et de maisons, il y a aussi plus de verdure naturelle, plus
20 de prairies, d'asiles ombragés de bocages, des contrastes plus fréquents et des accidents plus rapprochés. Comme il n'y a pas sur ces heureux bords de grandes routes commodes pour les voitures, le pays est peu fréquenté par les voyageurs, mais il est intéressant pour
25 des contemplatifs solitaires qui aiment à s'enivrer à loisir des charmes de la nature, et à se recueillir dans un

[1] This was long considered the first use of the much-debated word in French. Littré so gives it. It has since been proved that it occurred in translations and lesser known writers as early as 1675 (cf. François, "Romantique," *Annales J.-J. Rousseau,* 1909, Vol. V, pp. 198-236. Morize, *Revue d'Histoire littéraire de la France,* 1911, Vol. VIII, p. 440; Delaruelle, *ibid.,* p. 940).

silence que ne trouble aucun autre bruit que le cri des aigles, le ramage entrecoupé de quelques oiseaux, et le roulement des torrents qui tombent de la montagne. Ce beau bassin, d'une forme presque ronde, enferme dans son milieu deux petites îles, l'une habitée et cultivée d'environ une demi-lieue de tour; l'autre plus petite, déserte et en friche, et qui sera détruite à la fin par les transports de la terre qu'on en ôte sans cesse pour réparer les dégâts que les vagues et les orages font à la grande. C'est ainsi que la substance du faible est toujours employée au profit du puissant.

Il n'y a dans l'île qu'une seule maison, mais grande, agréable et commode, qui appartient à l'hôpital de Berne, ainsi que l'île, et où loge un receveur avec sa famille et ses domestiques. Il y entretient une nombreuse basse-cour, une volière, et des réservoirs pour le poisson. L'île, dans sa petitesse, est tellement variée dans ses terrains et ses aspects, qu'elle offre toutes sortes de sites, et souffre toutes sortes de cultures. On y trouve des champs, des vignes, des bois, des vergers, de gras pâturages ombragés de bosquets, et bordés d'arbrisseaux de toute espèce, dont le bord des eaux entretient la fraîcheur; une haute terrasse plantée de deux rangs d'arbres borde l'île dans sa longueur, et dans le milieu de cette terrasse on a bâti un joli salon où les habitants des rives voisines se rassemblent et viennent danser les dimanches durant les vendanges.

C'est dans cette île que je me réfugiai après la lapidation de Motiers. J'en trouvai le séjour si charmant, j'y menais une vie si convenable à mon humeur, que résolu d'y finir mes jours, je n'avais d'autre inquiétude sinon qu'on ne me laissât pas exécuter ce projet qui ne s'accordait pas avec celui de m'entraîner en Angleterre, dont je sentais déjà les premiers effets. Dans les pressentiments qui m'inquiétaient, j'aurais voulu qu'on 5 m'eût fait de cet asile une prison perpétuelle, qu'on m'y eût confiné pour toute ma vie, et qu'en m'ôtant toute puissance et tout espoir d'en sortir on m'eût interdit toute espèce de communication avec la terre ferme, de sorte qu'ignorant tout ce qui se faisait dans le monde, 10 j'en eusse oublié l'existence, et qu'on eût oublié la mienne aussi.

On ne m'a laissé passer guère que deux mois dans cette île, mais j'y aurais passé deux ans, deux siècles, et toute l'éternité, sans m'y ennuyer un moment, 15 quoique je n'y eusses, avec ma compagne,[2] d'autre société que celle du receveur, de sa femme et de ses domestiques, qui tous étaient à la vérité de très bonnes gens, et rien de plus; mais c'était précisément ce qu'il me fallait. Je compte ces deux mois pour le temps le 20 plus heureux de ma vie, et tellement heureux, qu'il m'eût suffi durant toute mon existence, sans laisser naître un seul instant dans mon âme le désir d'un autre état.

Quel était donc ce bonheur, et en quoi consistait sa 25 jouissance? Je le donnerais à deviner à tous les hommes de ce siècle sur la description de la vie que j'y menais. Le précieux *far niente* fut la première et la principale de ces jouissances que je voulus savourer dans toute sa douceur, et tout ce que je fis durant mon séjour ne fut 30 en effet que l'occupation délicieuse et nécessaire d'un

[2] Thérèse Le Vasseur (see note p. 201).

homme qui s'est dévoué à l'oisiveté. L'espoir qu'on ne demanderait pas mieux que de me laisser dans ce séjour isolé où je m'étais enlacé de moi-même, dont il m'était impossible de sortir sans assistance et sans être bien aperçu, et où je ne pouvais avoir ni communication ni correspondance que par le concours des gens qui m'entouraient; cet espoir, dis-je, me donnait celui d'y finir mes jours plus tranquillement que je ne les avais passés; et l'idée que j'aurais le temps de m'y arranger tout à loisir fit que je commençai par n'y faire aucun arrangement. Transporté là brusquement, seul et nu, j'y fis venir successivement ma gouvernante, mes livres et mon petit équipage, dont j'eus le plaisir de ne rien déballer, laissant mes caisses et mes malles comme elles étaient arrivées; et vivant dans l'habitation où je comptais achever mes jours, comme dans une auberge dont j'aurais dû partir le lendemain. Toutes choses, telles qu'elles étaient, allaient si bien, que vouloir les mieux ranger était y gâter quelque chose. Un de mes plus grands délices était surtout de laisser toujours mes livres bien encaissés, et de n'avoir point d'écritoire. Quand de malheureuses lettres me forçaient de prendre la plume pour y répondre, j'empruntais en murmurant l'écritoire du receveur, et je me hâtais de la rendre, dans la vaine espérance de n'avoir plus besoin de la remprunter. Au lieu de ces tristes paperasses et de toute cette bouquinerie, j'emplissais ma chambre de fleurs et de foin; car j'étais alors dans ma première ferveur de botanique, pour laquelle le docteur d'Ivernois m'avait inspiré un goût qui bientôt devint passion. Ne voulant plus d'œuvre de travail, il

m'en fallait une d'amusement qui me plût, et qui ne me donnât de peine que celle qu'aime à prendre un paresseux. J'entrepris de faire la *Flora Petrinsularis,*[3] et de décrire toutes les plantes de l'île, sans en omettre une
5 seule, avec un détail suffisant pour m'occuper le reste de mes jours. On dit qu'un Allemand a fait un livre sur un zeste de citron; j'en aurais fait un sur chaque gramen des prés, sur chaque mousse des bois, sur chaque lichen qui tapisse les rochers; enfin je ne vou-
10 lais pas laisser un poil d'herbe, pas un atome végétal qui ne fût amplement décrit. En conséquence de ce beau projet, tous les matins, après le déjeuner, que nous faisions tous ensemble, j'allais, une loupe à la main, et mon *Systema naturae*[4] sous le bras, visiter un
15 canton de l'île, que j'avais pour cet effet divisée en petits carrés, dans l'intention de les parcourir l'un après l'autre en chaque saison. Rien n'est plus singulier que les ravissements, les extases que j'éprouvais à chaque observation que je faisais sur la structure et l'organisa-
20 tion végétale, et sur le jeu des parties sexuelles dans la fructification, dont le système était alors tout à fait nouveau pour moi. La distinction des caractères génériques, dont je n'avais pas auparavant la moindre idée, m'enchantait en les vérifiant sur les espèces communes,
25 en attendant qu'ils s'en offrît à moi de plus rares. La fourchure des deux longues étamines de la brunelle, le ressort de celles de l'ortie et de la pariétaire, l'explosion

[3] *Flora Petrinsularis,* an account of the flora of the Ile de Saint-Pierre which Rousseau was planning to compile.

[4] The famous *Systema naturae, sive regna tria naturae systematice proposita* of Linnaeus.

du fruit de la balsamine et de la capsule du buis, mille petits jeux de la fructification que j'observais pour la première fois me comblaient de joie, et j'allais demandant si l'on avait vu les cornes de la brunelle, comme La Fontaine demandait si l'on avait lu Habacuc.[5] Au bout de deux ou trois heures, je m'en revenais chargé d'une ample moisson, provision d'amusement pour l'après-dînée au logis, en cas de pluie. J'employais le reste de la matinée à aller avec le receveur, sa femme, et Thérèse, visiter leurs ouvriers et leur récolte, mettant le plus souvent la main à l'œuvre avec eux; et souvent des Bernois qui me venaient voir m'ont trouvé juché sur de grands arbres, ceint d'un sac que je remplissais de fruits, et que je dévalais ensuite à terre avec une corde. L'exercice que j'avais fait dans la matinée, et la bonne humeur qui en est inséparable, me rendaient le repos du dîner très agréable; mais quand il se prolongeait trop, et que le beau temps m'invitait, je ne pouvais si longtemps attendre, et pendant qu'on était encore à table, je m'esquivais et j'allais me jeter seul dans un bateau que je conduisais au milieu du lac quand l'eau était calme; et là, m'étendant tout de mon long dans le bateau, les yeux tournés vers le ciel, je me lais-

[5] *Habacuc.* The story referred to is told by Louis Racine who says that his father once handed La Fontaine a copy of the Minor Prophets, when the two men were at a church service. Some of the prophets seem to have been unknown to the fabulist. For many days after, when La Fontaine met any of his acquaintances on the street, he greeted them with the remark: *"Avez vous lu Baruch? c'était un grand génie."* Rousseau was mistaken in believing that the story concerned Habacuc. (Walckenaer, *Vie de La Fontaine,* 1824, p. 405.)

sais aller et dériver lentement au gré de l'eau, quelquefois pendant plusieurs heures, plongé dans mille rêveries confuses,[6] mais délicieuses, et qui, sans avoir acun objet bien déterminé ni constant, ne laissaient pas
5 d'être à mon gré cent fois préférables à tout ce que j'avais trouvé de plus doux dans ce qu'on appelle les plaisirs de la vie. Souvent averti par le baisser du soleil de l'heure de la retraite, je me trouvais si loin de l'île, que j'étais forcé de travailler de toute ma force
10 pour arriver avant la nuit close. D'autres fois, au lieu de m'écarter en pleine eau, je me plaisais à côtoyer les verdoyantes rives de l'île, dont les limpides eaux et les ombrages frais m'ont souvent engagé à m'y baigner. Mais une de mes navigations les plus fréquentes était
15 d'aller de la grande à la petite île, d'y débarquer et d'y passer l'après-dînée, tantôt à des promenades très circonscrites au milieu des marceaux, des bourdaines, des persicaires, des arbrisseaux de toute espèce, et tantôt m'établissant au sommet d'un tertre sablonneux, couvert
20 de gazon, de serpolet, de fleurs, même d'esparcette et de trèfles qu'on y avait vraisemblablement semés autrefois, et très propres à loger des lapins, qui pouvaient là multiplier en paix sans rien craindre, et sans nuire à rien. Je donnai cette idée au receveur, qui fit venir de Neu-
25 châtel des lapins mâles et femelles, et nous allâmes en grande pompe, sa femme, une de ses sœurs, Thérèse et moi, les établir dans la petite île, où ils commençaient à peupler avant mon départ, et où ils auront prospéré sans doute, s'ils ont pu soutenir la rigueur des hivers. La

[6] This fondness for revery is generally recognized as one of the distinguishing features of the romantic school.

fondation de cette petite colonie fut une fête. Le pilote des Argonautes n'était pas plus fier que moi menant en triomphe la compagnie et les lapins de la grande île à la petite, et je notais avec orgueil que la receveuse, qui redoutait l'eau à l'excès, et s'y trouvait toujours 5 mal, s'embarqua sous ma conduite avec confiance, et ne montra nulle peur durant la traversée.

Quand le lac agité ne me permettait pas la navigation, je passais mon après-midi à parcourir l'île, en herborisant à droite et à gauche, m'asseyant tantôt dans les 10 réduits les plus riants et les plus solitaires pour y rêver à mon aise, tantôt sur les terrasses et les tertres, pour parcourir des yeux le superbe et ravissant coup d'œil du lac et de ses rivages, couronnés d'un côté par des montagnes prochaines, et de l'autre élargis en riches et 15 fertiles plaines, dans lesquelles la vue s'étendait jusqu'aux montagnes bleuâtres plus éloignées qui la bornaient.

Quand le soir approchait, je descendais des cimes de l'île, et j'allais volontiers m'asseoir au bord du lac, 20 sur la grève, dans quelque asile caché; là, le bruit des vagues et l'agitation de l'eau, fixant mes sens et chassant de mon âme toute autre agitation, la plongeaient dans une rêverie délicieuse, où la nuit me surprenait souvent sans que je m'en fusse aperçu. Le flux et le re- 25 flux de cette eau, son bruit continu, mais renflé par intervalles, frappant sans relâche mon oreille et mes yeux, suppléaient aux mouvements internes que la rêverie éteignait en moi, et suffisaient pour me faire sentir avec plaisir mon existence, sans prendre la peine 30 de penser. De temps à autre naissait quelque faible et

courte réflexion sur l'instabilité des choses de ce monde, dont la surface des eaux m'offrait l'image, mais bientôt ces impressions légères s'effaçaient dans l'uniformité du mouvement continu qui me berçait, et qui, sans
5 aucun concours actif de mon âme, ne laissait pas de m'attacher au point qu'appelé par l'heure et par le signal convenu je ne pouvais m'arracher de là sans effort.[7]

Après le souper, quand la soirée était belle, nous allions encore tous ensemble faire quelque tour de pro-
10 menade sur la terrasse, pour y respirer l'air du lac et la fraîcheur. On se reposait dans le pavillon, on riait, on causait, on chantait quelque vieille chanson qui valait bien le tortillage moderne, et enfin l'on s'allait coucher content de sa journée, et n'en désirant qu'une
15 semblable pour le lendemain.

Telle est, laissant à part les visites imprévues et importunes, la manière dont j'ai passé mon temps dans cette île, durant le séjour que j'y ai fait. Qu'on me dise à présent ce qu'il y a là d'assez attrayant pour exciter
20 dans mon cœur des regrets si vifs, si tendres et si durables, qu'au bout de quinze ans il m'est impossible de songer à cette habitation chérie sans m'y sentir à chaque fois transporter encore par les élans du désir.

J'ai remarqué dans les vicissitudes d'une longue
25 vie que les époques des plus douces jouissances et des plaisirs les plus vifs ne sont pourtant pas celles dont le souvenir m'attire et me touche le plus. Ces courts moments de délire et de passion, quelque vifs qu'ils puis-

[7] This passage needs merely to be versified to make a romantic poem. To have written *Le Lac* Rousseau needed only to have lost Elvire.

sent être, ne sont cependant, et par leur vivacité même, que des points bien clair-semés dans la ligne de la vie. Ils sont trop rares et trop rapides pour constituer un état; et le bonheur que mon cœur regrette n'est point composé d'instants fugitifs,[8] mais un état simple et permanent, qui n'a rien de vif en lui-même, mais dont la durée accroît le charme, au point d'y trouver enfin la suprême félicité.

Tout est dans un flux continuel sur la terre. Rien n'y garde une forme constante et arrêtée, et nos affections qui s'attachent aux choses extérieures passent et changent nécessairement comme elles. Toujours en avant ou en arrière de nous, elles rappellent le passé, qui n'est plus, ou préviennent l'avenir, qui souvent ne doit point être: il n'y a rien là de solide à quoi le cœur se puisse attacher.[9] Aussi n'a-t-on guère ici-bas que du plaisir qui passe; pour le bonheur qui dure, je doute qu'il y soit connu. A peine est-il, dans nos plus vives jouissances, un instant où le cœur puisse véritablement nous dire: Je voudrais que cet instant durât toujours.[10] Et comment peut-on appeler bonheur un état fugitif

[8] It would seem as if de Musset in his *Souvenir* intended directly to challenge this statement, as he challenges Dante:

"Ce fugitif instant fut toute notre vie;
Ne le regrettons pas."

[9] A favorite romantic and indeed lyric mood. See Shelley's *To a Skylark*:

"We look before and after
And pine for what is not."

[10] See Goethe's *Faust,* I, Studierzimmer:

". . . Werd ich zum Augenblicke sagen,
'Verweile doch, du bist so schön.'"

qui nous laisse encore le cœur inquiet et vide, qui nous fait regretter quelque chose avant, ou désirer encore quelque chose après?

Mais s'il est un état où l'âme trouve une assiette assez 5 solide pour s'y reposer tout entière, et rassembler là tout son être, sans avoir besoin de rappeler le passé, ni d'enjamber sur l'avenir, où le temps ne soit rien pour elle, où le présent dure toujours, sans néanmoins marquer sa durée et sans aucune trace de succession, sans 10 aucun autre sentiment de privation ni de jouissance, de plaisir ni de peine, de désir ni de crainte, que celui seul de notre existence, et que ce sentiment seul puisse la remplir tout entière; tant que cet état dure, celui qui s'y trouve peut s'appeler heureux, non d'un bonheur 15 imparfait, pauvre et relatif, tel que celui qu'on trouve dans les plaisirs de la vie, mais d'un bonheur suffisant, parfait et plein, qui ne laisse dans l'âme aucun vide qu'elle sente le besoin de remplir. Tel est l'état où je me suis trouvé souvent à l'île de Saint-Pierre, dans mes 20 rêveries solitaires, soit couché dans mon bateau que je laissais dériver au gré de l'eau, soit assis sur les rives du lac agité, soit ailleurs, au bord d'une belle rivière ou d'un ruisseau murmurant sur le gravier.

De quoi jouit-on dans une pareille situation? De 25 rien d'extérieur à soi, de rien sinon de soi-même et de sa propre existence; tant que cet état dure, on se suffit à soi-même, comme Dieu. Le sentiment de l'existence dépouillé de toute autre affection est par lui-même un sentiment précieux de contentement et de paix, qui 30 suffirait seul pour rendre cette existence chère et douce à qui saurait écarter de soi toutes les impressions sensuelles et terrestres qui viennent sans cesse nous en distraire, et en troubler ici-bas la douceur. Mais la plupart des hommes agités de passions continuelles connaissent peu cet état, et ne l'ayant goûté qu'imparfaitement durant peu d'instants, n'en conservent qu'une idée obscure et confuse, qui ne leur en fait pas sentir le charme. Il ne serait pas même bon, dans la présente constitution des choses, qu'avides de ces douces extases ils s'y dégoûtassent de la vie active dont leurs besoins toujours renaissants leur prescrivent le devoir. Mais un infortuné qu'on a retranché de la société humaine, et qui ne peut plus rien faire ici-bas d'utile et de bon pour autrui ni pour soi, peut trouver, dans cet état, à toutes les félicités humaines des dédommagements que la fortune et les hommes ne lui sauraient ôter.

Il est vrai que ces dédommagements ne peuvent être sentis par toutes les âmes, ni dans toutes les situations. Il faut que le cœur soit en paix, et qu'aucune passion n'en vienne troubler le calme. Il y faut des dispositions de la part de celui qui les éprouve; il en faut dans le concours des objets environnants. Il n'y faut ni un repos absolu, ni trop d'agitation, mais un mouvement uniforme et modéré, qui n'ait ni secousses ni intervalles. Sans mouvement la vie n'est qu'une léthargie. Si le mouvement est inégal ou trop fort, il réveille; en nous rappelant aux objets environnants, il détruit le charme de la rêverie, et nous arrache d'au-dedans de nous, pour nous remettre à l'instant sous le joug de la fortune et des hommes, et nous rendre au sentiment de nos malheurs. Un silence absolu porte à la tristesse. Il offre une image de la mort: alors le secours d'une imagination riante est nécessaire, et se présente assez naturellement à ceux que le ciel en a gratifiés. Le mouvement qui ne vient pas du dehors se fait alors au dedans de nous. Le repos est moindre, il est vrai, mais il est aussi plus agréable quand de légères et douces idées, sans agiter le fonds de l'âme, ne font pour ainsi dire qu'en effleurer la surface. Il n'en faut qu'assez pour se souvenir de soi-même en oubliant tous ses maux. Cette espèce de rêverie peut se goûter partout où l'on peut être tranquille, et j'ai souvent pensé qu'à la Bastille, et même dans un cachot où nul objet n'eût frappé ma vue, j'aurais encore pu rêver agréablement.

Mais il faut avouer que cela se faisait bien mieux et plus agréablement dans une île fertile et solitaire naturellement circonscrite et séparée du reste du monde, où rien ne m'offrait que des images riantes; où rien ne me rappelait des souvenirs attristants; où la société du petit nombre d'habitants était liante et douce, sans être intéressante au point de m'occuper incessamment; où je pouvais enfin me livrer tout le jour, sans obstacles et sans soins, aux occupations de mon goût ou à la plus molle oisiveté. L'occasion sans doute était belle pour un rêveur, qui, sachant se nourrir d'agréables chimères au milieu des objets les plus déplaisants, pouvait s'en rassasier à son aise en y faisant concourir tout ce qui frappait réellement ses sens. En sortant d'une longue et douce rêverie, me voyant entouré de verdure, de fleurs, d'oiseaux, et laissant errer mes yeux au loin sur les romanesques rivages qui bordaient une vaste étendue d'eau claire et cristalline, j'assimilais à mes fictions tous ces aimables objets; et, me trouvant enfin ramené par degrés à moi-même et à ce qui m'entourait, je ne pouvais marquer le point de séparation des fictions aux réalités, tant tout concourait également à me rendre chère la vie recueillie et solitaire 5 que je menais dans ce beau séjour! Que ne peut-elle renaître encore! que ne puis-je aller finir mes jours dans cette île chérie, sans en ressortir jamais, ni jamais y revoir aucun habitant du continent qui me rappelât le souvenir des calamités de toute espèce qu'ils se plai- 10 sent à rassembler sur moi depuis tant d'années! Ils seraient bientôt oubliés pour jamais: sans doute ils ne m'oublieraient pas de même; mais que m'importerait, pourvu qu'ils n'eussent aucun accés pour y venir troubler mon repos? Délivré de toutes les passions 15 terrestres qu'engendre le tumulte de la vie sociale, mon âme s'élancerait fréquemment au dessus de cette atmosphère, et commercerait d'avance avec les intelligences célestes, dont elle espère aller augmenter le nombre dans peu de temps. Les hommes se garderont, je le 20 sais, de me rendre un si doux asile, où ils n'ont pas voulu me laisser. Mais ils ne m'empècheront pas du moins de m'y transporter chaque jour sur les ailes de l'imagination, et d'y goûter durant quelques heures le même plaisir que si je l'habitais encore. Ce que j'y 25 ferais de plus doux serait d'y rêver à mon aise. En rêvant que j'y suis ne fais-je pas la même chose? Je fais même plus; à l'attrait d'une rêverie abstraite et monotone je joins des images charmantes qui la vivifient. Leurs objets échappaient souvent à mes sens 30 dans mes extases; et maintenant, plus ma rêverie est profonde, plus elle me les peint vivement. Je suis souvent plus au milieu d'eux, et plus agréablement encore, que quand j'y étais réellement.[11] Le malheur est qu'à mesure que l'imagination s'attiédit, cela vient avec 5 plus de peine, et ne dure pas si longtemps. Hélas! c'est quand on commence à quitter sa dépouille qu'on en est le plus offusqué!

[11] This mood and idea were immortalized by Wordsworth in *I wandered lonely as a cloud* of which see last two stanzas, and seem to have suggested the famous passage on the origin of poetry in "emotion recollected in tranquillity" in Preface to second edition, *Lyrical Ballads*.